FUNDAMENTALS OF
GUERRILLA WARFARE

FUNDAMENTALS OF GUERRILLA WARFARE

ABDUL HARIS NASUTION

[FACSIMILE EDITION]

With an Introduction by
Otto Heilbrunn

FREDERICK A. PRAEGER, *Publishers*
New York • Washington • London

FREDERICK A. PRAEGER, *Publishers*
111 Fourth Avenue, New York 3, N.Y., U.S.A.
77-79 Charlotte Street, London W.1, England

Published in the United States of America in 1965
by Frederick A. Praeger, Inc., Publishers

Library of Congress Catalog Card Number: 65-20502

Printed in the United States of America

INTRODUCTION

OTTO HEILBRUNN

General Nasution, the Indonesian Defense Minister, develops in this book his theory of guerrilla and antiguerrilla warfare. Much of the book is based on his country's and his own experience in the war of independence against the Dutch (1945–49).

All the ingredients for this conflict had been provided by Indonesia's involvement in World War II. In February and March, 1942, the Japanese had attacked South Sumatra and Java. The Dutch, unpracticed in modern war, were quickly defeated. Because of their performance, they lost prestige in the eyes of the Indonesians, who became convinced that they, too, could beat the Dutch easily, should they ever reimpose their rule over the islands.

Three factors made the Dutch-Indonesian conflict almost inevitable:

1. The Japanese had promised self-government to the Indonesian people in order to secure their cooperation. As a first step, they formed the Central People's Organization (later replaced by the People's Loyalty Organization) and the Central Advisory Board, which was to be consulted before the Japanese made important decisions. In the last days of the war, they also set up an Indonesian Independence Preparatory Committee. These organizations, all chaired by Sukarno, spread, by propaganda, the desire for self-government and independence among the people, and three and a half years of Japanese occupation deepened the almost general resentment against foreign rule.

2. The Japanese formed and trained an Indonesian-officered home guard, the Peta, which was meant to fight off an Allied invasion; 120,000 strong in 1945, it became the nucleus of the Indonesian Republic's Army. There were also a number of youth organizations that had received some military training from the Japanese. Finally, an anti-Japanese underground movement had sprung up.

3. The Japanese appointed Indonesians to fill the higher civil service posts vacated by the Dutch, and these officials acquired administrative experience.

Thus the Indonesians had been provided, as their leaders believed, with the national will to independence, the military means to achieve it, and the administrative ability to sustain it (Cf. pp. 15 and 101).

On August 17, 1945, Sukarno and Hatta declared the Republic of Indonesia independent, and Sukarno became President. Twelve days later, the People's Security Corps, subsequently called the People's Security Army, was formed from Peta units and youth organizations.* In a number of clashes with the Japanese, the Corps managed to secure arms. However, not all the armed irregular organizations were then or subsequently amenable to army control (Cf. pp. 151–52, 162–63, 168, and 189).

The British had landed in Java in September, 1945,† and Dutch contingents returned with them to the islands. The Indonesians soon fought against Dutch, British, and Japanese. The British strongly advised the Dutch to negotiate a settlement with the Indonesians and left the islands in due course. A truce between the Dutch and Indonesians was concluded on October 14, 1946. The Linggadjati Agreement was initialed on November 15, 1946, and concluded on March 25, 1947. By this agreement, the Republic was recognized as the *de facto* authority in Java and Sumatra; a United States of Indonesia was to be set up, consisting of the Republic, the State of Borneo, and the State of the Great East (Celebes and other islands); and both sides were to work for the establishment of a Dutch-Indonesian Union.

While these negotiations were being conducted, fighting continued, but on a much reduced scale. The main theaters of operations in the conflict were Java, Sumatra, Bali, and two areas of Celebes; in Borneo and elsewhere, the Dutch had little trouble in securing control.

Differences about the implementation of the Linggadjati Agreement prompted the Dutch, whose forces now totaled about 130,000 men, to start on July 20, 1947, their First Police Action, as they called it, or the First Dutch Aggression or Colonial Attack, as it has

* The name of the Army of the Republic (Java and Sumatra) was subsequently changed to Indonesian Republican Army and later to Indonesian National Army.

† The British occupied Java and Sumatra, while Australian forces were responsible for the eastern half of Indonesia.

2

been named by the Indonesians. The Dutch had hitherto held in Java only the cities of Batavia (Djakarta) and Bandung, the corridor between these cities, and the area around Surabaja, and in Sumatra the area around Padang and Palembang. They now aimed at extending their control and destroying the Republican Army. They had some success in their first aim: In Java they gained about half the island, leaving the Republic in control of the western tip and the east-central area. The Dutch thus acquired the most fertile rice areas in Java, and they also took possession of the oil regions in Sumatra. But they failed in their second aim: The Republican Army, whose strength had increased to over 500,000 men by the incorporation of irregular forces, often managed to withdraw from the big towns, where it lost much of its arms and equipment, and moved to the safety of the hills and mountains. Although these forces lacked proper leadership, the Dutch were unable to annihilate them or to pacify the occupied regions.

On Australian and Indian initiative, the U.N. Security Council intervened; both sides in the dispute ordered a cease-fire on August 4, 1947, but Dutch operations continued. Owing to further United Nations activities, the so-called Renville Agreement was signed and a truce announced on January 17, 1948. The Agreement envisaged the formation of a United States of Indonesia, of which the Republic was to be a constituent state, and the people were to decide by plebiscite whether they wanted to join the Republic or another state within the Union. Until the United States of Indonesia was formed, the Dutch would retain sovereignty. The cease-fire line agreed upon left the Dutch in possession of their gains, while the Republic was obliged to withdraw 35,000 troops from behind the line.*

The Indonesians feared another attack and started to reform their armed forces. The total strength of all their fighting groups in the unoccupied areas was now 470,000 men. For reasons of economy and rationalization, the Army strength was reduced to 160,000 men by demobilizing the less well-armed and less well-trained army units

* George McTurnan Kahin, *Nationalism and Revolution in Indonesia* (Ithaca: Cornell University Press, 1952), is an invaluable study of the Indonesian political scene. L. H. Palmier, *Indonesia and the Dutch* (New York: Oxford University Press, 1962), is a shorter account. Cf. also Alastair Taylor, *Indonesian Independence and the United Nations* (Ithaca: Cornell University Press, 1960).

3

and a number of irregular semi-independent units. The Army also suppressed a force of almost 25,000 Communist-armed rebels (Cf. pp. 38, 52, and 106).*

The Indonesian Army decided to rely no longer on conventional defense for which it was not organized and equipped. It was held that two kinds of troops were required in another conflict with the Dutch. First, the regular army, well-armed and operating in battalion strength, would be quick on the move to fight where required, hit the enemy sharply in his rear, and extend the areas under Republican control.† Second, there would be the less well-armed territorial militia for local guerrilla duties; it would tie down the enemy and "guarantee the presence of permanent resistance in each outlying district" (p. 111).‡

However, time had run out before the reorganization could be effected. Negotiations following the Renville Agreement broke down in December, 1948; the Dutch repudiated it and, without warning, began the Second Police Action on December 19 with three divisions in Java and three brigades in Sumatra. On that day, Sukarno and Hatta were captured in Jogjakarta, but the Republican government did not cease to function. The Dutch, supported by their air force, paratroops, and tanks, quickly gained possession of the remaining Republican cities in Java and Sumatra and the connecting roads, yet they could not acquire control of the countryside. Nor did they succeed in smashing the Republican forces. Especially in Java, the Indonesians survived the onslaught intact by refusing to fight pitched battles and by disappearing into the countryside (Cf. pp. 180–81),¶ and although they had neither aircraft nor

* Nasution refers to this incident, which took place in September and October, 1948, as the Madiun Affair.

† Nasution often refers to such attacks as "Wingate" actions. However, the operations of the Chindits who fought under the command of Major General Orde Wingate behind the Japanese lines in Burma in 1943–44 and the "Wingate" actions are not strictly comparable. The Chindits wanted to create favorable opportunities for exploitation by their main forces at the front, while the Indonesians, who had neither main forces nor a front, wanted their "Wingate" forces to expand the territory under their control. Both types of forces, however, inserted themselves into, and operated in, the enemy's rear for extended periods.

‡ In January, 1949, at Nasution's instigation, village guerrillas were organized in Java as third line troops. For their duties, cf. p. 170.

¶ The people's reaction to this policy was not always favorable.

heavy arms, they succeeded in spreading their guerrilla "pockets" all over the islands and in re-establishing their control over much of West, Central, and East Java and South Sumatra.* The Dutch, less than 150,000 strong but greatly superior in weapons, had to cope not only with the mobile battalions† and the militia but also with the village guerrillas, and, since the Dutch were fighting in the midst of a mostly noncooperative population, their numerical strength was insufficient to pacify the islands.‡ Thus a stalemate was reached. Once again the U.N. Security Council intervened, and, with American prompting, negotiations between the warring parties were reopened on April 12, 1949. In July, Sukarno was released from captivity; a cease-fire was concluded on August 1; on the twenty-third of that month a conference began at The Hague; and on December 27, 1949, the Dutch transferred sovereignty to the Republic of the United States of Indonesia. The troops of the Royal Netherlands Army left the islands for good.

The most prominent architect of the military resistance was Nasution. Born in North Sumatra in 1918, he was educated at the Royal Military Academy (Bandung) and commissioned in the Netherlands Indies Army in 1941. During the Japanese occupation, he worked in the civil administration and led civil defense forces in Bandung. After the proclamation of independence, he was appointed to a minor Staff position. From 1946 to 1948, he commanded the Siliwangi Division, the crack division of the Indonesian National Army and formed from irregular troops. In 1948, he became Chief of the Operational Staff of the Armed Forces. His special task was "to analyse experiences of the first colonial attack in order to draw up more accurate guides against the possibility of aggression for the second time. This analysis led to a specific concept concerning the structure of our defence and military organisation, as well as

* In Sumatra, the Indonesians still applied linear defense tactics at first.

† Since the reorganization of the army was not concluded before the second outbreak, army attacks were carried out mostly by small units which did not have much striking power, and their contribution to the war effort was limited.

‡ Whether the naval blockade of Indonesia that the Dutch maintained would have changed the issue in the long run is difficult to determine; as a short-term measure, it did not produce results. The Indonesian countermeasure—their scorched earth policy, which led to the destruction of sizable Dutch investments —was probably more effective.

5

to new ideas and guiding lines for our troops" (p. 105), and these ideas are reflected in the book. When the Second Police Action started, Nasution was Commander of the Army and Java Territorium, where most of the fighting took place. In 1950, he became Chief of Staff, Indonesian Army, was suspended in 1952 for advocating the dissolution of the Provisional Parliament and the holding of a general election, and was reappointed in 1955. From 1957 to 1959, he was Chairman of the Joint Chiefs of Staff, and, in 1959, he became Minister of Defense. Since 1960, he has held the rank of full general.

The book, written in 1953, does not merely contain variations on a theme by Mao Tse-tung but is the product of independent thought. Nasution properly distinguishes between auxiliary guerrillas, who assist the regular army in its operations, and other guerrillas who fight on their own—independent guerrillas, as we call them. There are two types of auxiliaries: those who harass the enemy in wartime, as the French *maquis* and the Soviet partisans did in World War II, and those who operate in peacetime in countries for which an invasion is planned, as North Korean guerrillas did in South Korea immediately before the start of hostilities. "It is common strategy in recent years," Nasution says, "to employ cold or secret war during peacetime to eat away a potential enemy from the inside so that he can be invaded and subjugated easily and rapidly" (p. 49; cf. p. 18)—a possible pointer to events to come in Southeast Asia. The independent guerrillas, Nasution goes on, either achieve a deadlock, as the Indonesians did, and international political pressure may bring the war to an end, or they must form a regular army and beat the enemy in the field, as the Chinese and the Viet-Minh did.

Mao had already stated that even if the guerrillas form a regular army, guerrilla elements are still needed to achieve victory. Nasution supplies the reason why. "A guerrilla war, sufficiently active behind the front line of the enemy, can engage an enemy ten to thirty times its number. Thus the enemy . . . is forced to decrease the number of troops used in the actual front line. . . . At the right time [our regular] army can go over to the offensive in order to destroy and annihilate the enemy's army as a result of the guerrilla's activities. . . . In this way the British expeditionary army together with the Spanish guerrillas defeated Napoleon's army in Spain" (p. 17). In that war, the French had numerical superiority over Wellington's forces, but the guerrillas tied down so many of the French in places away from the battlefield that on the battlefield itself he achieved numerical equality and won two brilliant victories in 1812 and 1813. In 1954, General Vo Nguyên Giap used the same strategy; his guerrillas tied down superior numbers of the enemy, and he had numerical superiority over the French Union Forces throughout the battle for Dien Bien Phu.

Nasution is the only guerrilla leader who also has practical experience in counterinsurgency operations, many of which were carried out after independence had been granted (Cf. pp. 73, 100, and 103). There is no doubt that the parts dealing with antiguerrilla war are the best of the book.

He strikingly sets the scene by his characterization of anti-guerrilla and ordinary war: The first consists largely of constructive efforts, the latter is largely destructive (p. 54). "The guerrilla movement is only the result, not the cause of the problem" (p. 73). "The anti-guerrilla movement must be able to realize what are the politico-ideological and socio-economic problems that give rise to and nourish such guerrilla resistance" (p. 55) and then decide "how . . . the anti-guerrilla fighter [can] win back the people . . ." (p. 73) "so that the guerrilla will be cut off from his 'base' " (p. 100). The antiguerrillas "must demonstrate political, psychological, social and economic skill in order to win the hopes and faith of the people gradually" (p. 100). This can be achieved only if "the anti-guerrilla movement brings to the people a better ideology or at least an improvement of their fate" (p. 55). "If we do not succeed in winning the people, all military and police activities, although they may be perfectly executed, will be in vain because such activities strike only the effect not the cause" (p. 100).

Elsewhere in his book, Nasution somewhat underestimates the importance of antiguerrilla victories in the field; the population must, after all, be convinced that the antiguerrillas will win in the end; otherwise it will not support them. But on the whole, Nasution enunciates sound principles, some of which were wrongly ignored in antiguerrilla wars that had not yet ended or not even begun when the book was written.

7

His military doctrine of antiguerrilla war is equally sound. "Essentially, anti-guerrilla warfare is a 'patrol' warfare" (p. 103), as was confirmed by the ferret forces in Malaya, the commando units in Greece, and the combat patrols in the Philippines. Nasution emphasizes that the antiguerrilla must be superior in mobility, flexibility, aggressiveness, and skill, and he rightly stresses the importance of military intelligence. He advocated the use of helicopters before they were employed with such good effect in Cyprus. "The nature of anti-guerrilla measures must be offensive, aggressive, and active" (p. 62), he says, and the troops must not allow themselves to become immobile in their guard posts and small fortresses, as the Japanese did to some extent in China, the Dutch in Indonesia, and the French Union forces in Viet-Nam. The population must be encouraged to provide its own security, as was done so effectively in Malaya and Kenya. And last but not least, "the treatment of guerrilla fighters must be tactful" (p. 58)—a rule that was followed in Malaya and that made the amnesty there so successful but that was disregarded in Algeria and greatly influenced the outcome of the struggle.

We should pay special attention to Nasution's concept of the science of war, a topic that he raises three times in his book (pp. 13, 51, and 93). The science of war, he says, not only consists of the knowledge of tactics, strategy, and logistics, but also embraces political science, propaganda, economics, and sociology. It embraces, in fact, all facets of the art of turning the population against the enemy.

The guerrilla often has an advantage over his opponents because he is trained in, and has as a rule mastered, this art.

FUNDAMENTALS OF
GUERRILLA WARFARE

In Memoriam:
The late General R. Sudirman
and the late General R. Urip Sumohardjo
Fathers of the Indonesian National Army

TABLE OF CONTENTS

III. THE MOST IMPORTANT INSTRUCTIONS TO GUERILLAS (1948 — 1949).

FOREWORD.

This edition "Fundamentals of Guerilla Warfare and The Indo. nesian Defence System Past and Future" is just an introduction to the book "Indonesia's War of Independence", which I am composing. I hope that this brief information will give an understanding to others of the development of our guerilla movement in order that they may evaluate its shortcomings and perfections. It also will provide material for future study, especially bacause it was taken from our own experiences. In any event, in the immediate future we must use anti-guerilla tactics within the country to fight rebel movements and we must use guerilla strategy if our country is attacked by a foreign aggressor. Our present situation which is full of moral and material defects is the result of revolution and sufferings during recent years, the instability and weaknesses of our government, and the cold war which rages in the midst of various crises which cause demoralization and disintegration. This situation cannot be improved and made more stable in the near future. If we should be attacked from the outside within the next ten to fifty years, we will not be able to put into the field a modern armed force to defend our archipelago because we still need about ten years to establish our modern land force and we may need about twenty of thirty years to establish a modern navy. All these must be accomplished together with the necessary technical progress. This is the reason that so long as our foreign policy is independent and neutral we must build our armed forces with our own power, which means we have to emphasize a people's guerilla resistance in the defense of our country.

We have had many experiences with guerilla warfare, but we must not stop training for it because to stop means to deteriorate. Principles of our past experiences must be used for the realization of our purposes in the future by blending all possibilities of improvement and progress which we might obtain. Guerilla warfare needs preparation, organization, education, regulations, etc. That is why we have to use the present time to avoid the bad experiences we have often had in the past, such as organizing, preparing and adapting our way of thinking after war has broken out when it is too late to correct the many shortcomings which exist. We have had bitter results caused by mistakes and errors of organization, ideas, rules, preparations, etc., which in a critical moment must be changed, resulting in failures.

In order to give more information to civilian readers this explanation is presented in a non-technical manner.

In preparing this edition I would like to express my thanks for the aid given by the General Staff of the Army, the Ministry of Information, the former Sambas brigade, Major Darsono, Commandant of the First Battalion of the Djakarta Military District Command, Captain Sutjipto, Lt Susidarto, and Messrs. Djamal Marsudi and Maladi who submitted pictures and other material which I needed.

Also I wish to thank the Topography Department of the Army which gave me valuable assistance.

I hope this book will prove useful for the country in general and the army in particular.

Djakarta, 1 May 1953.

The Author.

———

I. FUNDAMENTALS OF GUERILLA WARFARE.

1. War in this century has become a total people's war.

In such a war it is not only the two armed forces which fight. War has become wider and deeper for a number of reasons, among them technical progress. War in the present time has a total quality, and all the people with all their possessions and resources must be used in order to achieve victory. All available sources must be utilized. To defeat the enemy not only does one have to destroy its armed forces, but also must crush its political institutions and social economy. Modern warfare moves at the same time in the military, political, psychological and socio-economic fields, so that the nature of the attack is total. This is also the case of the victim who is attacked, who uses a total people's defense.

The armed forces cannot ensure victory in war when the political, economic, social and psychological fronts are not strong enough to ward off and overcome the enemy. That is why the leaders in a war are not only military leaders, but also commanders of total people's movements. However, one must realize that the final result of war is determined by the two armed forces. Actually the enemy has lost when his armed forces are defeated. For the victory of the armed forces a necessary condition is a strong political, psychological, social and economic front. Therefore all phases of a nation's life are involved in this type of war.

To make the victory of the armed forces easier, the cold war, or the psychological war, is waged before as well as during the hostilities. Psychological war has two purposes: to weaken and if possible to destroy the morale of our enemy; and also to nurture and strengthen the will of our own people. Psychological war creates fifth column elements within the enemy's country and also provokes him so that enemies fight among themselves, creating a chaos which destroys their unity and disrupts all defense activities against the attack from outside.

Besides these actions the political war must always try to decrease the opponent's allies and to increase his enemies, but to do the opposite for ourselves. Economic war must try to destroy the enemy's resources and tools of production while aiming at strengthening our own. It must confuse the enemy's production with strikes and air raids while we prevent such attacks on ourselves. Economic defense also includes the increasing of our own

11

production as much as possible. The war effort is not carried on by the armed forces alone, but it has become an effort of the entire nation and occupies all phases of the citizens' life. Each phase contributes to the war effort and cannot be ignored.

Because of the above reasons the attacker launches a lightning attack to break down the organization of the enemy before he is able to concentrate all his forces and resources for total defense. Countries which neglect their war preparations become victims to such an attack and consequently it is too late for them to mobilize the total defense of their country. This danger is faced by democratic countries who usually are the ones attacked and who then find it too late to mobilize for defense.

At present most nations use this total war, and indeed, every victim of an attack uses total defense also. In the past war, the greatest war in world history, Germany and Japan, as well as the Allies — America, Russia and England — all used this kind of total war.

During the Indonesian revolution which we recently experienced, the Dutch made total attacks on us, and we answered with our total fight. The Dutch made maximum use of their ten million people for this war and mobilized their armed forces as they had never done before. The Dutch made use of political, psychological, economic, and military offenses alternately and together.

Dutch political activities succeeded in winning the towns in Java and Sumatra through a cease fire agreement and the Linggadjati agreement in 1947, wich gave them time to call up and organize their armed forces from Holland. The first Dutch military action presented opportunities for each cultural group to become a state and so to surround and diminish the prestige of the Republic of Indonesia while plundering the rice growing areas and the plantations, the harbours and the means of communication. The Dutch political action of the "Renville" agreement resulted in the evacuation of guerilla pockets, a feat their military action could not achieve. Dutch psychological activities divided our domestic front by endless disagreements and provocations. Their economic blockade starved and drained the Republic's areas.

We, in principle, also orginized our total people's defense although in not so orderly a way as our enemy who had an excellent organization. We had many deficiencies due to lack of military and political co-ordination, and lack of disciplined strategy. Thus our enemy had the opportunity to defeat us sector by sector even though

12

at first our position, politically and militarily as well as psychologically and socio-economically was much stronger and the necessary elements for winning a war were on our side. The Dutch could enter Indonesia only with the help of the British and Australians, and at the beginning were only able to control their own camp area. Our people's revolution controlled de facto almost the whole of Indonesia and the weapons we seized from the Japanese were enough to equip several of our divisions. At the same time all the means of production were controlled by us.

Even though we have the above advantages, our total people's defense was still just a slogan and not a concrete effort as yet. Our total people's defense was not unusual because our enemy and other nations, big and small, who wished to save their independence and sovereignty from aggression have used this kind of system also.

From the above we see that wars are not only fought by armies alone but are conflicts in which whole nations and peoples are engaged. Wars no longer are waged only on the battle fields but take place everywhere although the final decision of victory or defeat depends on the outcome of the military forces. The science of war does not only consist of military sciences such as tactics and logistics, but includes military policy, politics, psychology and economics. Thus, once again, we see that the field of war does not consist any longer of military actions alone, but is comprised of politics and economics also. The leader in war does not only concern himself with military matters, but also must direct operations in other fields. The qualifications needed by such a leader are not only expertness on the military side, but knowledge in both the political and economic fields.

It is the people who fight, not just the armies. It is the people who declare war and determine peace and create their armed forces. The military leaders must always remember this: they are like the spearpoints of the people and are directed by the people. That is why the army is now an army of the people and no longer a separate entity.

The people train themselves and from the people there emerges and are sent out young men to carry arms when the people consider it necessary to fight. It is to the people themselves that these young men will return when the war is over. The people mobilize the young men to fight and then demobilize and rehabilitate them again when the war is over.

13

For the purpose of establishing efficient machinery to regulate this change a compulsory militia is set up. Also, in a total war, compulsory military training along with other training is set up for civilians.

2.   Guerilla warfare is the war of the weak against the strong.

When a nation is attacked from outside it tries to defend itself. To defend oneself does not mean to ward off or prevent blows alone. This is only passive defense which allows the aggressor to remain strong enough to renew the attack. Defending oneself should mean eliminating the threat of further attacks or in other words, to destroy and conquer the attacker.

Democratic nations are usually forced into a war because they are attacked; they do not start wars. When they have armies as strong as their aggressors, with equal fighting capacity, they are able to defend themselves in a war. Usually, however, the aggressor is ahead in every phase because he has had opportunity for more preparation. Consequently he goes into battle with greater power in places and at times of inadequate defense so that his initial advances are extremely rapid.

On the other hand, the victim of attack is caught unprepared and tries to make up for lost time. He struggles to hold back the enemy as long as possible by retreating gradually in order to gain time and room to mobilize and organize forces strong enough to launch a counter-attack. Before reaching that point, however, he is always on the defensive and defends himself by escaping the attacks of the enemy until the right moment when he has assembled enough forces to go over to the offensive. It is only in this final offensive that the enemy can be defeated, destroyed, or struck in such a way that in desperation he simply surrenders.

That is what history tells us about wars. In the past war, Japan attacked America who gradually retreated while at the same time collecting her power. Finally she was able to thrust forward in an attack on Japan that resulted in Japan having to surrender unconditionally. This was the case also when Germany attacked Russia who fell back while collecting greater strength and who ultimately was able to change the direction of the war; instead of the Germans seizing Moscow it was the Russians who seized Berlin.

When we were attacked by the Dutch in 1947, 1948 and 1949, we were not in a position to do as America and Russia did in the

14

above examples. Within a short time the enemy was able to seize all important cities and roads. We failed to collect enough troops to attack Djakarta and force the Dutch to their knees in unconditional surrender. The reason that the Dutch were finally willing to withdraw their forces from Indonesia was not because they were defeated by our army, but because they were weakened and stymied by us so that there was no longer any hope for them to destroy the Republic. When their efforts to do this were frustrated, international pressure hastened the transfer of sovereignty.

Actually, the TNI (Tentara Nasional Indonesia, i.e., Indonesian National Army) was no match for the Dutch Army. Although in the year 1945 many of our young men had military training and in Java alone we had about 60 PETA (Defenders of the Motherland) battalions and even though we had captured enough weapons from the Japanese to equip several divisions, we were not able to organize our army properly. This was so not only because of a shortage of time and skill but most of all because our national strategy neglected the military-strategic factors. Within one and a half years the Dutch were able to mobilize a modern army of 130,000 men, a feat we were unable to equal even though our forces were several times larger. We were forced to use infantry troops which fought in platoon and company strength. Our heavy weapons were captured or destroyed during the fighting in the big cities and in the outskirts before the main action of the war commenced.

When we re-appraise the situation it is clear that we had sufficient time, forces, and equipment to raise modern battalions and regiments with their reserve weapons at the time of the formation of the TKR (Tentara Keamanan Rakjat—People's Security Army) if the government had kept working along a definite plan. The trained forces from the PETA, Heiho (Indonesians who were trained by the Japanese), and KNIL (Royal Netherlands Indies Army) were enough for several dozen infantry battalions with the necessary equipment. There was lacking, however, the required leadership at a higher level. There was sufficient infantry equipment and more artillery available than the KNIL ever possessed in Indonesia. We also had armoured cars and small tanks in the big cities in the initial stage of the revolution.

On further analysis we will see that the Dutch needed two years in which to mobilize their army since they had to start from scratch. The 130,000 men who fought against us, apparently, were the most they could raise. This was indicated by statements made by the Dutch Minister of War in the Second Chamber, and also by the Chief of the General Staff himself. In addition to this, the Dutch were limited by our guerilla activities and were forced to restrict their occupation to several towns. Thus, they had to recognize our administration in the rest of the country for fear of an outbreak of extensive guerilla war.

This, however, is only a backward observation. At that time our government did not know precisely how much equipment we had taken over because each area acted independently in the beginning. In those times it was very difficult for headquarters to control army units and districts, each of which maintained its own sovereignty. For these reasons the growth of the army was largely determined by local conditions and powers. It was without a definite plan of development based on a definite plan of strategy which would have utilized time, forces and weapons more effectively.

It is quite common that in a time of revolution with emotions raging, we are not permitted orderly discussion, planning and reconstruction — except when there is competent leadership able to overcome this situation.

Because of the fact that we were unable to raise a regular army equal to the Dutch, we were forced to rely on guerilla tactics exclusively. This was unlike the actions in China and Vietnam where in addition to guerilla attacks, attacks by regiments and divisions were used to capture cities and to drive the enemy as far away as possible. We used guerilla warfare not because we believed in its "ideology" but because we were forced into it and could not establish a modern, organized force equal to the Dutch. Our guerilla fight was still in a period of weakening the enemy and we could not yet destroy him even section by section.

That is probably the reason why the leaders of the country did not entrust the entire fight to the military, but always chose the political way to find an agreement with the enemy, while at the same time threatening the use of guerilla war, scorched earth and international political pressure.

The case of the Red movement in China and the war of the Vietminh in Indo-China was different. Here, without compromise, a war was fought to defeat the enemy and army divisions were organized phase by phase to drive the enemy away.

3. Guerilla warfare cannot, by itself, bring final victory; guerilla warfare can only hope to weaken the enemy by draining his resources. Final victory must be achieved by a regular army in a conventional war, because only such an army can stage an offensive of the nature that will subdue the enemy.

The principles of warfare clearly state that only by means of an offensive can the enemy be defeated because he can only be destroyed by being attacked. Napoleon said: "Do not go on the defensive, except when there is no other way. When you face this problem you must fully realize that you do this only to gain time to concentrate your reserve forces and to trick the enemy away from its base of operation, without changing your aim. That is to launch an offensive against the enemy."

A defensive cannot defeat an enemy; this can only be done by an offensive. A defensive action serves temporarily to prepare and await the correct time for the offensive.

As is explained above, we will be forced to stage a temporary defensive since the enemy has attacked us first. So if we are not able to come forward with an equal force, or when our numbers are less, it will happen that the enemy will gradually succeed in seizing part of our territory. The most that we can control is what we can secure behind our front line. In the territory occupied by the enemy our regular war stops, and the enemy is able to control all important centres and communications. The only thing left for us to do is to make pockets between the enemy's positions. It is here that guerilla warfare can best be used by the remnants of the main army or by partisans from the people. A guerilla war, sufficiently active behind the front line of the enemy, can engage an enemy ten to thirty times its number. Thus the enemy becomes exhausted and is forced to decrease the number of troops used in the actual front line and whom we have to fight with our regular army. At the right time this army can go over to the offensive in order to destroy and annihilate the enemy's army as a result of the guerilla's activities carried out by army units and partisans behind the enemy's frontline.

In this way the British expeditionary army together with the Spanish guerillas defeated Napoleon's army in Spain. This was also the case with the Russian guerillas behind the enemy's front lines who helped the Red Army's operations by which the Germans were finally thrown back. The famous Red victory at Stalingrad was also due to assistance from guerillas operating behind the German defense lines. Traffic was unsafe, bridges were destroyed,

17

telephone wires were cut, convoys were put under fire, guard posts were attacked at night, small troops were ambushed, etc. Such guerilla activities greatly exhausted and weakened the invading German army.

In North China the Japanese aggressing army faced similar harassments by guerillas. Railroad tracks were destroyed, vehicle convoys fired on and blockaded, roads mined, guard posts destroyed, patrols ambushed, buildings blown up or burned, etc. Even the Japanese quarters were dynamited and telephone wires were continually stolen, rolled up and hidden by the guerillas and the telephone poles burned. The results of the guerilla activities were so successful that it was impossible for the Japanese troops to advance during the day unless they moved in regimental strength, and all movements at night were practically eliminated.

In Spain as well as in Russia and China, guerilla actions were not carried out helter-skelter merely for the sake of destruction, but these movements were designed to assist the regular army, the backbone of the resistance movement, in its operations. For this reason such guerilla activities were not isolated, but they took place according to the needs of the operation of that army. They were completely co-ordinated although the guerilla units had freedom of action. They moved separately but co-ordinated their attacks, storming one and the same enemy according to a single plan of strategy.

Thus, guerilla activities behind the enemy front line can be helpful to the regular army's defense. They are equally useful in facilitating the regular army's offensive because they disrupt the enemy's lines of communication before the regular army begins the attack. The Allies used guerilla activities behind the German and Japanese fronts in order to hasten their downfall. French partisans were famous for their services which caused confusion in the rear of the German army while the Allied Army was pushing from the front. Their contribution was as important as the bombardments by the air force behind the German front lines. For the same reasons guerilla units were put into action in Malaya and the Philippines to disorganize the Japanese from the rear. They were so effective that the aftermath (of their work) has not been solved up to this time.

Today it has apparently become a custom to start guerilla activities during peacetime in those countries for which an invasion is planned. This is done not only by means of a secret Fifth Column as the Germans did in the Netherlands, but also by secretly encouraging and arming opposition factions in the country which will be the victim of the attack. In the "cold war" the future enemy is placed under attack in peacetime by guerilla warfare. This domestic struggle is an important facet of today's total war. The enemy is eaten away from within so that he easily subjugated. Certainly such guerilla activities can only be successfully carried out when there is fertile atmosphere in a particular country to nurture such a movement, for example, when there are social schisms, poverty — in short when there is dissatisfaction. We can realize the meaning of such civil war as is rampant in all South East Asian countries at this time, Indonesia not excepted.

The examples taken above concern guerilla units which assisted the regular army in its operations, relieved the army's burdens in the defensive or accelerated the speed of operations on the offensive. The guerilla units did not contain the main force of resistance, but were only an auxiliary force to alleviate, to speed up and to aid the main force. A good example are the Vietminh guerilla units of today which assist in the regular army's offensive.

Our situation when we were attacked was different. In our fight for independence we were not able to put an army into the field with an organization equal to that of the enemy. The Dutch attacked with three brigades in Sumatra and with three modern divisions in Java. We had more divisions and brigades, but they were divisions and brigades in name only; their content and organization were not worthy of the name. We were not able to put up organized resistance along a definite front; we were forced to allow the enemy to occupy the cities and highways, in short, to let the enemy move unhampered wherever he wished. We may remember the sarcastic remark directed at our army headquarters at that time that "the Dutch Staff was touring through Java." We may recall that at that time the politicians also criticized us for not being able to defend the capital of Jogjakarta. In such a situation the whole territory in general terms was officially occupied by the enemy, so that General Spoor was able to remark at the turn of 1948: "...the operation has come to an end. We only have to clear up the remnants, a task which will take only two or three more months."

Because we were the weaker party we had to fight an extensive guerilla war. With our "wingate" operations we infiltrated in all directions so that from the coast of Bantam to the coast of Besuki there was one single chain of hundreds of guerilla battle fields with intensive fighting. The Dutch had to disperse their divisions into hundreds of stationary detachments and were thus frustrated

19

in their attempts to annihilate the Republic of Indonesia and the Indonesian National Army, to dominate the whole island, to set up their federal government, to start economic reconstruction, etc. In short, they finally came to a dead end and relinquished their original aim.

In our case the guerilla units did not assist the regular army as in the examples cited above. Guerilla tactics were the main source of our power in war, a total guerilla war using non-cooperation and scorched earth which was successful in bringing to a deadlock the enemy's colonial war. I say 'bringing to a deadlock' because our guerillas did not defeat the enemy in the sense of destroying or wiping out the enemy from Indonesia's soil. We only frustrated their attempts; we did not defeat them in the usual military sense of the word.

We mainly defended ourselves and we used guerilla warfare in such a way that their efforts came to a stalemate. We were on the defensive as Napoleon said, only because we were forced into it. The enemy's efforts came to a stalemate because when we evacuated the towns and started to build pockets in which the civil adminis- tration and military organization remained intact, we took care that we were not destroyed by them. We maintained a rigid policy of non-cooperation and only a small number of not respected traitors collaborated with the enemy and they could not establish a self-sustaining government. We maintained a scorched earth policy so that their economic reconstruction failed. Later we harassed them as much as possible, exhausted them by means of ambushes, confusion, infiltration, etc. Although these were aggressive actions we were still on the defensive. We could not seize towns or maintain ourselves for a long period against attacks by the army. We let the Dutch "tour through Java"; we could not destroy their isolated posts nor their passing convoys.

The fact that the enemy finally surrendered, that he was willing to recognize a return of all the areas to the Republic and the TNI, that he was willing to transfer sovereignty under several conditions and was willing to withdraw his troops, all were hastened by inter- national political pressure. Consequently we did not have to prolong our guerilla war which at a certain point would have required a regular army to launch an offensive.

Indeed, in most cases in history guerilla wars only tire the enemy. Usually it is the regular army, either of the country itself or of an ally, which carries the offensive to defeat an aggressor. For example, the German army in Russia was defeated not by guerilla actions but by the Red army; the Nationalist Army in China was not defeated by guerilla units but by the People's Liberation Army, the regular army. Guerilla warfare strategically carried out is defensive. A victory in a war can only be achieved by an offensive, carried out by an organized army, an army equal or greater in force than that of the enemy.

If in our own war of independence we did not receive political support from outside, we would have had to obtain a victory in the military field and we would have had to fight a long and terrible war like the revolutionary war in China or the Vietminh War of Independence. This is so because to obtain a victory we must go over to the effensive with a force that can match the enemy's. Prior to this stage of the war we must able to continue on the defensive, as seen in other examples of a common war, in which we must maintain a permanent front and thus can control and occupy a base territory. At this stage we must already have an equal force, a regular army as strong as that of our enemy.

Before we reach the defensive stage we must fight a total guerilla war to progress in such a way that two aims will be realized. First, the guerilla fighters as the weaker party must prevent themselves from being pursued, encircled, and exterminated by the enemy. They must avoid frontal fighting, open fighting and any other kind of fighting in which the enemy is in an advantageous position because of his greater numbers. Secondly, guerilla units must develop from weak into strong units. This is only possible when in battle they are able to destroy the enemy piece by piece and then seize the equipment of the enemy who has been wiped out. Thus the guerilla decreases the strength of the enemy and adds to his own weapons. Therefore, a guerilla fighter must fight with real economy. He only engages in a battle if a gain is possible. He must calculate his gain and losses like a good businessman. For this reason there must be no useless battles in which the enemy is only pricked or annoyed. Moreover, the guerilla must avoid useless loss of life of the guerilla fighters. The guerilla unit must be very thrifty with its forces for the loss of one machine gun means more to a guerilla unit than to a large enemy force just as one rupiah means more to a pauper than to a rich man.

Therefore guerilla units should not fight just to show courage as has been often suggested by our leaders and by propaganda of the past in such slogans as "refuse to retreat, go on attacking, go on destroying." In that way we lost tens of thousands of weapons and ammunition in fighting in the towns and outskirts of the cities.

21

What is more, almost all of the equipment and almost everything else was lost before the real war started.

4. A guerilla war is usually an ideological war. Guerilla warfare is a total people's war.

In the example of Indonesia in the last chapter, the guerilla war was the main nucleus of all the war efforts, not just a means of support, as shown in the other examples. Therefore it is obvious that such a war demands greater time and immeasurable sufferings and loss of energy. Indeed a guerilla war is far from easy or simple but on the contrary requires or demands greater endurance and ability.

The history of guerilla wars shows plainly enough how deep both mentally and physically is the resulting destruction. Participation in guerilla activities supplants the usual habit of obeying laws and customs with the habits of carrying out underground movements designed to confuse the enemy, waging scorched earth policies, sabotage, setting up self-instituted courts, etc. These are effected by a small group or by an individual, not in the framework of the usual social organization and not according to the ordinary principles of law.

The resulting internal and external destruction is so great that in countries where guerilla war was fought it is apparent that several decades are needed to repair the damage. In the meantime confusion reigns in all fields. Those territories where guerillas were operating in the last war have not been pacified up to now. Moreover, in their new relationship to the ideological war and colonialism, elements of the cold war between West and East have been added. The guerilla war in Indonesia did not end with the withdrawal of the Dutch troops; it continued on as a civil war which was equally vehement.

In the areas which suffered most from guerilla activities which rose and fell like the tide, traditional standards and institutions, governmental administration, social structure, etc., underwent many upheavals, and now require great and enduring efforts to be restored to a stable condition. In fact, a guerilla war, especially as cited in our last example, is very demanding. It requires the greatest ability given voluntarily from the professional guerilla fighters, as well as from the people who assist them. The first requirement is ideological strength on the part of each guerilla fighter and the ability to carry out guerilla activities properly, not only urged by a feeling of duty towards the country but because of personal desire. Guerilla soldiers are not only required to carry arms as our soldiers in an ordinary war, but they are soldiers carrying an ideology. They are not only pioneers in the battle but above all pioneers of an ideology.

History has sufficiently proven that a guerilla war always precedes an ideological fight. The oppressed people, the colonized, the tyrannized people raise their fists threatening to eliminate the cruel oppressor, the tyrant and the colonizer. The suffering of a fight, however great, is light when compared with the misery of cruel oppression, colonization, and tyranny. The misery is usually widespread and the people are forced to suffer a long time. The aims of resistance are not only supported by a few agitators, but by many people. The resistance movement involves all the people.

The ideology of the spirit of freedom serves as the source of strength and willpower to initiate a war against a strong enemy with well organized troops. Once this ideology has ignited the total people's war which has been smouldering in the hearts of the people, they make use of any and all available weapons to begin the struggle. From this mass of people in revolt the guerilla fighters usually emerge, and at this point the mass movement changes into a guerilla war and later develops into a regular war. Thus, usually the guerilla fighter is conceived and grows out of an oppressed or colonized people. In some cases a guerilla movement may develop from the remnants of an army together with a nucleus of people from a nation occupied by an enemy invader who desires to oppress and colonize them.

Only a strong ideology, a strong inner spirit, can make a guerilla war explode. That spirit must be sufficiently courageous to tread the long and difficult road of suffering up to the moment when the enemy in power is finally defeated. Only a clear awareness and a conscientious devotion to the ideology of the guerilla movement can bind the fighter to his duty since he is free to sever his connection any time. Twice during our struggle for freedom guerilla warfare was waged and we saw how many so-called "guerilla fighters' left the occupied cities to hide in the kampongs or even surrendered to find protection from the enemy. There are some of these "guerillas" who now during peacetime scream that they were the best patriots and revolutionaries, and today they are still living comfortably in our midst. They did not have enough inner strength to participate in the guerilla war for which one needs a great amount of ideological consciousness and resoluteness of soul.

Governments which do not have popular support or are not rooted in the people's ideology cannot hope to obtain the people's

23

cooperation to fight a guerilla war on their behalf if their countries are attacked. The people's attitude will either be one of apathy or they will fight at a later time for their own sake. The former Netherlands Indies government had planned a guerilla war after the regular army was defeated by the enemy and before the arrival of Allied assistance. However, the guerilla war failed to develop except on the island of Timor near Australia. As General Imamura said: "The greatest defeat of the Dutch resulted from the fact that they could not win the Indonesian people as their allies." The colonial government could not expect from their colonized people the willingness to fight a guerilla war. On the other hand it was easy for the Japanese to activate a people's guerilla movement against them as happened at Atjeh in 1942.

There were no German guerillas when the Allied army invaded in 1944 — 1945 since the people were tired and fed up with their oppressive government. Although we had a violent guerilla war just recently, it will depend on the political situation whether there is enough spiritual basis for a guerilla war in the future. If the people continue to be disappointed and miserable, if the government only brings happiness for a small group of corrupt officials, if the government is not the choice of the people, it would be a waste of time to plan a guerilla war to defend the country against a future aggressor.

As has been shown above, an intense ideological fight is usually the strongest motivation for a guerilla war. It is the desire to free itself from the chains of tyranny and domination that compels a colonized nation, no longer willing to be humiliated, to actively oppose the oppressor. When the enemy recruits its army to put down the rebellion it is only effectively opposed by force in the form of a guerilla movement. The guerilla movement is a small and simply armed unit of force, and is supported, maintained and protected by the people so that it may compete with the large, fully equipped and organized army of the enemy. The fighting spirit which is burning in the heart of the guerilla, as well as in the people he has sprouted from, inspires him with the strength to carry out penetrations of the enemy and to withstand difficult trials, such as enemy bombardments and all the cruel retaliatory measures to which his family is subjected, including the burning of villages and the torture of civilians. This spirit gives him the strength to carry those heavy burdens with a willingness which would not be possible if he fought because he was forced to, as for example by a country's laws or rules. This willingness to suffer is only possible because of the holy call of his own heart.

24

For this reason a member of a guerilla army, fighting for an ideology, can not only be used as a country's tool to be ordered to carry a gun; but also as an ideological pioneer, he must be active in ideological matters and in politics. How can he be the vanguard of an ideology or fight for a political aim if he is merely a tool to be ordered around with no voice in political decisions. It is not sufficient for him to be merely acquainted with political matters, but he must champion and propagandize for them. An army which is merely a country's tool to be given instructions does not have the inner strength to withstand a violent guerilla war.

It is the first duty of a guerilla movement to maintain the spirit, nourish the ideology, and especially to bolster the spirit of resistance in the people. Guerilla strategy should not place emphasis on combat actions alone but must also consider the importance of the guerilla's politico-psychological and socio-economic facets, including propaganda, non-cooperation policy, scorched earth policy, infiltration, etc. Guerilla war should be understood in a wider meaning as including other things than just armed fighting. What is more, armed operations are not mainly directed at military targets, but often have political, psychological and socio-economic goals. Examples of the latter are raids on cities to punish collaborators, raids on production centres to cause chaos, ambushes of vehicles, burning of buildings and cutting and stealing of telephone wires.

Differing from the ordinary soldier who is only faced with combat, the guerilla is also directly involved in an economic, political and psychological war. The guerilla people are not in the same position as the people behind the front line who in the military term become "war workers" in a regular war. Guerilla people, besides having to work hard, must also directly face mopping-up operations of the enemy, raids, burnings, imprisonment and other sufferings, and often cruel reprisals, because the enemy is not able to capture the guerillas themselves. The village people of a district are directly involved in the fight against the enemy, and only a firm inner discipline, rooted in an ideology, can strengthen the people so that they will gladly endure the misery of the fight and will hide, nurse and serve guerilla fighters as if they were their own blood children.

Actually a guerilla war means a total people's war which has a far more intensive and extensive meaning than a total war in the ordinary sense.

It was exactly for the purpose of making the guerilla war a total people's war that in the years 1948-1949 we organized a military form of guerilla government, consisting of the administrative units at village level (desa), underdistrict (onderdistrik), regency (kabupaten), territory (daerah), and provinces (gubernuran), each headed by a military commander who was also chief of the total guerilla administration in that area and who operated with full support from the civilian bodies.

Such a total war could be waged in any desa, underdistrict, district, territory and province. The leadership would be in the hands of one person at each level who would preside over the political-psychological war which uses as weapons non-cooperation and non-fraternization, scorched earth and crop destruction and economic war on enemy-owned plantations. Every guerilla area was engaged in an autonomous political and economic war. The government administration was "guerilla-ized" and the government officials received cars to play "hide-and-seek" with the enemy patrols. All government affairs were "guerilla-ized" — the judicial courts and police, the levying of war taxes, information services, public health, education, manufacturing, communications, etc. In guerilla-izing that way the enemy was foiled in his attempt to destroy the organization of our own country so that it was not possible for him to replace it with his government. All the while our side kept the wheels of government going to serve the needs and the struggle of the people.

In this framework of total warfare the leadership could recruit and plan a strategy of the whole people for one aim. However, the leadership must fulfill the absolute requirement for guerilla war which is, that it must be rooted in the people. Our guerilla government using specially trained workers, known as territorial cadres, took care that the foundation, that is, the people, remained intact and in good morale.

5. Guerilla war does not mean that all the people are fighting.

As has been explained, the guerilla fighter is a champion of the people's ideological struggle which lives in the hearts of the people. If the ideological foundation and roots are not there, there will be no support for a guerilla war. The guerilla soldier is rooted completely in the soul of the people, and therefore, the guerilla movement can only prosper if the people serve as its foundation.

Our leaders always compare the guerillas to fish and the people to the water, using the example from Mao Tse-tung's teachings. The Chinese leader has explained that the "water" must be nourished in its natural political and socio-economic climate to

26

ensure the proper development of the guerilla fighter who "swims" in it.

Therefore, it is very important for the guerilla soldier, being a leader of the people's fight for freedom, to maintain that favourable "climate" with the people. Since he is fighting for the people, his actions must have the immediate appreciation and approval of the people. We cannot profess to be fighting in the people's interest when in practice our actions consist of annoying or hurting the people. The relationship in regard to the people must be kept as perfect as possible. The guerilla soldier should not be allowed to have a special position above the people, as often happens in the case of so-called fighters with whom we have had experience in the past.

In other words, guerilla war is a people's war; the guerilla is born and bred in the midst of the fighting people, the guerilla fights with the help, care and protection of the people. The guerilla is a loyal soldier of the people.

It is not necessary, however, that all the people should actively participate in guerilla warfare in its special sense. In its general meaning, a guerilla war is a total people's war, a military, political, socio-economic and psychological war. For specialized active guerilla services to hit the enemy with armed attacks and sabotage, according to Lawrence, only two percent are guerillas and ninety-eight percent are people sympathetic to the cause; two percent do the fighting and ninety-eight percent give assistance; two percent are active and ninety-eight percent passive guerilla fighters.

Of importance also is the quality of the guerilla fighters. One group consisting of brave, spirited guerilla soldiers, skillful in their task although small in number, are more useful than a armed mob. In the Boer war in South Africa guerilla troops were able to hold off the English army which was thirty times larger. Five to six thousand Red guerillas in Malaya were able to engage a hundred thousand British soldiers and police. We have seen ourselves, how the RMS (Republik Maluku Selatan) guerillas were able to fight TNI (Tentara Nasional Indonesia) troops at an average of one platoon against one or two battalions. In the revolt in the South Moluccas one battalion of rebel troops engaged eight battalions of our Republic's troops, but they could not be annihilated, even though they were pursued until we tired of chasing them.

One small guerilla party equipped with light weapons but trained intensively can effectively engage a force ten to thirty times larger and can compel it to disperse, rendering it impotent.

In the history of our fight there were many suggestions of an "armed people" and "revolt of the masses". These slogans must be understood as slogans, because it would be wrong to think that we were aiming at making all the people active guerilla fighters, something which is not possible, not necessary, in addition to being inefficient. Revolutions by armed masses are usually unsuccessful in defending themselves. It is true that it is quite easy to agitate the masses to become violent, but it is equally true that a mob tends to break and become easily confused so that it becomes difficult to lead. A single success can quickly ignite the spirit of the masses but one failure can cause this spirit to tumble and can even break it entirely. The masses are easily confused by rumours.

Generally our armed mass revolts in the big cities did not result in military gains. Armed mass movements took place in Djakarta, Bandung, Semarang and Surabaja. Only the one in Surabaja had any historical importance. In all the other instances we were badly beaten and ultimately driven out of those cities. By operating systematically the enemy could gradually master a situation, while we were forced to flee, leaving behind men and material of immeasurable value for our guerilla activities which took place later. The above cited examples of upheavals of masses first of all have psychological meaning, showing our willingness to fight as a nation. However, the leadership failed to organize those skilled fighters into a nucleus to fight the long guerilla war which was required.

A guerilla war also needs economic implementation. Therefore a people engaged in a guerilla war must adapt their organization [to existing conditions] by assigning duties to each guerilla, the number of active guerilla fighters being decided by the situation and the ability to equip them.

Based on these considerations we planned our organization after having studied past experiences in our first guerilla war. We assigned village guards to defend the people who are usually armed only with knives. The villagers could carry out certain duties to assist the army, such as communication, transportation, acting as guides, patrolling, etc. In every military district there was set up one territorial company or one battalion armed 1 : 3 or 1 : 5 who were responsible for the guerilla resistance of the whole district and were permanently stationed there. In every military residence we set up one or more mobile combat battalions which could be integrated into a larger unit. These battalions were armed 1 : 1 and

28

were given weapons for the offensive. Thus the above comprise the duties for active guerilla warfare.

Apart from the above there are other duties of the people which are regulated by the guerilla government. These include such things as furnishing of supplies and maintenance, passive resistance, non-cooperation, etc. For these purposes we set up territorial cadres at every government level who stimulated and guided the people for such resistance.

We can not expect to obtain the highest amount of efficiency because of several reasons most of which are of a political and psychological nature. In war time, however, we experienced radical shifting and rapid organizational development under the direct pressure of war necessities. The number of guerilla fighters always decreases at the start of the war and always increases at the end of the war. That is why we had an excess of soldiers and militia which was necessarily reflected in the supply of provisions and the rehabilitation of ex-soldiers after the war.

We have already had experiences with the excesses of "an entire armed people". There were 470,000 members of fighting groups in those areas of the Republic where there was no fighting after the Renville agreement and they became an unbearable burden for the government which had just lost its "surplus areas" and was in the grip of a tight Dutch blockade. The people of the villages had to suffer, as it was they who were forced to care for these non-productive fighters on an "all-ensured basis". Corruption by the trusted leaders of the troops was easy. The national struggle was used as a cover for all kinds of personal and group interests. In the first and second military clash between the Dutch and the Indonesians we witnessed how the number of fighters declined, but how the number soared again after the battle was over. After all these years the people and the government continue to be burdened from the results, and the problem of what to do with veterans has become intolerable. It is difficult to determine the number of those who are true veterans. These true veterans have suffered because of those who call themselves fighters and who have swelled the number of veterans claiming benefits. We have seen that in the capital of Djakarta alone approximately 70,000 were registered after the transfer of sovereignty. In those times many offices and businesses complained for weeks because many of their personnel left the cities to join the fighting groups. Often the countryside had a shortage of young men to carry out the work or to plant the fields because they had left to join the guerilla units so that they could call themselves veterans.

It often happens when "all the people are armed" that it is not we who carry out guerilla activities against the enemy, but the enemy who carries out guerilla activities against us because we are not able to plan and control such large numbers.

6. A guerilla war must not consist of unorganized destruction.

We have already explained how important efficiency is, especially in the case of a guerilla war. It is common that among guerilla fighters everything that is organized is held in abuse. Many sneered at discipline, theorizing, regular training, regulations, strategic planning etc. It is true that a guerilla group does not need so many rules and regulations as are usually found in a regular army, but this does not mean that rules and standards, essential for military discipline, are not necessary at all. In the initial months of the revolution our fighters did not want to salute in the military way; they did not want rank; they did not want to admit the importance of any international organization.

Guerilla fighters must also have discipline, must have organization, must train, must study military tactics and must have planning and calculations. Guerilla troops must also have leaders who can command obedience.

Guerilla war must not be taken to mean that everyone can fight as he wishes, or that everyone can organize his own troops and plan his own strategy, or that they can act independently. Furthermore, a guerilla should not think that he has to continuously destroy, to always look for an enemy or to always be on the offensive.

How great were the setbacks our struggle suffered and how great the amount of confusion and difficulties that befell us in the past because we played the role of the guerilla too long. Take for example the longhaired warriors who were roaming along Malioboro Street in Djogjakarta, with pistols on both hips and bullets hanging at their waists and around their shoulders! How many difficulties did we have to cope with on the battle front because each kind of troops wanted to carry out its own strategy and each wanted to outdo the others in courage, thus thinking themselves clever! How much did the people suffer because they had to feed various kinds of troops! How many were the headaches of the General Staff which had to solve the disagreements between various units because there was no unified command! How unstable was the country because of the multiplicity of troops overlapping each other! On how many occasions was the enemy able to infiltrate its agents among our groups and play us off one against the other!

Guerilla warfare also requires training and study of military science. Such shortcomings on our side made many of our operations useless and many other times frustrated them. There was even a period when military science was labeled colonial, and it was believed that a war only required courage for victory. How many of our boys died in vain because of the mistakes of our commanders who urged them to go on hopeless attacks, to fight with bamboosticks against tanks, to fight with grenades against artillery, etc.! The bodies of our boys were seen lying in the street where they had died, mowed down by machine gun fire from British tanks while attempting to attack them with nothing more than sharpened bamboosticks.

The battles in the cities which were not under any leadership took a large number of lives, many of which were taken unnecessarily. Furthermore, at the same time tens of thousands of weapons were captured by the enemy. It became a fad to give orders over the radio, thus directing enemy artillery and mortars to our troops which resulted in the large scale and unnecessary slaughter of troops that could have been useful later on in the struggle. Because we lacked organization, planning and leadership, the enemy's task of wiping out our troops at the initial stage of the revolution was made much easier. The enemy was given the opportunity to crush our units one by one.

The cry "defend every inch of land" often compelled the troops to fight statically and frontally, afraid to maneuver in order to draw the enemy out in the wrong direction and attack his flank and rear. There should have been some troops who fired their weapons while other troops advanced from their original positions under cover of this fire.

To organize, to plan, to work scientifically, as is usually done in an army, is in a revolutionary period often mislabeled a foreign or colonial practice. Without organization, strategic planning, proper tactics, etc., many defeats will be suffered.

In the year 1945 we had enough weapons and ammunition to equip several divisions and approximately 150,000 young men in Java and Sumatra who had been trained in the PETA, Heiho, and KNIL. We can imagine how violent our guerilla war would have been if all the available trained soldiers and weapons were fully equipped and organized into battalions and regiments approximately equal to the enemy. If we had organized — not as we did on Java into a dozen brigades and fourty regiments of T.R.I. — but instead, had as combat troops only fourty battalions so that

31

then there were only two or three completely equipped regiments in each province and two or three battalions in each residency, we could have distributed the surplus weapons among the village militia so they could conduct partisan warfare. Although we had the opportunity to organize in this manner, we did not have time enough to use that opportunity because the guerilla fighters would not follow orders. It was impossible to agree on a single plan or an effective leadership in an atmosphere of authoritarianism, paternalism and extreme individuality.

Because there was no cool planning from the start we wasted time, which could have been used in improving our organization and training, on fighting battles at the outskirts of the cities and on demarcation lines.

Guerilla-mania is the greatest and the most dangerous enemy of the guerilla movement. Guerilla-mania does not allow disciplined planning and leadership; it brings the operations against an organized enemy to defeat; it causes inefficiency and chaos in our own camp and results in a weakening of our positions. A guerilla movement should by its own nature become more disciplined, more organized, better trained and skilled, able to advance to a higher degree of organization and as a prime condition to achieve victory in war. Guerilla-mania creates confusion for the people, from whom provision and assistance are requested without limits or discipline. Moreover, guerilla-mania and non-existence of organization or discipline facilitates guerilla warfare among ourselves. Small matters and personal disagreements easily cause guerilla war to flare up among ourselves, especially if utilized by the enemy or opposition, as we have often experienced, so that we clawed at each other in the face of a threatened hostile aggression. Guerilla-mania has in essence the effect of a counter-guerilla movement, as in a revolution where there develops a counter-revolution. Leaders who allow guerilla-mania to sprout forth in the ranks of their followers not only add to the inefficiency and paralysis of a guerilla army but they make it easy for the enemy to play one against the other and hit us one after the other, and in this way give them the opportunity to undermine the original revolution with a counter-revolution. In order to avoid guerilla-mania it is necessary to have strong and experienced leaders with the necessary authority. Weak leadership which cannot control insubordination adds to the growth of guerilla-mania.

Guerilla troops must appear undisciplined to the enemy so that he continues to misjudge them and be worried concerning the condition and aims of the guerilla troops. However, the guerilla figther must respect and discipline himself towards his own leaders so that they can use him to the fullest benefit. Certain elements of the revolt may advocate frenzied guerilla attacks against the opponent hoping that this will cause quarrelling among the guerillas themselves which cannot be controlled by the government. These elements on the other hand extinguish all guerilla-mania within their own ranks and discipline harshly the army and people as soon as the authority of the guerilla government it has subverted has been overthrown. It is obvious that such elements which advocate and conduct guerilla-mania in our own camp are a dangerous enemy.

We have already pointed out the suffering caused by lack of discipline and order on our side. "Keep on destroying, do not retreat one inch, concentrate all weapons on the front, etc." — such attitudes cost us dearly in valuable weapons and in thousands of dedicated young men who sacrificed their lives in vain. In addition much equipment was lost that was vital for the continuation of the war. It must above all be realized that the examples given are contrary to the principles of guerilla warfare which aim at avoiding the force of the enemy when he has a superior power, and only attacking the enemy in his weakest spots. As the experience of the Chinese guerilla shows the odds should be ten against one.

7. A guerilla movement has its base within the people. The people support, care for and conceal the guerillas and spy for them.

The guerilla movement can carry out its duty only because the people act as its storehouse and repairshop. With the assistance of the people the guerillas can obtain information concerning the enemy's break-down of communications, troop movements and types of force because the people live around the enemy and associate closely with him. To have a sympathetic people working with the guerillas is almost as if the doors of the enemy's General Staff and [living] quarters were left open. The guerilla troops always know the enemy's situation immediately. On the other hand a sympathetic people keep the guerilla's secrets from the enemy. The people conceal guerillas so that, for example, they can move about disguised as ordinary civilians. The people are ready to suffer tortures inflicted by the enemy in order to preserve the guerilla's secrets. General Sudirman liked to relate the story about Commander Diponegoro when he was pursued by the Dutch. As he passed a hut a woman came out and immediately wiped out the traces of his horse. When the enemy came the Commander's tracks could not be seen and no one would admit having seen him. This also happened to Major Imam Sukarto, the commander of the

Darmawulan brigade, who joined the guerilla fighting in Besuki. He happened to be in a village when the KNIL carried out a raid and he hid for hours behind a stone. The villagers were ready to suffer any kind of punishment to keep his hiding place secret. We see the superiority of the Atjeh guerilla who resisted the Dutch attacks for thirty years and later was active in the underground movement. This movement erupted at times and in 1942, shortly before the Japanese landed, rose and wiped out the colonial power.

The work of intelligence and counter-intelligence, so important in a war, is well ensured for the guerilla movement which has its base in the people because the people are able to infiltrate the enemy so that the guerilla movement has voluntary eyes and ears everywhere.

With the help of the people an intensive propaganda war can be conducted. All news aimed at causing confusion, panic and errors among the enemy can rapidly be disseminated. All rumours are carried by the sea of human beings. The best channels of communication in the community — houses of prayer, city halls, religious institutions, etc. — are available to the guerillas. Pamphlets and news of the guerillas are distributed rapidly and widely by the people. This propaganda war is very important on the one hand to frustrate the enemy's propaganda directed at our people, and on the other hand to disorganize and disturb the enemy's peace of mind. However, the guerilla and his territorial cadres must effectively control their own system. Thus the enemy will not be able to infiltrate it with his own propaganda which will not appear to come from him and will cause confusion among the people. In a society which is not sufficiently prepared and disciplined secret propaganda can sprout up easily. We have in our own experience seen such things as a soldier who "happened" to find on a train a letter addressed to a certain T.N.I. officer; the finder opens and reads the letter, discovering that it contains secret orders from the Dutch intelligence to the unfortunate officer. The letter is brought to the headquarters of the soldier and rumours about the officer start circulating. We have experienced many such examples in the past years and our community is easily provoked and takes quick action without due consideration. There was a Dutch leader who once stated that the Republic could be brought down by provocation for it would result in slander, distrust, and murder among us. Anonymous letters, secret pamphlets, rumours, "secret" documents, all these would be able to defeat us in this branch of psychological war.

The Japanese occupation was successful in its propaganda war in Indonesia. Venerable Indonesian leaders joined in this propaganda for a Greater East Asia, and advocated that Indonesians become war workers and voluntary workers, even more than the Japanese themselves urged. The Japanese helped foster different secret organizations, which apparently competed with and opposed them, and which joined with Indonesian groups in opposition. The Japanese acted as supporters of every party so that they got all kinds of information about each one. They could even play one against the other. There were many of such Japanese achievements, including Kenpei, Kaigun, Bepang, etc.

Thus we see that the propaganda war was one of our weakest points in the past and will continue to be a weakness in the future because of the lack of intelligence of our community. In the guerilla war propaganda among people must be neatly arranged through the available channels: Firstly to defend our united front, and secondly to confuse the enemy's mind.

Sabotage against the enemy must be intensified by the people. All occasions for sabotage must be used: infiltration of the barracks, offices, enemy houses, etc. Sabotage of the occupation force's administration, of vehicles, supplies, the tearing up of railway tracks, blowing up oil supplies, setting fire to warehouses, cutting telephone wires, etc. There are many things that can be done to sabotage the enemy's war efforts and attempts at pacification. Sabotage can be employed so widely that the enemy distrusts every inhabitant and feels threatened everywhere, even in his sleep. Sabotage was continually carried out by the Atjeh people long after the Dutch defeated them.

It is common practice that an occupation army takes harsh measures against sabotage. Collective punishment, extensive torturing, even the elimination of whole kampongs and the machine-gunning of the people on a mass basis is common. Therefore, a people at war must be prepared for all the consequences so that the people's spirit will remain unbroken and will allow the guerilla army to launch even harsher measures against the enemy. The solidity of the common front of the guerillas and the people depends greatly on their ability to remain welded together. If there are any groups who surrender because of the pressure of the enemy's cruelty, the rest will easily follow their example.

The cruelty exhibited by Westerling in South Sulawesi was successful in extinguishing the guerilla war there and in paving the way for the Den Passar Conference, at which Sukawati, Tadjuddin

Noor and Nadjamuddin fought for the presidency. This situation was possible because the political front was divided. After Ratulangi and his followers were exiled, the Dutch gradually were able to break the front of non-cooperation so that the number of leaders and officials who were traitors increased. They even divided and dissolved P.N.I. (Partai Nasional Indonesia) which was set up by Tadjuddin Noor and his followers. The non-cooperative political front was broken and Westerling's cruel measures crushed the guerilla troops which had become isolated.

Once again, it must be said that a guerilla war needs a very strong fighting ideology for the people are ready to engage in a guerilla war only if there is such an ideology. The responsibility of the leaders in maintaining the people's spirit is extremely heavy. On one side the enemy offers pleasantness to the leaders, on the other side it intimidates the people with a show of harshness. This is a very dangerous form of psychological war for a people at war. It separates the leaders from the people and isolates the guerilla fighters from the people who act as its base, so that later the guerillas can be defeated little by little with either cruelty or pleasing offers.

It has been stated above that guerilla troops do not have services for maintenance usually found in an army. A guerilla war has no front line and guerillas have no rear as a regular army does. A guerilla army evades, retreats and disappears, dispersing in all directions and mingling with the people in order to elude enemy pursuit. That is why it cannot be crushed. It suddenly assembles and attacks when the enemy is withdrawing, is isolated, sleeping, exhausted, etc. When the attack is finished the guerillas disappear, not waiting for the arrival of enemy reserve troops. The guerilla emerges to attack everywhere and he disperses while withdrawing.

Since the guerilla has his starting point in the people, he prepares himself while hiding among the people. The guerilla has his roots everywhere, wherever there are people and wherever there are hiding places. The headquarters of the guerilla move according to the needs of the operation. The guerilla is very mobile and can live and rest everywhere.

The guerilla fights best in the midst of his own people, on his own territory, and to protect his own motherland. The people become his people, his friends, and his relatives, always willing to support and maintain him. He knows the people and the terrain down to the last detail. He operates in his own kampong and defends his own territory.

This is why the maintenance of the guerilla troops depends exclusively on the people. The people supply provisions and his food, thus he is able to live anywhere without being revealed to the enemy. He receives medical care everywhere; the people assist in transporting his supplies, they are ready to become his messengers for purposes of communication, they help entertain him and they aid his family. It is the people who take on themselves the responsibility pertaining to his maintenance.

It does not mean, however, that the people should give and serve him in all instances. As a guerilla fighter for the people he must attempt to make the people's burden as light as possible. If the defense of the people means excessive demands on the guerillas, their desires easily become hard to control. They become demanding in asking for provisions and help from the people. It is possible that the guerilla fighter may begin to feel that it is his right to be cared for and aided by the people. It is possible that his family will feel that it has priority in everything. This is how the perversion of a fight starts. The popular nature of the army fades away and it becomes feudal in character, something despised by the people. The guerilla begins to feel that the people should treat him as if he were a privileged person. At this stage he is no longer a people's fighter but a people's parasite, even a people's oppressor. At such a point the people will themselves go on a guerilla war against him. The people who formerly acted as his parents will turn on him and he will be annihilated by both them and the enemy.

Therefore, the matter of the amount of aid and provisions required from the people must be limited so as to remain as light a burden as possible. The guerilla fighter should attempt, as much as possible, to provide for his own needs by such means as stealing from the enemy's supplies. Moreover the guerilla fighter who does not fight every day must try to help the people with their work. Depending on the location and the availability of free time he could help in the paddy field, help maintain security in the village, use some of his energy to aid in the public health program of the people, help improve the level of learning of the people and, in general, help wherever possible. He must share his surplus food and supplies with the people. In this way the guerilla fighters continue to be considered as the people's own children. In these attempts to help the people the guerilla should not, however, forget or neglect his real duties. He should be on the alert and always be ready to improve his fighting ability

37

because in the last analysis a trained, disciplined, effective and efficient army is needed to win the war.

It is very important that there be a system and discipline in the relationship with the people. This is quite easy if there are guerilla cadres in every locality to act as intermediaries on the part of the people. These cadres must regulate and organize the aid to be both given to and received from the people. Guerillas should not act thoughtlessly so that they will create burdens and hurt the people unnecessarily.

To organize all these kinds of assistance from the people, to organize the people to become the base and service shop of the guerilla war, we need a guerilla government to execute everything on the basis of a guerilla war· During the Madiun Affair the rebels formed a national front government. The Darul Islam guerilla movement at first set up an "Islamic Council" with the purpose of improving the ways of the "National Committee" which we set up in the beginning of the revolution. In both of the above examples it was their intention to form a government which would reflect more accurately the desires of the people and, therefore, they wanted to remove the "National Committee."

Whatever may be the case, experts are gradually needed to organize all of the people's resistance against the enemy, to utilize sabotage and espionage as well as assisting, protecting and taking care of guerilla fighters. This is the work of the territorial cadres, in charge of the resistance of the people, who are active in military, community and governmental matters. These cadres were installed after our first guerilla war experiences and can be compared with the political cadres of a revolutionary movement who engage in guerilla activities. These cadres help, prod and urge on the district and village chiefs in carrying out their work for the guerilla government, guerilla community and guerilla economy. With these cadre workers a foundation is established within the people to spark a guerilla war.

8. The enemy's arsenals are the guerilla's source of weapons.

Many people say that guerilla warfare is impossible without an outside source of supply. We remember how the Russian guerilla was supplied from the air by the Red army, how the guerillas in Malaya and in the Philippines were armed by the Allies. The problem of equipment is indeed one of the serious matters for a guerilla movement. Theoretically the guerilla move·

ment must increase its arms, while attempting to decrease those of the enemy. Thus the guerilla forces must continuously grow while the enemy withers.

To accomplish the above, the arms and ammunition of the guerilla troops must necessarily come from the enemy. If aid does not come from an outside country or an allied army, which can supply aid in a continuous stream, then after the supplies that have been stockpiled are exhausted before the guerilla war can start, then the enemy must become the guerilla's supply store. The Reds in China called Chiang Kai-shek their "supply master."

The problem of arms and ammunition is a very important and difficult one in a guerilla war. For this reason nations which face the possibility of an occupation of their country in war time must prepare scattered supply stores throughout their country before the war starts. They must arrange to have supplies smuggled in from abroad. Every bit of aid from abroad must be utilized. This phase must be worked out by the political leaders. A guerilla troop cannot carry out guerilla warfare if it is out of ammunition and explosives.

However, whether or not a guerilla army has sufficient equipment or a surplus of equipment is not a necessary requirement for the guerilla troop. A guerilla war is precisely a war of the small opposing the big. The guerilla's strength lies in the fact that he carries out the guerilla war effectively, and appears and disappears wherever circumstances demand. He always determines when and where he appears and disappears, and when and where he attacks. When the enemy advances and is strong the guerilla withdraws. When the enemy retreats and is weak and exhausted the guerilla emerges with surprise attacks. The use of proper strategy and tactics is the guerilla's strength and his enemy's weakness.

Therefore, the guerilla must understand how important it is to be thrifty in men and ammunition. The more powerful one is the enemy who has many more forces. The loss of one geurilla fighter does not mean the same as the loss of one soldier to the enemy. The firing of one bullet without reason means little to the enemy.

For these reasons the geurilla troops must decide their operations only after careful planning. They should not defend or attack only to be putting up resistance or attacking. When one is overcourageous there is bound to be disaster in the end. One

39

should attack only when there is a good chance of winning, when the enemy is temporarily weak because of isolation, because the enemy is fatigued, or because the enemy is careless. When this is true, the attack will really result in the destruction of the enemy or will make the enemy serve as the guerilla's "supply master". When there is no such chance the guerilla should withdraw and disappear. It must be explained to the people so that they will not misunderstand, so that there will be no sneering that the guerilla fighters only withdraw, and that the guerilla fighters are cowards. On the other hand the tendency of some groups to pretend to be guerillas must be eliminated. These would-be guerillas take advantage of the struggle, and masquerading under the name of guerillas move from place to place, wherever they are safe, under the pretext of tactics. They are parasites, impostors and traitors to the people. A guerilla war requires both discretion and firmness to prevent and exterminate both the extremes of aggressivenness and of reluctance to make battle.

It is also very important to control unnecessary audacity on the part of units who interpret slogans as laws of strategy and tactics. Slogans such as "Defend every inch of land," "Never withdraw," "With courage to die" and "Living torpedo" are only designed to bolster the spirit and are not intended as laws for battles. Such exaggerated interpretations will demand a very high price and can cause the guerilla war to fail at a later date.

It is clear as has been explained that not every "John Doe" can become a guerilla fighter. The requirements for a guerilla are high, higher than for most ordinary soldiers.

Our earlier efforts to seize equipment from the enemy have not been considered of much importance. Generally the equipment that we used during the guerilla war was left over from the Dutch and the Japanese—supplies which we already had before the guerilla war started. Here and there we succeeded in seizing a few arms, but these did not amount to much and it did not happen very often. On the contrary it is obvious we have not been successful in our attempts to prevent loss of equipment. We should not lose our arms in battle. We should be careful that our equipment, stored here and there for use, does not fall into the enemy's hands. Several times the enemy was able to discover and capture our supply dumps because we were not edequately prepared to disperse them to safety and to scatter the supplies as would have been correct in our guerilla condition.

If the guerilla movement has no outside ally to aid it, it has to obtain its equipment from the enemy it is to continue the guerilla war. What is more, we remember that a strategic guerilla war is merely a defensive one in order to defeat the enemy at some later time. The guerilla war must be carried to a higher level and be supplemented by an ordinary war, using equipment equal to that of the enemy. We have, thus, clearly shown that the enemy's storehouses must become the guerilla troop's own stores.

It was fortunate in our case that we did not have to bring the war to such a desperate level because our domestic and foreign policies were able to use the results of our guerilla war to achieve minimum aims.

However, for the future, when the Indonesian people have to wage another guerilla war, it is necessary to realize beforehand the difficult problems that will arise in securing equipment. It must be remembered that Indonesia desires to pursue an independent foreign policy and thus stands alone from the start. Also, because of our geographic situation, islands separated from each other and from other countries by oceans, there are difficult problems to be solved in maintaining supplies in a future war. The guerilla wars we have just gone through did not force us to face this vital question.

To carry out an attack systematically and to seize the enemy's equipment and destroy him if necessary—the military aims of guerilla war—one must understand the need for a combat team which is strong enough to destroy an equal enemy. Often the guerilla leaders neglect this all important side and are satisfied with defensive resistance only. Often our guerilla commanders and brigadiers are only coordinators between the guerilla troops of one pocket and those of another, and are not able to conduct attack movements, except "general attacks," which only result in panic and do not cause the enemy any permanent damage.

9. Summary of guerilla war strategy and tactics.

Many among us, including our former and present leaders, continue to praise and honour the guerilla, the guerilla war, and the total people's defense as an effective remedy to defeat every aggression against our country. For this reason it is necessary to evaluate objectively the strategic meaning of guerilla war. A guerilla war can be dreadful and violent, it can tie up and paralyze an enemy ten times larger than the guerilla force. However, strictly speaking a guerilla war is strategically defensive and is not able to defeat an enemy. For defeat it is necessary to have a regular army which is incorrectly termed by our people as "international," i.e., its ideas are not indigenous to the Indonesian people. This term is incorrect and is the result of agitation born of an atmosphere in which we are distrustful and uneasy of all things which are not national.

Only by means of a regular army which can bring the war to a final decision and through strategic offensive can the forces of an aggressor be defeated. The guerilla army assists the regular army in achieving this decision by a war of attrition and by squeezing out the life blood of the enemy wherever he may be. This is the guerilla's function, and if there is no regular army, but only guerilla troops to carry the fight, the decision of a victory in war must be sought through ways able to liquidate or crush the enemy who at this point is already tired and frustrated, weary, and at a loss as to what to do. This does not mean that he is defeated; at the most he is willing to make a compromise.

Theoretically, guerilla troops must operate so ruthlessly and dexterously that they both seize enough equipment from the enemy and have sufficient time to gradually build up a regular army which can develop and enlarge so that it can face the enemy on "an equal basis." This is the hardest and most difficult means of conducting a guerilla war and is usually experienced by a nation which revolts against a colonizing, tyrannizing government. The spirit to oppose colonialism and tyranny awakens a rebellious movement and this gives birth to small guerilla troops who by their skillfulness gradually gain experience in organization and as they mature grows into a regular army. In the first stages more attention is given to political and psychological activities until more area has come under the control of the guerillas. In the meantime the guerilla troops grow in strength and are employed to harass the enemy's army. From this stage [the guerilla] moves on to an ordinary war until in the end the enemy is defeated.

In many cases guerilla war is only used to assist a regular army whether it belongs to the country itself or to an ally. The strategy and tactics used by guerilla fighters in either of the cases are the same.

The guerilla strategy serves to engage the enemy as much as possible, to tire out and to squeeze out his blood and to make him jittery. This is all the guerilla can hope to do since it is not intended that he defeat the enemy army. Indeed the guerilla cannot openly oppose except by attacking suddenly with a large concentration of force and disappearing again as rapidly as possible. It is not right to say that the movements of the guerilla are advances and retreats, which give the impression of a back and forth movement. The guerilla emerges and disappears, pops up and down everywhere so that the enemy cannot locate him but feels that attacks come from everywhere.

The strategy of the guerilla is to force the enemy to spread out in all directions and to tie him down as much as possible by forcing him to set up permanent bases. Thus, the enemy is spread out, broken up, and nailed down, while the guerilla fighters can continue to sap his strength. Large groups of the enemy must be avoided or at most annoyed like being pinched everywhere. Small enemy groups must be surrounded and destroyed and their equipment seized. The most important targets are convoys, trains, telephone exchanges, etc., which the enemy needs behind the front lines in order to serve the battle fields. Political and psychological aims in this guerilla war are to punish collaborators who are in the service of the enemy, [to sabotage] the apparatus of the occupation administration, etc.

To be able to emerge and disappear without trace but always with effective results guerillas need a "base" in the midst of the enemy position, and must be served by the people who are available in all the places that the constantly moving guerilla fighters stay. These "bases" must be chosen in such areas where the land and people fulfill certain conditions. The terrain must be difficult for the enemy to cross, must contain enough hideouts and escape routes for the guerillas, and be inaccessible to the enemy with his heavy equipment. The area should be a place where the guerilla could force the enemy to face him on equal terms in regard to weapons and troops. The terrain must be familiar to the guerilla fighters and the land must be inhabited by spirited people believing in the same ideology as the guerillas or at least friendly to the guerillas. The conditions as to land and people are most favourable if the guerilla troops are based in their own village among their own relatives.

Guerilla fighters need the most complete and recent information about their enemy. The information should not be outdated. The guerilla troops must be able to avoid the mopping-up operations of the enemy and must always be able to choose the right targets in order to inflict the greatest injury on the enemy. For this reason guerilla troops need secrecy, mobility and flexibility. Thus they can appear and disappear whenever and wherever their operations wear out, weaken and confuse the enemy. This is only possible when they receive aid, protection and care from the peoples These conditions are thus found in the areas which are controlled by the guerilla troops, meaning their own base areas. Thus one must not reject the guerilla tactic of luring the enemy into their pocket area. Often leaders who do not understand have pointed to it as a sign of weakness if a guerilla was not able to defend "his area." It is true that in a guerilla war the enemy is not prevented from entering any area. It is even true that he is lured into such areas that are difficult to pass and that are some distance away with the purpose of tiring him, lengthening his lines of supply, thus creating opportunities for the guerilla troops to attack and destroy him. Do not expect a linear defense by the guerilla in regard to his pockets of resistance. This is why it is wrong when a guerilla government administration is established. Every pocket must be prepared to receive and face the enemy's patrols in a game of cat and mouse.

The guerilla character is reflected in the desa administration, communication, people, etc., who at any time can evacuate. The commando posts and communication posts are operated in this way. The offices of the district chief and village chief, the guerilla clinic, the guerilla kitchen, etc., must meet this requirement. In order to implement this "civil resistance" in the right guerilla manner, guidance from the "territorial cadres" is needed.

The guerilla state of mind penetrates all guerilla government offices and the people as a whole, which from one place to another is able to avoid the enemy's mopping-up operations and maintains the people's spirit of resistance. For this reason [bases] have to be simply set up, mobile and flexible. Our villages have already mastered the skill of playing "cat and mouse" with the Dutch patrols.

A guerilla war is only effective if the guerilla troops really can destroy targets and seize equipment. Guerilla troops playing cat-and-mouse with the enemy will eventually become fatigued from being pursued so long. It is necessary to follow a plan of tactics to annihilate the enemy piecemeal. Annihilation and seizure of the enemy's equipment can only be accomplished by systematic battles carried out at calculated places and times. Often the commanders of the guerilla troops are content if they continue to survive the encircling actions and raids of the enemy, often by temporarily dividing and dispersing the men who find safety individually and reassemble after the enemy has passed. Such passive defense is certainly not adequate. We must concentrate forces tactically at places and times where the target is suitable as has been explained above.

44

To do this, it is necessary that each commander delegate authority to subordinate officers as in a regular army. Guerillas do not always fight in small units, but at certain times and places must assemble and fight in a larger unit. An enemy target of one platoon must be attacked by a combat team of one company or more, a target of one company must be attacked by one batallion. Only in this way is an enemy immobilized, because unless he moves in a larger force he is in constant danger.

The war in Indo-China has proved that persevering guerilla fighters can raise their army to the division level and that even though its equipment was not very modern compared with that of the enemy, by using guerilla warfare and supported by a burning spirit they could gradually change from the defensive to the offensive, in spite of the fact that the enemy had complete control of the air.

10. The principle requirements for a guerilla war are a people who will give assistance, sufficient geographic room, and a war of long duration.

In summary it becomes obvious that there are several essential conditions which need to be fulfilled to reach victory in a guerilla war. These are: a people to give the guerillas assistance, a favourable geography and a long war. These conditions have been explained before. It is natural that the aiding people should be strong of heart, determined in their ideology, firm in the spirit of freedom, and tough in enduring the hardships of a long struggle. Those people who are only outwardly inspired during peacetime, those who are accustomed to a soft life and are not familiar with the simple life, are of little help in a guerilla war. The geographical condition demands that the territory in which the guerilla troops operate is sufficiently large and difficult to travel over. Its terrain should consist of few highways, many mountains and hills, and if possible, forests and undergrowth. These are the hideouts for the guerillas and it is here that they are most difficult to be reached. It is here that the enemy's superiority in technology and equipment is of little avail to him. He is not in a more favourable position because of his modern weapons and means of transportation. The two sides face each other as simple infantry.

It is common we feel confined when we look at a map because a map is a small, incomplete picture of reality. Pockets and corridors which look narrow on a map prove quite large in reality. Arrows pointing out the direction of the enemy's movement and his posts, appear to cover the face of the map, but in reality they are only spots in an area more than sufficiently large. An encirclement apparently closed on the map still allows enough of an opening in reality. These facts were experienced by us during our fight for independence.

In order to fulfill the third condition, that of a long war, it is necessary that the people and the guerilla army are truly determined, and will patiently fight while suffering until victory is achieved in the final battle. The people, and the leaders especially, must be firm in resisting the enemy's intimidation which is alternated with enticing persuasion. They must firmly refuse to collaborate, must continue non-cooperation and must prefer further sufferings rather than receive employment from the enemy, protection of their homes by the enemy or have their cities pacified by the enemy. We witnessed the breakdown of the guerilla front at the end of 1946 in South Celebes because the leaders in the end dropped their non-cooperative attitude, an action which caused the isolation of the guerilla movement and allowed Westerling to succeed in destroying it. A firm attitude to continue the guerilla struggle can only come forth from a spirit of freedom, a spirit of struggle and a simple way of life.

Many experts have stated that there is another factor contributing to a successful guerilla war: foreign aid in the form of equipment, brought in by an ally through the air, over seas or over land, through smuggling or other similar operations. The task of the guerillas would indeed be easier if they were given such supplies as were regularly delivered in the past war in West Europe and the Pacific. The Allies dropped from the air and smuggled by ships many supplies of arms to the partisans. From the previous analysis, however, we saw that one of the main qualities of a guerilla was that he must make the enemy's warehouse his own. One example of failure of a guerilla was is shown by the German guerilla movement in 1945 when Germany was occupied by the Allies and there was no hope of help from abroad. The principle reason for failure here was that the people were exhausted and a feeling of despair was everywhere. The grip of the secret police had killed off all initiative and dynamic energy in the people.

The guerilla and anti-guerilla war will in the future assume a more important place in the study of warfare, and must always be taken into consideration. Preparation and education for guerilla and anti-guerilla war is required in addition to ordinary military education. On the other hand, for an army which is considering guerilla war, the above is not sufficient since it is limited only to the preparation for guerilla war. The army must be well trained as a regular army to engage in both guerilla war and in anti guerilla war. The situations which it may have to face will be varied and changeable. The army must be able to adapt itself to both situations so that it will be able to cope with conditions in all phases of the development of the war.

Another condition that must be fulfilled as completely as possible is that of adequate preparation in peacetime. We must be certain that no matter what area of our country is occupied, the enemy will be opposed by a guerilla movement in that locality. Even though its planning may be local the guerilla movement will not be separated from the overall war and the strategic operation of the headquarters of the armed forces. It is necessary that the army make preparations for the execution of its duties in relation to the guerilla war. These preparations are of course not complete in every detail; they are only basic plans and preparations. Preparations of an educational nature include those which aim at teaching the guerilla units the skills of guerilla and anti-guerilla activities, as well as those necessary for the erection of educational centres in certain areas to exclusively train young men in people's resistance. Also necessary are forces designed especially to train agents for propaganda, sabotage, communication, paratroops, intelligence, etc. Such training is very important. Material and equipment, such as armament, ammunition, explosives, means of communication, must be readied and scattered over the areas where the guerilla has bases. Special preparation should be made for subversive activity in cities, intelligence, sabotage and propaganda. We certainly must realize that such intensive and extensive preparations can only be disclosed (?) during the first stages of the war or threat of war.

In establishing a guerilla organization, it is necessary that in addition to the preparations of their own army, as has been explained above, the guerillas must make efforts to organize and educate the people in each area. The people must carry out various tasks in the field of passive resistance, such as intelligence and espionage, propaganda and communication; and activities in the field of active resistance, such as sabotage and guerilla tactics. Since these are difficult tasks, it is essential that rigid psychological and physical conditions be fulfilled. A few well trained nuclei are more valuable than many unorganized mobs.

The regular army itself must prepare to disperse and form guerilla troops when and if it is separated from the main force, and it must be able to re-unite these guerilla units into a regular army for the ordinary war. It must be able to engage in different kinds of warfare when circumstances require. It must conduct a guerilla war using combat teams in company, batallion and regimental strength. It must be trained to fight in a regular war in the usual arrangement of companies in a batallion, batallions in a regiment and regiments in a division. To carry out the above great mobility on foot is required so that the force can move rapidly over any type of terrain.

In the last world war Russia had its separate guerilla headquarters subordinate to the Supreme Command of the Armed Forces. It was from here that the regional commanders in various areas received instructions and here strategic and tactical coordination with the regular army units was arranged. Here provision for supply to guerilla troops operating behind the enemy's lines was organized. Usually supplies were dropped from the air. There were even secret airfields operated for the benefit of guerilla fighters.

In the case of Russia, because only part of the country was occupied by the enemy, the guerilla headquarters was still in the area controlled by Russia. If the whole area is occupied, as happened with our Republic, the Supreme Command must be able to operate in pockets of the occupied area. Of course the communication between the leadership and the subordinate units is more difficult. It is necessary to establish a system of leadership and communication which is suited to the condition of being in a pocket, and which is at the same time mobile and underground. Another solution is to transfer the supreme command to a friendly country; however, in this case its value for the guerilla fighters' morale is less since they desire the leadership to be in their midst.

The condition of the terrain on the larger islands of Indonesia is suitable for the conduct of guerilla warfare; there is sufficient land although it is not comparable with the expanses of the European and Asian continents. There are many mountainous and jungle areas where passage is difficult and there are few roads. The country has many wet and dry ricefields which produce food and the rivers and forests yield fish and game. Even on the island of Java, which is one of the smaller islands, the most thickly populated and with the most roads, it was shown that there was ample opportunity to conduct a guerilla war even with combat teams at batallion strength. The cities and highways were in the hands of the enemy, but the villages and pathways and narrow footpaths were the guerilla's possession. The guerillas were even able to blockade the occupied cities.

Being an archipelago, Indonesia is difficult for the enemy to enter from abroad since he has to cross the ocean. Also, during a guerilla period, communication and transportation from abroad are made difficult and regular supplies are cut off. An enemy who can cross the ocean to attack us will also be able to control the sea communication of our archipelago. This does not mean that we can not sneak, as guerilla fighters, from island to island, or even from abroad in spite of having to sail in small boats. In the past we have been able to smuggle guerilla fighters in and out of Java, Kalimantan, Celebes, Moluccas, Malaya, Philippines, etc. We were able to penetrate the modern and fully equipped Dutch coast guard.

The people are in general in the best position to defend the freedom of their territory against outside aggression. However, in South East Asia it has been proved that this condition has been easily utilized by a foreign enemy to wage a guerilla war against some of us. There is enough political, economic, social and psychological chaos in our young nation and there is enough misery and ignorance everywhere which can be used to raise guerilla forces to fight a guerilla war against us in our rear. Such troops in a future war will certainly be equipped and activated as completely as possible by the enemy. Such non-direct attacks, such jabs from the rear, can always spread and become a civil war and in this way relieve the task of the aggressor's army. It is common strategy in recent years to employ cold or secret war during peacetime to eat away a potential enemy from the inside so that he can be invaded and subjugated easily and rapidly. Especially young and backward countries like ours are subject to becoming victims to such a plan.

For this reason, in order to fulfill the main requirement upon which a victory in a guerilla war rests, namely that of passive and active aid from the people, there must be stable conditions within the country prior to the war.

There are those who say that a guerilla war brings more disaster than blessing, arguing that a guerilla war is indeed destructive in nature. The destruction is intensive and extensive, not only materially because it uses sabotage and scorched earth, but also what is more, it causes psychological, political and social damage. A guerilla fighter is bred on a spirit of destruction and is not easily repatriated into the community as an ordinary citizen. If one is accustomed to using harsh and brutal measures, he does not easily change and become a tactful and patient man again.

49

If one is used to being active in underground activities, he is not easily moved to pay attention to legal rules. Most standards and values common in law-abiding countries and ordered societies have tumbled down and many have become old fashioned. The spirit of revolution, of guerilla warfare and of scorched earth is aimed at destroying the whole existing religious, legal, socio-economic order which forms the organization of the dominating power. How can the guerilla accept again a legal, political and socio-economic situation since to him it has the taint of the old system? Many nations and countries, in fact, continue to be chaotic years and decades after a guerilla war overturns and rubs out the ethical, legal standards which are normally found in a society. Burning, sabotage, killing and kidnapping at the expense of the enemy have a heroic value. To have participated in guerilla activities makes it difficult for one to adapt oneself to an ordered society, a society based on law.

Experiences in guerilla war have shown that retaliatory measures from both sides become increasingly cruel. The spirit of revenge drowns out sound reasoning and the sense of fair play. The anti-guerilla units retaliate against the people collectively because they aid or hide the guerilla fighters. The anti-guerilla units torture the members and relatives of guerilla troops to make them fearful; sometimes whole villages are burned to the ground. The guerilla fighters take revenge by being even more inhuman; every collaborator and every enemy soldier who falls in their hands is tortured just as mercilessly. Be that as it may, it must be remembered that guerilla activities are not the final aim; they are merely an effort to defend an ideology, to defend freedom, the principles of human rights and the holy rights of a nation, which determine the future of generations to come. Every nation desiring to continue as a nation, if it does not want to be subjected by another, must defend itself. A nation is fortunate if it has sufficient military power and war potential to fight a regular war. However, if that is not possible because it lacks military forces, the nation must resort to guerilla warfare, a type of warfare meant to be fought by a small against a large party, with all of the necessary consequences. "Peace loving but above all freedom loving" is the slogan of every selfrespecting nation. The histories of guerilla wars have shown that nations with a strong spirit to defend their freedom have gained back their freedom in the end by waging a guerilla war, although sacrifices were very great and the destruction to the whole life of the nation immeasurable. Filled with this victorious spirit, such nations have been able to overcome the damage suffered by the fighters and the country. No sacrifice, if pure and sincere, is in vain!

As our own people are concerned and who, as part of their task of maintaining their sovereignty and freedom in the near future, will need to conduct a guerilla war, it must be realized from the start that a guerilla war means suffering. A guerilla war fought while pursuing an independent foreign policy will receive no outside support and must be necessarily a long war. These facts must always be borne in mind in order to defend and maintain freedom which has been achieved at such a high cost of lives and so much suffering by the people.

11. A total people's war needs a unified leadership, not only at the national level but also down to the local level.

Today, war is a total people's war. A war must be concluded with the defeat of the enemy's military forces, but to accomplish this it is also necessary that the enemy be attacked in the political, psychological, economic and social fields. In a total war it is necessary that all phases of the people's life are defended. This can only be done properly when all of the people's potential energy is activated. War is an effort undertaken by a nation to achieve a definite aim—to defeat the enemy. There is really only one strategy in war, of which the military, political, psychological and economic strategies constitute parts. Therefore, there is no independent military strategy, no independent political strategy, nor are there independent psychological or socio-economic strategies. It has been explained in the first chapter that it is not the armies any longer who fight but two entire nations. The science of war does not only consist of the knowledge of tactics, strategy and logistics, but also embraces political science, propaganda, economics and sociology. It is not sufficient for the leaders to merely be tacticians as in earlier times, but they also are required to master matters dealing with political war, economic war and propaganda. The leader in a war who restricts himself to military affairs will be a failure because he will be powerless in the political, propaganda and economic wars which are the foundation for victory in a modern war.

To achieve this aim a leadership is required that is absolute in character and that, as we have been shown from experiences in history, should be centrally controlled. In former times it was the king who served as the absolute leader, but in the past war we saw various governments assume the same power. The total

51

people's war in Russia was led by Marshall J.V. Stalin who held the post of Premier, Party leader and Supreme Commander. The Nazis in Germany were organized in a total people's war with Hitler as the Head of the State, Leader of the Party and Commander in Chief. The British were led by Winston Churchill who held the posts of Prime Minister and Minister of Defense and who was de facto Supreme Commander and Leader of the combined Chiefs of Staff. The United States was led by F.D. Roosevelt who was President, Head of the Cabinet and Supreme Commander and who was directly Leader of the Joint Chiefs of Staff. These leaders were at the same time the political and military leaders. They were not merely symbols of the total people's war but they were its real, active leaders. They were able to coordinate and unify all sectors of the war—military, political, psychological, social and economic—in order to obtain the one aim of the war, decided upon by the representatives of the people. The original constitution of the Republic of Indonesia proclaimed in 1945 that the posts of President, Prime Minister and Supreme Commander are all held by one man. The emergency condition in which the life and death of the state hung in the balance necessitated such a total leadership and demanded that the leader in war should not only be constitutional and symbolic but genuine and active, being a political, military, psychological, social and economic leader. Every time our country is in danger, and the Parliament is able to convene, as happened on 3 July and the Madiun Affair, the parliament transferred all power to the Head of State.

It is common that a nation takes such measures as concentrating leadership at the highest level when danger threatens the life of the state. In this way a complete concentration can take place in an ordinary war at a national level so that the top national leadership can still communicate with the outlying areas and troops.

In a guerilla war, in those areas occupied by the enemy, or when the whole territory is occupied by the enemy, because organized resistance has broken down leadership must be decentralized. Guerilla war is then conducted on a regional basis. A total people's war is carried out regionally and is only directed and coordinated by the national leadership. The military, political, psychological, economic and social war are conducted on a regional basis. Complete decentralization is an essential feature of guerilla war. It is a mistake that a country engages in guerilla war and does not decentralize the total leadership. We suffered somewhat in West Java from such a mistake during the first guerilla war. This disrupted the attempt to make the war a total people's war. The same mistake was made which resulted in the proclamation by the guerillas in Kalimantan to promote Hassan Basri as their military governor.

In the second guerilla war on Java we used to the fullest such a concentrated form of leadership. The lurah became the top official of all the village, the K.O.D.M. (Commander Military Sub-District) of the sub-district, and the K.D.M. (Commander Military District) of the Kabupaten, the K.M.D. (Commander Military Area) of the residency, the Military Governor of the territory and the headquarters for the island. The civilian employees under the Governor, Resident, Regent and District head were integrated into the guerilla government.

In drafting the rules for a system of defense, and we hereby think mainly of guerilla war as playing a major part in it, we must keep in mind that the quality of leadership and authority will shape the nature of the guerilla war. Rules which divide the leadership at the national level will prevent the unification and activation of the sum of all war efforts. This means that the total people's war is prevented from coming into being, that the seeds of defeat have been planted from the beginning. In the event of a guerilla war, the laws and rules that are drawn up must be consistent with the fact that a guerilla war is regional and is fought in pockets. A decentralized leadership is thus called for. If this requirement is overlooked, then the anti-guerilla enemy carrying out its conception of total war with its stress on politico-psychological, socio-economical aspects, rather than military espects, will hit and destroy sector by sector. Westerling's successful terror in South Celebes can be attributed to the fact that it was based on the results of a cleverly guided, politico-psychological and socio-economical war. This first caused the whole non-cooperative front to collapse and then was responsible for the Den Passar conference where those who had championed cooperation as well as those who had championed non-cooperation were competing against each other for the position of "president".

We can say the same about the law which prepares for the concentration of power at the top level as a temporary measure. A war situation or emergency situation, when the life of the state is endangered, can force a nation to put aside temporarily the usual laws, the usual rights and duties, or even the constitution, in order to facilitate the organizing of a total people's war. The authority of the people only goes so far as to allow them to decide on war or peace, which leads to the next step: the state of emergency, the key for the preservation of democracy.

We have gained some experiences already from the short struggle for our independence. The unity and unanimity of leadership is a necessary condition for a perfect total people's war.

12. The anti-guerilla war must aim at severing the guerilla fighters from their base within the people, and must therefore emphasize political, psychological and economic actions. The guerilla must be opposed with his own tactics consisting of offensive actions carried out in a mobile, flexible fashion.

The anti-guerilla war is an attempt at pacification. It consists largely of constructive efforts while an ordinary war is largely destructive.

In studying guerilla war it is best to conclude with an analysis of anti-guerilla strategy which eliminates the total people's resistance, whether it takes the form of active guerilla fighting and sabotage, or whether it is of a more passive nature, such as underground movements, propaganda, and intelligence. Every invading army must be prepared for the existence of guerilla troops behind his front lines. However, in the case of young countries in South East Asia, they must constantly be on the alert for guerilla activities in their territory in peace as well as in war· These countries which are backward in all aspects and which have suffered terribly as a result of their history and which have come to know about guerilla activities and underground movements, are still experiencing internal guerilla movements. The unstable conditions of these countries and peoples, the political, economic and social chaos and their demoralization and confusion are all easy targets for hired guerillas who work for the interests of foreign and domestic circles. The unstable conditions give birth to a fifth column and a civil war within the boundaries of the victim nation. Domestic political quarrels make use of guerilla activities and underground resistance. Anti-guerilla responsibility in its broad sense is a responsibility that never ends for many countries, especially for the young countries that have emerged in the last two centuries. (Balkan, Middle East, South America, South East Asia) It is clear that any future enemy of ours from abroad will utilize to the utmost guerilla movements and underground movements to weaken us from within, to break us to pieces and to cause our collapse.

54

Guerilla war carried out as a resistance movement of the people is of a total nature. Therefore, the anti-guerilla war also must assume a total character. This means that the anti-guerilla movement must be able to realize what are the politico-ideological and socio-economic problems that give rise to and nourish such guerilla resistance For the aggressor it is easy to see these problems. But for the governments facing them on a day-to-day basis as a domestic war it is difficult to analyze the situation. They are unable to be objective enough to recognize the sources of guerilla strength or the roots with which the guerilla is nourished and secured. Such a country is not able to oppose the guerilla with a system and organization of an equally total nature in all phases of the guerilla war. The main aim of anti-guerilla strategy is to separate the people from the guerilla. Only on this basis can an anti-guerilla operation of a military nature be successful. The elimination of the guerilla bands is of a secondary nature.

The reasons which spur people to revolt and start a guerilla war are varied. Very often it is to defend or seize national independence as happened in Spain against Napoleon, in Russia against Napoleon, in China against Japan, in America against Britain, in the Arab countries against Turkey and in South East Asia against colonialism. Sometimes it is a fight of a people who are oppressed by their own national government as were the Red revolts in Russia and China. Sometimes it is for lesser reasons, such as provincialism and political differences of opinion as we are experiencing in Indonesia. The source of these inner forces must be studied and understood. The crux of the problem is whether the anti-guerilla movement brings to the people a better ideology or at least an improvement of their fate, an improvement which can be felt directly. An anti-guerilla war in the interest of colonialism or domination cannot be successful except when the people involved are already divided and shattered among themselves by internal conflicts such as endless controversies among the leaders, dictatorship, corruption and all such things that disgust and demoralize the people. A healthy people, vital from within, cannot be colonized or tyrannized unless they are entirely destroyed.

Such an internal affair can be compared to two brothers with different ideologies and different sets of values. The basis is a political controversy at times accentuated by socio-economic and psychological problems. That is why victory in this field, i.e., the political field must be ensured. Unless the truth of the ideology of the anti-guerilla group is demonstrated, the guerilla will win in the end. Maybe for a temporary period they can be forced underground or made to withdraw by military force. But if their soul is not defeated the ideology will continue to grow and in time it will metamorphosize and reappear as a revolt or guerilla movement at a time when a domestic or foreign situation occupies the thoughts and energy of the government or weakens the position of the government in power. It is thus shown, especially in the case of an anti guerilla movement during the period of a domestic war, that its political, socio-economic and psychological measures are essential and necessary conditions to paving the way for a successful military operation, such as the elimination of guerilla troops. The political-ideological victory and the socio-economic and psychological victories are the foundation on which a military victory must be achieved.

All operations are conducted within the framework of a total over-all plan in which it is clearly decided which are the more important, and which are the mere technical operations. A military operation has never been shown to extinguish guerilla opposition of a significant nature.

The manner in which anti-guerilla fighters behave towards the people greatly influences the course of events. When the German army invaded the Ukraine in Russia the people received them with joy because there had already been discord between the Ukraine and Russia. However, Hitler and his Gestapo ignored the principles of guerilla war and they were extremely cruel. They even expressed their intention to enslave the Ukraine nation. Gradually the people rose up and organized themselves in a guerilla movement that became more and more active until it made the position of the German army hazardous. The Red army attack on Stalingrad was made possible largely by the disturbances that the Ukraine guerillas inflicted upon the German army. The atrocities permitted by the generals in Napoleon's army in Spain, including torturing of the people, violating the honour of the women, and public executions of rebels, created an intense people's resistance which aided the British army in defeating the French in that territory. The Japanese occupation army in China also experienced the same reactions from the people making its occupation very difficult.

To ensure the right attitude and good behaviour of an occupation army and an anti-guerilla army is a primary condition for conquering the guerillas. Desires must be bridled, the spirit of revenge must be controlled and cruelty must be avoided. Collective arrests, collective punishment, and the burning of civilian house because these civilians assisted or hid guerilla fighters become the most potent weapons to serve the guerilla cause since it makes them appear even more as the people's protectors or avengers against tyranny and injustice. On the other hand, the anti-guerilla members must work for true justice and virtue. They must practice justice in action, maintaining the principles of humanity, and everything that creates and increases the feeling of appreciation and respect of the people. The most important thing is to please the people. This is the basic anti-guerilla strategy. Only in this way will the guerilla forces lose their allies, their bases, and their "institutions" which take care of them and give them protection. Only in this way can the guerilla be shorn of his strength.

A knowledge of the people, their ideas, their customs and their problems becomes an excellent weapon in the hands of the anti-guerilla; but just to know them means only to be in the possesion of the weapon; the weapon must be utilized to the best possible advantage in order to gradually win the people's heart and to weaken the guerilla's ties with the people. The people adhere to certain ideas, nurture certain desires and needs and look forward to obtaining certain ideals. They will be able to discriminate which side can guarantee the achievement of their aims and needs of which side can better provide these needs, and it is the side which can furnish them that will finally be supported. This side then will gain the final victory. A guerilla war is in principle merely an ideological war.

It may happen that the anti-guerilla side will show expertness and skill in psychological war and achieve a tactical conquest over part of the population, but such a victory is only important in that the troops gain time; it is not decisive. It creates an advantageous opportunity to prepare for the main fight, but it does not mean that victory has been achieved. The psychological war, mentioned above, is the one that intimidates, frightens the people, divides the leaders of the people among themselves and separates the leaders from their followers. It professes to free the people from the deception of their leaders and from the coercion of the guerillas. Such statements will only be successful if they are true, or when the leaders and guerillas are not perfect. However, when the people and the guerilla movement are really united, because their fight is sincere, such efforts are useless.

In this connection it is very necessary that the anti-guerilla side stir up the people's forces by using the people's leaders. The anti-guerilla activities will prove a failure if they only operate with an army, especially a foreign army or a mercenary army. It will prove a failure when the people's forces cannot be encouraged to support its cause. Anti guerilla efforts must be aimed at attracting the influential leaders of the people to their side by using all kinds of maneuvers. If possible the people must not directly feel the coercion and needs of the anti-guerilla side, but these must be channelled through the medium of the people's leaders. The ordinary life of the people should not be disturbed; their customs and religion should be maintained. Finally the ideal situation would be that the people would actively participate in their own security, defend their house and premises against the guerilla and actively inform on guerilla movements. At this stage it is clear that the guerilla movement has been severed from most of the people; the guerilla movement has lost its popular appeal. The benefits of this phase, however, will be lost at once if the anti-guerilla forces are improper, unfair and undisciplined in their actions. Actions that do not concern the main aim of the fight, but only the interests of an individual or clique, although they may happen only a few times, can pain the people's heart greatly. The people cannot place their faith in a person or group who fights for high ideals if that person nor group itself has a low character and behaves cruelly.

In connection with this matter the attitude towards and treatment of guerilla fighters must be tactful, and in accordance with the high ideals and fine spirit of the anti-guerilla, but at the same time they must be firm and resolute when neccessary.

The psychological war attempts to obtain information about the tensions and discords among the people, especially among the leaders or between the leaders and the followers. This knowledge can be used to divide them, but if only rumours and slanders are used it will not aid in the success of the anti-guerilla activities. This is the most vulnerable weakness of the guerilla. The knowledge must be transmitted to the guerilla side that only the leadership and not the rank and file are the guilty ones. It must be emphasized, however, that in carrying out such psychological moves the slander and provocation will only be of temporary value. As soon as the truth about such slander and provocation comes out, it will eventually harm the side which has used it. Against a leader with a clean and meritous fighting record, slander and provocation are of no avail. They may temporarily have some effect, but eventually they will strengthen his position.

A war of ideas must be fought on the basis of actual facts and must be transmitted to the people and to the followers. Indeed, it often happens that both sides use slander, provocation and rumours in a very cheap manner. On the other hand, any trite controversy or negligence on the part of the guerilla based on true happenings can be used with good results by the anti-guerilla group.

In this connection it is clear that guerilla prisoners must be treated with justice and decency. It is wrong to label them without further thought as terrorists or extremists, or to call them bandits, agitators, etc. Only when a large group of guerrillas have been imprisoned is there a chance to crush the remnants who stubbornly refuse to surrender. It is most important to win the hearts and thoughts of the guerilla members themselves, especially those who are caught, by displaying an attitude that is right and fair, by proving that the aim of the anti-guerilla is higher and by other further attempts to change their way of thinking. In this connection it is clear that if the anti-guerilla party is in the possession of facts about its own vices and does not correct them, then such attempts will prove unsuccessful.

With the explanation above it is clear that activities in the political-ideological, socio-economic and psychological fields are important; they are not separate activities but they form one set of efforts. Only progress in these fields can form a basis for a military solution because a military anti-guerilla solution without these necessary conditions will not give successful results. Military actions are only an auxiliary part of the main operations. The records of anti-guerilla activities sufficiently prove their failure because they accentuated mainly the military operations. On the other hand, do not think that a military solution is unnecessary. Every guerilla movement has a nucleus which will refuse to surrender and besides, military guerilla actions can only be opposed by purely military opposition, such as guarding places which are significant targets for the guerilla, protecting the people, and above all pursuing the guerilla troops and destroying them in battle. It is urgent to lay stress on the fact that to destroy them with military might as stated above, will always fail as long as the guerilla fighters can conceal themselves among the people and call for help, as long as they have their base within the people. It is this that is not primarily a military matter, but largely a matter of political, psychological and socio-economic concern.

In the military field, movements must be carried out swiftly; aggressive attacks must be launched suddenly and unexpectedly. In short, the anti-guerilla troops must use the same tactics as the guerilla troops. The requirements for successful guerilla warfare, such as mobility, flexibility, aggressiveness and skill must be surpassed by the anti-guerillas. Since a guerilla is not satisfied with only retreating, but must destroy, this should also become an anti-guerilla tactic. The guerilla can only be beaten and conquered by his own method of fighting. It is true that anti-guerilla enterprises demand far more forces than the guerilla activities and it is important that an excess of forces be available to the anti-guerillas.

The usual arrangement of infantry units is not suitable for this anti-guerilla task. Anti-guerilla units should be light, they should carry light equipment, at the most a light mortar or machine gun, radio communication that is light and easy to handle. It is important that they can be transported rapidly, either by air or on the road to such areas where guerilla units are reported. It is of paramount importance that they can walk fast on the field of operation, and are able to go on long distances for a considerable time and at great speed while surmounting all kinds of natural barriers such as underbrush, mountains and hills, rivers, etc. They should be quick on their feet and have great endurance. Thus these fast teams, moving for days on isolated terrain must be equipped with provisions which can follow them. On the one hand, it is important to carry sufficient provisions, on the other hand, the team must be light in order to be mobile. For this reason they should live, as much as possible, from the terrain itself or if this is not possible supplies should be airdropped.

It is important to know the terrain of the operation. Accurate and complete maps are necessary and all efforts should be made to obtain information about the terrain. Therefore, newly arrived troops cannot be assigned to anti-guerilla warfare in an unfamiliar area. They need time to become acquainted with the area, to study it carefully and to obtain skill in that locality. The skill to move swiftly through an area is one of the guerilla's greatest advantages, and must also be mastered by the anti-guerilla troops. They must be able to move through areas which ordinarily are impossible to pass. To accomplish this, units must specialize in certain areas and transfers from one unit to another should be avoided as much as possible, since it takes a long time to become thoroughly familiar with an area.

The more modern anti-guerilla teams employ radio sets, airplanes and helicopters to meet the requirements for an anti-guerilla campaign more perfectly. From the air the commander can study the terrain. Planes can drop anti-guerilla paratroops at any place and they can also drop supplies limited only by the type of terrain which is not always suitable for dropping. A helicopter can land people and supplies practically anywhere and can land and remove wounded fighters. Light radio sets are perfect for connecting the commander with his troops and the troops with each other. The only disadvantage to such modern tools if not used with sufficient strategy, is they will serve as a warning to the guerilla fighters, so that they can disappear or can go out of the area.

Because of the requirement of mobility efforts have been made to organize special infantry companies who receive commando training and are trained for parachute jumping so as to produce the perfect anti-guerilla team equipped with the most appropriate weapons for a movement against such guerillas. What is more, this mobility becomes a means of avoiding the necessity of stationing detachments of troops everywhere to guard against the guerilla. The TNI which is still in the initial stage of its organization has used planes to transport guerilla troops and supplies to distant, isolated patrols. Several suggestions have been made to concentrate all activities on commando troops which could appear anywhere as the "perfect" guerilla. They can be flown anywhere to wipe out guerilla troops. Apart from the fact that the secrecy of the movement is lost by the approach of an airplane and the technical difficulties involved in dropping supplies and transporting the wounded, the most important matter of anti-guerilla war has not received ample attention. This is that it is very difficult to know where the guerilla troops are located and is not easy to detect them. Even though the perfect forces may be available, the question is "where to strike." This is one of the strengths of the guerilla troops. They can spring up and disappear at any place at once. It is certain that the existence of such highly trained anti-guerilla troops can aid the efforts of the regular infantry if the targets are clearly known, but this is seldom the case. It becomes a very mobile reserve combat troop for the regular infantry and this is the only advantage.

It is sufficiently clear that the command in such anti-guerilla activities must be decentralized. The commander of each column on the move must be given wide authority and must be allowed much initiative. On the other hand these commanders must have many tricks in store and must be prepared to improvise. A high degree of individuality is desired.

A major problem is that of obtaining information on the whereabouts of guerilla units. When contact is established with the guerillas, it must be maintained so that the guerillas can be destroyed at a later date.

Intelligence about the guerilla fighters is extremely difficult to obtain because they move through the terrain and the people like lice. The anti-guerilla troops are like blind men let loose in the bushes, not knowing which way is north or south. It is therefore clear how important is such intelligence. It is necessary to gradually organize a wide net of intelligence in the society. It is necessary that intelligence groups be very mobile so that when they find traces of guerilla fighters they will be able to follow them without losing them. It is necessary that communication tools are of the best, when possible, small radio transmitters will do. These intelligence workers themselves need much equipment since they are the eyes and ears of the anti-guerilla troops.

The main effort must stress the formation of special anti-guerilla troops which are fast moving, aggressive and omnipresent. Then these very mobile troops need eyes and ears; these senses must also be highly mobile. Then a significant force for anti-guerilla activities will exist. Furthermore, stationary elements are also needed, including guards as well as intelligence and espionage quarters. Stationary does not mean that they wait passively but are actively patrolling and on the move. These elements cover the area like a net, but a net which does not try to economize on forces.

The nature of anti-guerilla measures must be offensive, aggressive and active. Every sign of passiveness, waiting, and defensive actions are wrong. It will take months to wipe out a guerilla force which is fast-hitting. Protection of significant places, escorting convoys and such actions which have basically a defensive meaning must be carried out with a sense of active attack. Protection will be effective only with active patrolling in different directions and at different times passing through and exploring the surroundings of the place which must be guarded. It is true that the guerilla must be fought in his own way, must be opposed with his own weapons, but this does not mean that there are no defensive tasks and stationary guards at all. Certainly, there must be defensive tasks to preserve security in the controlled areas and bases. There should always be stationary guards, guarding the important buildings. However, such duties must not be wasteful of personnel so that as many troops as possible can actively be on patrol. With all this moving the guerilla feels pursued and feels the narrowness of the area in which he moves. He feels pressed to defend himself and feels he has no opportunity to attack. Thus he is prevented from taking the initiative and can be pushed underground.

In the history of anti-guerilla warfare we often see the tendency for a defensive attitude because of the exactness of the hit-and-run

62

tactics of the guerilla, producing nowhere a feeling of security. For this reason people start putting up guards everywhere, at the military bases and along the roads. Such a defensive tendency results in a system of permanent bases and such a system needs many troops spread out over the guarded area which like a net, covers the area.

It requires many forces and expenses to maintain. Naturally one can feel safe in these bases but the whole army has become nailed down and made immobile. It is forced into a passive, defensive position. On the other hand the guerilla fighters have gained full freedom of movement and they completely master the area outside the guard houses. They have the initiative to spring up and attack everything. Thus, in the end, one feels that all places must be guarded and that there is a constant shortage of forces.

In the history of Atjeh, the Dutch were in the end so annoyed by guerillas that they concentrated their forces only around Kotaradja. When Commander van Heutz arrived, he put an end to the situation by going over to a strategy of fast moving attacks. He sprinkled posts over the territory to serve as bases for the active moving patrols. Investigators were sent from these bases. Patrols moved day and night at undefined hours and would make sudden appearances and invasions from directions not anticipated. Thus, aided by internal difficulties of the Atjeh tribe, pacification of the Atjeh territory could be performed.

Offensives and fast moving actions must have a final objective of destruction, also the policy of the guerillas. All operations should be aimed at destroying the guerilla bands, not just attacking and then retreating and allowing the guerillas to scatter. On one side active patrolling must be carried out to narrow the space and to shorten the time of movement for the guerilla so that as the degree of pacification advances he is compelled to go underground and is unable to rise up or move again as a troop. On the other hand the bands which are active must be chased and annihilated.

The difficulty is often not only to find out where the guerilla troop is located, but especially to take care that everything at the anti-guerilla's disposal will be used at the right time. This means that when opportunity comes, we must make use of it. Not only is this espionage work necessary but also when contact has been made with the guerilla troop, the guerilla troop will try to free itself and disperse. It is therefore important not to lose contact. The guerilla must be chased quickly and thoroughly without hesitation and without waste of time. This pursuit is a difficult but important task and is only successful when light and persevering troops are used. The chase must be continued until the attack. For this, physical strength and supplies must be available for a pursuit of many days. Mobile combat reserve troops must always be kept ready to move, to continue the chase and attack the guerillas who are being pursued by another anti-guerilla team. If the anti-guerilla force is strong enough the guerillas must be surrounded and wiped out. If the force is not sufficiently powerful, it is best to strike swiftly at the flank or rear of the guerillas. At least the troops in pursuit should be relieved by fresh troops. Troops must be stationed in such a way that distances and transportation cannot prevent the troops from helping each other. It is not often that guerillas are found in a compact group and every such occasion must be utilized to best advantage.

Combat troops are used also to invade suddenly in the middle of guerilla hideouts, such as those known to exist in the mountains and forests. Swift attacks will strike unexpectedly those territories considered as guerilla bases. These territories infested with guerilla nests must be patrolled intensively in all directions to make them free of guerillas.

The guerilla fighter must be separated from the people. The guerilla must be fought with his own tactics. This is the essence of anti-guerilla strategy.

For the colonial war, the Dutch recruited all their military power. Their war effort achieved a peak never before reached in their history. A modern armed force of approximately 150,000 tried to defend Dutch policy in Indonesia. Also, van Mook's leadership followed the correct policy to achieve the aim of the Dutch government. With only an initial force of several detachments of NICA, marines and a small air force, the formal sovereignty over the Indies, and under the aegis of the Allied Forces, he returned to Indonesia. At that time the government of the Republic had de facto control over the islands, was in possession of the complete administration, had an army of more than half a million soldiers with equipment seized from the Japanese army sufficient for several divisions, was supported by a revolutionary popular spirit which was widespread and deep, and possessed a conviction to carry out the consequences of the proclamation of independence. The skillfulness of van Mook, the combination of politics, military, economics and propaganda, and his influence behind the barbed wire in several internment camps, was increased through the Linggadjati agreement to Kalimantan, East Indonesia and the

64

large cities on Java and Sumatra, and later through the Renville agreement, to include two thirds of Java and one fifth of Sumatra. In addition he also created the federalist states, which were finally recognized by the Republic as representing two thirds of Indonesia and which until this day have come to fill two thirds of our temporary People's Representative Council. At the term of the year 1949 General Spoor stated: "The military operation has come to an end; only two or three months are needed to clean up the remnants of the armed bands." Political and military forces were coordinated and were extremely effective in an offensive of a total character. The Dutch political moves were successful in gaining the cities and they cleared the pockets of TNI soldiers. The military forces seized the areas of the different national groups for the erection of van Mook's states for a political offensive aimed at encircling and diminishing the Republic. The military offensive even captured Jogjakarta and made the Head of State and other leaders surrender.

This policy eventually was a failure; the guerilla war frustrated it and the diplomats seized the transfer of sovereignty. What was the reason? It was that the Dutch also made major mistakes in their effort to squash the revolt and the guerilla war of the Indonesian people. They were not successful in severing the guerilla fighters from the people. The Dutch measures even strengthened the ties as shown by the second colonial war of 1948-1949. The Dutch army could not use their military superiority because their land forces were forced to become immobile in hundreds of small fortresses spread among Republican pockets.

Indeed, we made many mistakes because we did not establish teamwork between the military and political leaders. We surrendered too soon politically, although militarily we did not need to do so, and at the same time we were waging guerilla war against each other; and although the raging civil war was sometimes hot and sometimes cold, and divided the national potential, yet the guerilla war was successful in frustrating the Dutch policy aimed at subjugating or annihilating the Republic and its TNI army.

In the military field the Dutch were eventually dispersed and nailed to hundreds, yes thousands, of stationary guard posts. In general they were tied to cities and highways and only seldom did they conduct a long and hot pursuit that would lead them to explore mountains and pockets, which indeed would have been disastrous for our morale. The most frightening thing for the

65

guerilla is a chase in the guerilla manner, cutting through pockets, not always being able to return to the base because these are the targets being combed by the enemy, and having to face the enemy at unexpected places. It was fortunate for us that the Dutch failed to conduct such operations. Guerillas must be fought with guerilla tactics.

But the strange thing was that after 1950 we assumed, whether consciously or unconsciously, the mistakes of the former Dutch army. We were not in a position to surmount the guerilla problem in all its aspects because the manner of our country's organization would not give us the chance. We did not draft one systematic plan of operation in all fieds, but we limited ourselves to military operations only. In many ways we did not pay enough attention to the factor of the people. Many of our measures resulted in increasing our enemies. We have allowed the guerilla movement to utilize the spirit of provincialism and religious adherence to help the guerilla cause, while we struck at them and made more enemies. More and more people became sympathetic towards the enemy and distrustful of us. Thus we did not divide the enemy among themselves, but we supplied them with friends. We did not attract more people to be active on our side, but instead made them join the other side.

It is not possible to ensure the success of political, psychological and socio-economic measures by means of military actions alone, for success depends on the quality of the political leadership.

We ofteen have blamed, as the Dutch did before us, the way anti- guerilla operations were conducted. We also ended up with thousands of stationary posts and we were eventually tied to the cities and highways and many times were not able to explore the pocket areas in the mountains, conducting ourselves as superiorly trained guerillas facing an enemy. Anti-guerilla fighters need action and more action without stopping their pursuit of the enemy.

II. THE GUERILLA AND OUR FUTURE WAR

1. Have your umbrella ready before it rains (keep your powder dry).

Many people have been predicting the outbreak of a third world war. The cold war has become increasingly warmer. It has turned into a real war in Korea and Indo-China and is a dangerous threat in the Middle East and Germany. The atmosphere has become such that both sides are competing in an armed race. One local conflict could begin a new world war. Of course we hope that a third world war will never occur; however, it is already with us in the form of a cold war throughout the world and as a hot war in several places of the world. Although we pray for the best we should keep our umbrella ready before it rains. It means that we have to prepare ourselves to defend our motherland if it is dragged into a war.

Also, in case a world war breaks out, it still remains for us to keep from being dragged into it. But whether we will get involved in a war or not is not entirely within our control. The last world war clearly demonstrated how neutral countries would be invaded by the great powers if strategy so required. It is true that presently we are not directly situated at the front which divides the two gigantic camps so that there is the possibility that we will not be immediately involved in the crossfire of a war. Nevertheless the geopraphical situation of our archipelago represents a very important strategic factor; the mineral riches and natural products of our islands would be ample reason for any warring power to be interested in our country.

In this connection it is very important for us to attempt to improve our internal situation and to prepare our defense. If the domestic situation is, as it is presently, pregnant with internal strife and sharp divisions, we invite interference from other countries that are strategically interested in such a chaotic atmosphere. Moreover, when we are better prepared for our own defense, this in itself will be an additional factor, helping a country decide whether to involve us in a war. Internal stability and adequate defense preparations are the foremost factors in keeping us from being dragged into a war.

We continue to pray that we will stay out of such a catastrophe, but we must roll up our sleeves and be ready for any eventuality.

67

We thus see clearly the obvious necessity of organizing and regulating our own country. This is an absolute condition if we are to defend ourselves against agression, and also if we are to stay out of a world war should it occur.

The foreign policy of every nation at war has as its aim to get as many allies as possible and to limit its enemies to as few as possible, and at the same time to bring about just the opposite for the enemy.

This was the situation in the past as well as in the present. The histories of wars have shown that countries pursuing a neutral policy attempt to stay neutral as long as possible and when they are invaded by one party, only then will they join the other party. There are alliances that are formally arranged and those that emerge spontaneously, since one party cannot allow its enemy to seize the territory of a neutral without question. Theoretically as well as historically this is the situation, but in the case of our country the fact is that everything is confused. Our independent policy is interpreted by some as being the ability to choose freely, and by others as having no alliances at all. The only thing that is clearly desired by everyone is to stay out of a war; but what has to be done if we should be invaded? Well, this is a question that most of us would like to avoid until the invasion has occurred. These then are more reasons why we should seriously roll up our sleeves and work hard to prepare for future eventualities.

What is the form or content that our defense must take? There are various opinions about that, each based on different reasons. When we look at a map of Indonesia, we see a geopraphical surface equal to that of Europe, and it becomes clear that in such an area it is very difficult to provide adequate defense everywhere at the same time. It is too long and too wide an area to set up a defense sufficiently well-knit to guarantee every point. From this we draw a conclusion; we first need a force (especially an air force) to observe as far and as carefully as possible the neighborhood of the archipelago to detect any approaching aggresor. We should attempt to destroy with our navy and air force an invading enemy before he lands and, in order to secure victory, we should also be prepared to invade the territory of our enemy or a least be able to bomb it sufficiently from the air. Secondly, if the enemy is able to land, all that remains for us to do is face the enemy with simple, local resistance. The vast area of the archipelago cannot be covered by sufficient defense preparations. We need a very mobile combat army to hit the enemy and crush him wherever he appears. This is a modern united army, which with local support can destroy the enemy. These are the conclusions which are drawn when we examine a map of our country. Similar proposals have been suggested as a basis for our defense. However, for the next ten or fifteen years, and maybe for a longer period of time, we will not be in a position to carry out such a plan because we cannot yet fulfill the necessary conditions.

The theoretical computation of the necessary strength is as follows: to pursue the normal policy of neutrality, it means that we and our ally must balance or be stronger than the enemy, whoever the enemy may be. To pursue a policy of non-alliance it means that we must balance any enemy or union of enemies. It is obvious at once that such conditions cannot be fulfilled in the world today.

To organize a proper armed force through our own effort, is something that takes time, personnel, material and finances that we do not possess. Such an organization requires quite a long time. Recent figures have shown that for an army a period of ten to fifteen years is needed to train a nucleus of technical personnel. For a navy, fifteen to twenty years are required. This all depends on whether the government considers it of overall importance or not. Technical skills are very few at this stage, a factor which makes it more difficult to organize a modern army. Technical-trained troops are few in number and we will need much time to increase them. Practically, our industry is only a repair industry. It is difficult to buy equipment because the producing countries need most of it for themselves and also because of the fact that the whole world is competing in an arms race. The purchase of arms has become a political matter. A government gives first to its own army and later to its friends. Also our purchasing capacity is very low. Even though our land is considered one of the richest in the world the national income is considered one of the lowest and our country's budget only amounts to a few thousand millions rupiahs (compared with the USA which spends yearly on its armed forces 46 thousand million dollars). In 1950, one American infantry division needed $ 74,300,000 to equip it, and the financing of its personnel for a year amounted to about $ 80,000,000. Weapons are quickly outdated, which means a change or substittution after four or five years. The figures on the air force and the navy are more startling. Now we see that we are far from the completion of an armed force which is adequate for the geopraphical situation of our archipelago.

For a period of ten years we will be limited to a simple defense on land, a regional defense, although we also should have mobile reserve forces in a limited number. These facts are not secret since foreign experts can analyse the situation by themselves and see our deficiencies. Strategic sea power and an air force are a matter of concern for many decades in the future. This is the harsh reality of our situation and it must be the basis for further work in solving the problem.

However, because we "love peace but love freedom more", we must not be discouraged by our own backwardness; we still have quite a good way out for our country's defense for the coming ten or fifteen years, if we seriously put our mind and bodies to the problems.

There are proposals, coming especially from other countries, that we should not prepare ourselves for a war to defend ourselves properly. The implication of this kind of propaganda is obvious: they are interested that we should not be strong. To prepare oneself to defend one's independence does not mean to instigate a war or to dislike peace, but exactly to avoid aggression because one loves peace. The umbrella must be readied before it rains; a weak country attracts aggression.

2. For the next ten years or more guerilla warfare will be the main item on our program of defense.

We are forced to use guerilla warfare when we are unable to defend an area by conventional means and the area is occupied by the enemy. There is no alternative left to us other than to use guerilla warfare in which all our people in the whole country participate, since we cannot prevent an enemy from seizing the roads and urban areas. We cannot defend an area successfully when we are not able to bring into the field an adequately equipped modern army, one equal to that of our opponent.

When will we be able to possess such an army? This depends on our ability to train an army and to buy and obtain the necessary equipment. Five or ten years are needed to train the soldiers necessary for a land force if assistance is brought in from outside to supply the instructors and the core of staff and officers for the initial stage.

A longer time is needed for the air force; and a regular land force without an adequate air force is worthless. In addition, to build a naval force with the proper technical training requires at least fifteen to twenty years.

We have up to this point considered only the training of personnel. If this is given priority and carried out under the best circumstances the pace can possibly be speeded up. To acquire the necessary equipment, equal periods of time are needed. It depends on how much we can spend for purchasing it, and on our political ability to buy equipment from countries which produce weapons. This is a question that never has been as thoroughly explored as it should have been by our government.

We may consider it a permanent factor of our strategy that guerilla warfare will be an important form of defense for us in the future. For the immediate future, however, guerilla warfare remains our chief form of defense, but gradually, parallel with the development of our army into a modern army, the importance of guerilla warfare will decrease, until at a certain point we will have a regular army. However, even when we have reached such a stage, our strategic position, because of geographical factors, is such that a modern enemy will have ample opportunity to land and invade our country because of our long shoreline and the fact that we are an archipelago. It is almost impossible to prevent a powerful aggressor from occupying parts of our territory. Wherever the area is occupied there is only one way for us to defend ourselves, namely, suitable guerilla warfare.

For this reason guerilla warfare will always remain our most important form of warfare. The natural features of our bigger islands offer the best conditions for guerilla warfare. The large area, the roads, mountains, and woods are satisfactory for a long guerilla war. There is only one question left: whether our people really want to conduct guerilla warfare? This depends on other factors of a politico-ideological and socio-economic nature. In a country threatened by division, plagued by corruption and suffering from poverty, one cannot expect the people to be willing to fight a guerilla war to defend themselves against an outside aggressor; on the contrary, the people will conduct a guerilla war against their own government. As long as the government is not the people's choice and not able to defend the people's interests, it is doubtful whether the people will have the desire and sincerity to wage a proper guerilla war to defend the country.

These factors touch the roots of the problem: the problem whether the people possess the above-mentioned capability, which has become more and more precarious since the transfer of sovereignty. A general disappointment prevails in all groups and on all levels. The belief and respect in the country decreases more and more. The country, especially the leaders of the country, are in a moral crisis.

A guerilla war in the total people's defense will be fought largely on land, in which the land forces as in former times play a major role. Many of our political leaders have suggested that not the land forces but the sea and air forces should be stressed because of our peculiar geographic condition and the fact that our ancestors were a sea-faring nation.

There is no denying that several decades from now we must become a maritime nation; we are inhabitants of an archipelago situated between two land masses and two oceans. It is obvious that we cannot reach that stage within twenty or thirty years, and for this reason it is wrong to think we should stress the development of a sea force within the next ten years.

If, for example, because of our technical abilities we are able to develop a modern navy, it still remains a question whether we should stress its importance. All three branches of the armed forces are needed. To gain victory over the enemy, he must be attacked and destroyed. Theoretically an enemy of our country can be defeated if we can annihilate him in his own country; to achieve this the sea and air forces would have to join and protect such an offensive. But the annihilation of enemy troops and the occupation of the enemy's territory can only be carried out by the army. If, for example, an enemy attacks Indonesia, he most probably cannot be stopped from landing, but once he has landed our army can start the attack and annihilate him with the assistance of the other branches of the armed forces. Although these are only theoretical problems, it is necessary to examine them so that we may have a complete view of the future, since voices from politicians have been heard recently, claiming that the army is of less importance than sea and air forces.

To return to the problem of a guerilla war in the future it is necessary for us to use to the fullest extent the expériences of the past, experiences which occurred at an important period in our nation's history and which hold many valuable lessons for us. Our people already have an organization which can be used as a foundation on which to develop a defense plan for the future, as they especially know ways and means to carry out a people's guerilla war. These can become the sources which supply material for our military development in the future. We are fortunate to have had our own guerilla history, the more so, because it served us as a tool to gain independence.

3. At present and in years to come we in Indonesia will continue to be engaged in anti-guerilla activities.

In the future we must continue to carry out anti-guerilla tactics. From the transfer of sovereignty up to the present time guerilla warfare has been raging in our country. Java, Borneo, Sulawesi and the Moluccas continued to be plagued with a guerilla war. In the Moluccas and Borneo great progress has been achieved in stopping the guerilla war. But in Java and Sulawesi the guerilla and anti-guerilla forces have reached a balance which „stabilizes" the atmosphere of resistance. One thing is clear: the guerilla war that is being fought between brothers cannot be ended in a short time, and considering the ways and results achieved in the past three years, it is very doubtful whether there is an immediate solution.

Our leaders realize that the present confusion within our country and within the people is rooted in the politico-psychological and socio-economic instability. In fact a people carrying out a guerilla war against the legal authority does it from dissatisfaction and thus points out the evils of that authority. Therefore, the "atmosphere" created by the people determines whether the guerilla thrives or not. The degree of violence of the guerilla war in our country, especially in Java and South Sulawesi, indicates clearly that the "atmosphere" of the people is politico-psychologically and socio-economically so bad, that the people's faith is transferred more and more to the guerillas and their fight. The people's faith and trust in the government becomes weaker as time goes on. The number of Darul Islam followers has increased because more and more people are choosing its side. This is a process that cannot be brought about by intimidation or coercion. This sympathy has deeper roots, which must be looked for in the hearts and thoughts of the people who evaluate every event as it really happens to them.

The guerillas have their roots in the people, and it is the function of the anti-guerilla movement to pull these roots out of the people. The guerilla movement is only the result, not the cause of the problem. The question is how can the anti-guerilla fighter give a concrete demonstration that he has a higher ideology? How can the anti-guerilla fighter win back the people and how can he rebuild trust and sympathy? These are the principal problems that our anti-guerilla war has to face, and they clearly show that efforts of a politico-psychological and socio-economical character are the more important facets in the strategy of maintaining security in our country.

We have a long distance to travel in solving these problems. I do not know how many years it will take and considering the deteriorating conditions that we have experienced since independence, it seems that the distance becomes greater every day. In the political field, there are still frictions between those for and against the results of the Round Table Conference of 1949 and there is still a wide gulf between the unitarians and the federalists growing even worse after the Dutch stopped meddling in our affairs. The fighters for independence are more and more forgotten men and many are still languishing in prison.

After independence, due to inefficient prison administration it took a great deal of time to determine whether prisoners were being held for political or criminal offenses and for this reason many prisoners who had been jailed by the Dutch for political crimes were forced to spend needless extra months in prison.

On the other hand, those who collaborated with the colonial power seemed to increase their control of the country. The people see how powerful many collaborators have become and the people find they can do nothing because these traitors of the Republic are supported by laws that resulted from the course of history since 1950. The revolution has not brought satisfaction, but dissatisfaction. The people do not have an elected parliament and president as yet, after seven years of independence. It is understandable how great the political and ideological dissatisfaction is among our people while the leaders avoid and avoid the solving of these problems.

Social-economic conditions have become worse for the people since 1950, except for a small favored group which continues to prosper. Living costs continue to rise, employer-labor disputes continue, production continues to fall, and the question of veterans' benefits remains a problem. Even independence has not solved the problem of famine.

The government administration is ill run and its ranks are swollen till they are not capable of efficient action. Officials are numerous but their quality is low. Corruption permeates the government and incompetent amateurs occupy important posts. Party and family favoritism have a tight grip on the government. There is no clear separation of powers among the various administrative ministries. Orderly administration is a prime condition, not only for any politico-psychological and socio-economic undertaking but also for political security within the country. To make the administration good and healthy will require a great deal of time and effort; it cannot be achieved by miracles. In this demoralizing atmosphere, spiritual standards and norms of decency are lowered. The evaluation of good and bad is more and more controlled by emotional desires. These symptoms are observed by the leaders themselves. Therefore the solution of the problem depends in the first place on these leaders applying the rules to themselves. One cannot expect improvement of the basic problems of security, order and peace in one or two years.

The technical steps that we have taken so far lead us to the same conclusion. The technical mistakes of the Dutch in combatting guerilla activities were unconsciously inherited and applied by us, even though we were ex-guerillas and should have realized the folly of such a course. The anti-guerilla movement should oppose the guerilla with its own weapons, which are: aggressiveness, mobility and flexibility. However, we have allowed ourselves to become immobile, nailed down to the cities and highways. The patrols that we send out are mostly of a routine nature and do not conform to the laws of guerilla warfare in exploring extensively the mountains and inland areas.

The immobile (permanent) character and the regular patrol routine are only of a defensive nature and leave time and opportunity to the skillful guerilla to escape. One cannot blame the troops entirely for these mistakes.

It is the situation which has lead to such features. A large army has of necessity to think in terms of quantity. After the exhaustion caused by a five-year guerilla war, there was no time for rest and proper training to adapt it to its new task. The soldiers who in the meantime have become thirty years of age on the average, experienced physical and psychological effects, which could not be avoided.

It has become obvious that the country is not yet ready to break through the problem of internal security. The reasons given above call for a longterm plan and a rather permanent organization in order to solve the problem of domestic security. The organization and education have to be adapted to the expected tasks, and cannot be of an incidental or provisional nature. Army units on active duty need special organization and training different from those of a reserve status. Working procedures among the chains of command must be regulated not in a casual but in a more permanent manner. The problem of the infantry, for example, which is under the responsibility of two great organizations, the infantry of the army and that of the mobile brigade, must most of all be handled objectively to avoid having two organizations doing the same duty.

Permanent character must be stressed in view of the international atmosphere which gives no prospect of easing in the immediate future. The conception of total war at the present has made war something of a more or less permanent character. Psychological warfare has become part of the terrible total war, whether in peace or in war-time. Southeast Asia for years has been a battlefield of the most violent cold war and its violence has not declined, but has increased in strength up till now. The cold war has helped to sharpen internal conflicts to the point where they have become civil wars, which more and more take on the character of a total war.

With this fleeting survey it is hoped that the anti-guerilla war in the present time will continue to demand attention and thought in the coming years. And the end of the anti-guerilla war cannot be separated from defense preparation problems because the end of this anti-guerilla war is an absolute condition to build up our country's defense in the future.

4. The guerilla war we were waging against the Dutch was militarily speaking of an immature nature.

If we examine the level on which our guerilla war was fought we have to conclude that it was only the initial stage of what actually must be achieved in order to gain victory in a war. A guerilla war is a form of resistance waged by a weak power against a much stronger oppressor. The weak one must remain on the defensive for a certain period, until he has inflicted upon the enemy such a loss that he is equal to him and is able to stage an offensive to defeat him.

Our guerilla war had only reached the defensive phase, and just the first stage of that phase, that is to say, our army was trying to keep from being destroyed by the enemy and it was engaged in organizing guerilla resistance, but we were not yet in a position strong enough to annihilate the enemy bit by bit. It was very seldom that we were able to destroy isolated enemy posts or patrols, or even their convoys which were protected by only one platoon.

We were mostly engaged in local guerilla wars; for example, within an area of a pocket we did not sufficiently carry out mobile attacks. We were too static and defensive. The enemy moved along in units as large as one platoon or one company, knowing that it, at the least, would be only harassed and not threatened with destruction because the offensive ability on our side was relatively weak.

This was caused by our lack or failure to organize and educate. A guerilla war needs a "first line" and a "second line". We already had a second line, which was guerilla resistance or partisan resistance, spreading out in every district. This resistance does not require many weapons. The purpose of the movements was only to engage and harass the enemy wherever he might be. But besides these units we need troops which are better organized, more fully trained and better equipped, and able to carry out destructive tactics on enemy troops.

In 1945 we had enough equipment and trained personnel to organize approximately ten complete regiments on Java, and enough forces and weapons to set up partisan troops which would be distributed among the districts. But instead we formed ten divisions and forty regiments of TRI (Tentara Republik Indonesia — The Indonesia Republican Army) and several dozen regiments of TLRI (Tentara Laskar Republik Indonesia — Indonesia Republican People's Army).

The attempt of what has become known as the "rationalization-reconstruction" of the army, reforming it into a number of battalions and brigade combat teams also failed in the end. The reason for this failure was that it was generally misunderstood that we were striving to build up as many battalions and brigades as possible so that the aim for greater efficiency became blurred. In the then ensuing guerilla war there were not enough combat forces to carry out destructive tactics. Our attempt to form several brigades or battalions to serve as combat teams left us with no other alternative than to resort to static defensive measures.

If every commander had only several battalions of combat teams and every territorial commander had one battalion of the same, trained and proportionately equipped, it would have made it impossible for the Dutch to patrol in troops smaller than one battalion, or set up a post smaller than one company so that we would have had more room to maneuver. Our battalions of combat teams should concentrate on attacking the enemy, while the resistance put up by the territorial forces and their partisans should engage and exhaust the enemy wherever he might be. Operationally we should have aimed at this, before the problem of rationalization and reconstruction had become a political question, involving loyalties which obscured the basic problem and made it impossible to solve.

Mindful of these conceptions and experiences, we cannot during the reconstruction that we are presently facing agree with some currents of thought and suggestions coming especially from the side of politicians, that we should not concentrate our efforts or even minds on developing more highly organized units, although the manpower, equipment and time are available. Therefore, our occasional anti-guerilla operations in open attacks show our inability to destroy the enemy. The pursuit of battalion 426 from Kudus at the border of East Java to West Java is full of such examples. Sometimes one company in their rear was confronted with several of our battalions and yet there were able to free themselves and flee to safety.

An enemy report from the commander of the Republik Maluku Selatan (South Molucca Republic) Samson, tells of leading his nine platoons against our six battalions which landed at Hitu and Tulehu in the first stages of our operation, and came to a deadlock on the northern part of the island.

"At the time of the landing on 28 September 1950, in Hitu and Tulehu the general line of defense in the Hitu sector ran from Mamala to Wakal. We were one platoon strong with one 7.7 Vickers. The commander, Sergeant-Major Lumanauw, and his men had been ordered by me to withdraw from West Ceram when his attack at Kottania, according to instructions, failed. At the time Piru and Kottania were already occupied by the TNI. When Sergeant-Major Lumanauw was forced to withdraw from the line of Wakal to Mamala because of superior enemy forces, I gave orders to discontinue the occupation of Asilulu-Hila, and, to strengthen the second line 200 miles east of the line Telaga Kodok to Hassal. Lumanauw was replaced by Adjutant Sopacua and I added two platoons of volunteer KNIL soldiers, who carried out the flanking attack west of Telaga Kodok via Gunung Damar. This attack threw the enemy back to Hitu. Later, for strategic rasons, the general line of defense was set for Oli from Hassal to Wanat and reaching as far as 150 miles east of Wanat. This sector remained under Adjutant Sopacua and his strength was still three platoons, one 7.7 Vickers and two 3-inch mortars seized from the enemy.

"In the Tulehu sector there were stationed at the time of the attack on 28 September 1950, one group consisting of special troops under the command of Corporal Patty, later strengthened with five volunteer KNIL platoons commanded by Sergeant-Major Rugebregt. Our troops were forced to withdraw to the second front line of Waitatiri which was 600 miles long. Later Rugebregt's troops were pushed back to 800 miles away from Passo village".

We admit that we received heavy blows from the RMS in the first stages immediately after the landing so that we were forced to send quickly several reserve battalions complete with an armored squadron and artillery, and only then could we break their resistance and seize the whole island. In later stages we gained more and more skill.

Of course, there were several examples in which we destroyed a somewhat equal enemy in an open battle. The Lucas battalion on 19 December destroyed an enemy's vanguard army one-half battalion strong in the vicinity of Bandjarnegara when they clashed with each other close to the demarcation line. There are other examples, but in general there are not many such instances.

5. We must as soon as possible develop a truly regular army.

Many politicians have lately suggested that we should stress the development of a guerilla defense for our sovereign state. With this suggestion they have denied the value of training and organizing a regular army or, using the worn-out term, an "international" army. Political and sentimental reasons ride along with such an objective problem as our defense. Such situations were often experienced during the period of the "Republic of Jogja".

We have already criticized and analyzed this at length so that we come to the conclusion that for the next ten years we must emphasize guerilla warfare and we must carry out anti-guerilla warfare. However, our analysis of what guerilla war is has shown that a guerilla war is only of a defensive strategic nature and is not able to bring a final, decisive victory. The guerilla forces must grow in the direction of becoming a regular army so as to be able to carry out an offensive in order to defeat the enemy.

Therefore, guerilla leadership must in time of war hasten to form regular troops as rapidly as the course of events will allow. How much better off we would be if we prepared before the war, rather than waiting until we are forced to do it while fighting a war.

We could, if we tried hard for five or ten years, form units up to the level of regiments or even divisions, though in limited number, which could become regular defense troops in certain areas.

The guerilla or partisan war, must be the responsibility of the people's partisan troops, which we can develop from the Pager Desa (Home Guards) and our territorial troops. These organizations can take over such guerilla duties in the same way we did when we had the T.N.I.

The army can then concentrate more on the organization of a regular army. Such an army, given the right training, should be able to turn to guerilla tactics when it is cut off from the main force. Whether it is a "regular" or "guerilla" army depends on the situation. It is a guerilla army when it is cut up; it is a regular army when it is given the opportunity to attack an equal target of the enemy.

Mao Tse-tung, for example, teaches that "in strategy we are one fighting against ten, but in tactics we are ten fighting against one". Although we are less strong than the enemy we must find such targets in which, with temporary concentrations, we achieve a superiority that enables us to destroy a smaller and divided enemy. Thus the guerilla must at certain places and times be able to carry out tactical offensives in a regular battle formation.

The problem of organizing a regular army according to "international" standards or concentrating all efforts on building a guerilla army is separate from the problem of emphasizing or neglecting the spirit. A guerilla army, as well as an army of international standards, must consider the soul of importance because this is the inner strength which enables us to risk our lives. To neglect this cardinal factor means to bring failure in the battle field. An army without a spirit is of no value.

On the other hand, spirit alone is not sufficient; there must be skillfulness and expertness. Morale and knowledge are both needed. Education and science will not harm morale. Morale with a good foundation will develop into something good as a result of such education. A systematic, military education will in the end not cultivate science alone, but precisely military character and behavior.

A nation is forced to carry out guerilla warfare because there is no other way and because it is not in a position to fight with an organized army. A guerilla war is a long, drawn-out and exhausting affair if one is to seize by military means — with no assistance from any allies — the final victory as we have already explained in the first chapter.

The lower the organizational level of an army, the more one has to carry out guerilla war, and the longer and the harder the course of war. The higher the organizational degree that we can put forward, the less the burden of a guerilla war we put on the people's shoulders. We resort to guerilla warfare because our territory is occupied by the enemy, because we are not strong enough to maintain a sufficciently firm front, and because our army has not yet reached a level high enough. This is a logic that must be realized with composure.

To accomplish the military duties of the present time it is necessary that the organization and its leadership make an efficient division of the responsibilities. In the development of this army there are two responsibilities which must be clearly separated from each other since they concern two kinds of subject fields not easily united. First, there is the task of preparing for an eventual guerilla war while completing the present anti-guerilla war. Second, we need to build up a modern land, sea, and air force on a long-term plan, for example, fifteen years.

For the first task there are more than enough T.N.I. forces — left over from the war of independence — which grew up in each area and gained experiences in those areas· They must gradually, after having reached the peak of activity in 1950-1951, be returned to their own area where they can better maintain security as they know the area and people. They must gradually return to their society, except for those who want to migrate to another area, so that back in their community they can serve as first forces when guerilla war must be prepared. Besides these, some of the veterans must be registered and re-organized into a reserve force, to be mobilized in times of emergency. Their rehabilitation must take place gradually, taking into consideration the socio-economic conditions in that area. There will be a time when each kabupaten (regency) has its own territorial batallion which can be mobilized, and a simple training depot where the kabupaten and the Pager Desa (Home Guards) soldiers as well as the territorial cadres can be trained periodically. One thing that our army has a special need of is a "territorial corps" (people's defense), whose members are to fill the positions at the sub-dictrict level and higher. For these we could use the present T.N.I. forces that have a sound foundation because of their participation and experiences in the revolution and guerilla war. There will then grow up, in the light of our traditions and experiences, a partisan guard of the kabupaten and desa (village) along a system of limited and selected obligatory training. I proposed such a plan in 1948 when we had to rationalize and reconstruct the army but there was no decision taken. There should be in the headquarters a leadership or inspectorate in charge of "territorial" affairs, such as the "second army", or the people's guerilla army. For this, there is need for special planning and education, which cannot be separated from the problem of rehabilitation of the forces back in civilian life in their commu nities.

On the other hand, T.N.I. soldiers who fulfill requirements are much needed for the permanent infantry battalions to carry out police and infantry duties in the coming years. The problem to be decided is whether there must be built up an infantry as part of the army or an infantry (mobile brigade) as part of the police. Essentially there is no difference in their task so that it would be wrong to set up two different bodies to do the same job. The army has too many infantry battalions and the police continues to recruit new mobile brigades.

Our second task, that of building modern military forces, needs its own particular opportunities on a long-term basis, undisturbed by the every-day worries of an anti-guerilla war and the preparat ions for a guerilla war. At the present time the A.U.R.I. (air force) and A.L.R.I. (sea force) are mostly training centers in character.

The A.D.R.I. (land force) should have been the same. From among the T.N.I. forces, those with sufficient qualifications must be taken as the nucleus. They must fulfill those conditions to become the professional core of the modern A.D.R.I. They will fill the positions of instructors, staff officers, and army department officials. They need foreign support and at a later stage they must go abroad to complete their training or specialize in a branch of the army.

The training of an expert core for the A.D.R.I. will require five or ten years, depending on how serious our efforts are. If the country gives priority to this problem it can be completed in a compara- tively short time. If it is done at the normal pace it will of course take more time. The A.L.R.I. also needs fifteen to twenty years, while the A.U.R.I. needs a shorter time.

For this reason it might be necessary to draft a plan for the development of a modern A.D., A.L. and A.U. (land, sea and air force) for a fifteen year period and the accomplishment of this project must receive special attention and not be disturbed by anti-guerilla problems, etc.

A division of tasks must be created within the organization. In the U.S., for example, there are separate headquarters for the training of land forces directly under the Chief of Staff. We have already planned headquarters for territorial preparations and training (of territorial units, cadres, and partisan depots) which would be the inspectorate for the people's defense, directly under the Chief of Staff. For the every-day leadership of the anti-guerilla war, there must be provided a staff, in line with its all-embracing character, in which all branches of authority involved must take part.

In this way a modern A.D.R.I. can be built up with ease together with a modern A.L.R.I. and A.U.R.I., while the "territorial" preparations follow their own way.

We have drawn the conclusion that a guerilla war alone cannot decide victory in war, but that this can only be achieved with an offensive by a regular army. In connection with proposals that our defense should be based on a guerilla war, we must again here stress that we must do our utmost to build up as soon as possible a regular army, preferably parallel with the development of a modern sea and air force. In defense anyone who relies mainly on guerilla war is thinking of getting support from an ally abroad because under such conditions he can hope to win the war. The followers of an independent policy, in the sense that they do not want to be allied to anyone, are contradicting themselves when they only rely on guerilla warfare for our defense. The followers of an independent policy should be the first ones to encourage the construction of a proper, regular army. After 1950, there was time, manpower and money available to build up a proper, regular army; therefore it was outrageous that we, especially the responsible leaders of our country, neglected to do so, unless it was intended not to maintain our independence against possible aggression. The problems of domestic security, the sentiments and policies of parties and individuals must be overcome when we are dealing with the defense of our freedom obtained at such a great sacrifice.

6. Organization and training for a future guerilla war.

It has been said above that a guerilla war is a burden carried by the people's partisans along lines that should continue the experiences and traditions which we developed during our war for independence.

For completeness' sake we will explain once more the relationship between the guerilla war and the total people's war to achieve final victory with the subjugation of the aggressor. To be complete we must form three "levels" of defense: resistance by the army, resistance of the partisans (people's guerilla army), and defense of the common people. Resistance is of an active nature while defense is of a passive nature.

In principle the army that we build is the same as those in other countries, it is "international," it has armed infantry, artillery, cavalry, etc., and it is organized in the usual units. Only our technical level, and the condition of the land and other special factors, give a special flavor to the strategy and tactics that we pursue, and also to the type of organization and training that we choose. Therefore, we should not hastily refuse everything that comes from abroad and reject the experiences of other peoples who have had more opportunities in their past than our young nation. The current of revolution, which causes sentiments and self-confidence to boil over, as has been the case in other well known revolutions in history, brings with it in its first phases those excesses that refuse everything which originates from a foreign country.

For a long time to come, the constitution of the land and the level of our technical skill will force us to keep our organization simple, with the infantry used as a "mass weapon." Percentage-wise our infantry will form a larger part of the armed forces than is the case in other foreign armies. The separated areas will more or less make our operations autonomous affairs. These will stress regional defense with each territory having a combat team suited to the situation of that particular territory. The Japanese army here had already provided for such a defense which was supported by preparations for a people's guerilla war.

The army that we are building is an "infantry" army that is organized into combat teams in each defense territory and consists of a batallion, regiment, or division carrying light equipment so that they can serve as fast moving combat troops. Besides these first line troops, there must be set up a large number of territorial battalions. The Japanese formed approximately sixty such battalions on Java.

For the next ten or fifteen years, in connection with the time needed for the growth of an air force and especially a sea force, and with our technical development, we still must pursue a defense policy covering the entire archipelago, treating it as if it were a continent. Some groups, looking too far ahead, wish to put more stress on the air and sea forces and keep a small and mobile army for combat purposes in any location of our archipelago whenever required. This is a problem of still many decades in the future.

The army then consists of infantry regiments, stationed in each region and, more specifically, within each ethnic group. A sound spirit of competition between the regions must be fully utilized to raise the standards of our army. Provincial pride must be constructively utilized and, above all, the "Wehrkreise" feature in our defense. During five years of fighting the army has grown regional-wise, and up to now each department of the army continues to laud the history of its growth and its struggle in that particular region.

In all the activity, and when our domestic security was at stake during 1950 to 1951, we were forced to relieve many territories of their troops. The Westerling affair, the Darul Islam, the Andi Azis affair, the AOI, the Republik Maluku Selatan. Ibnu Hadjar, etc., amidst the transfer of 30,000 KNIL soldiers from the Dutch forced us to shift troops on a wide scale in order to extinguish those threats to security, whether actual or potential.

It was the ingenuity of the leadership, after the planning for the development of the army started, to set up regiments in each region, regiments in each ethnic group, which absorbed all the troops originally from that area. This move also facilitated the demobilization of army members who did not want to continue military duty; moreover, it started the depot batallions for the training of regiments in each region, which were to maintain the fighting tradition in that region. In the beginning, the program for the development of the infantry intended to produce by 1953 a sufficient number of instructors for the depots of such regiments so that gradually regiments for Atjeh, Tapanuli, Solo, Besuki, Maluku etc., could be built. These regiments are to produce the needed infantry batallions with one school for cadres to serve several regiments.

This regional scheme should be balanced and it has been planned to establish an officers training school for the whole of Indonesia, where those officers now in the army will also obtain further training.

For several years to come these regiments will mainly consist of the TNI batallions left over from the war but gradually when demobilizations goes ahead—with ex-soldiers entering the reserve corps—the depot will produce more and more militia. As the TNI soldiers grow older, it is necessary that the militia be started as soon as possible so that there is a system of a popular army which is more in accordance with a democracy and a constitution than the army that we have now. It is possible that for some branches of the army for the time being a system of army cadres will be better because the required technical knowledge has been far from achieved by our people. The army plan drafted in 1951 will make such a militia possible in 1956.

Thus a survey to complete the overall view in which we stress regional development of a regular army is in accordance with the factors of geography and nationality and is more suitable for our defense. The regional character is more important in the organization and training of the people's guerilla force.

To come back to the crux of the problem of organizing and training for a future guerilla war, we must again stress the point that a guerilla war will have to be supported by the people's militia who as partisans can properly carry out duties such as the TNI accomplished during our fight for independence.

In the first phase of the national revolution every region formed a TKR (People's Security Army) to serve as a regular army and the home guards (laskar2) as partisans. But because they lacked proper leadership the TKR acted more like partisan troops and the home guards attempted to be on the same level as the army so that the difference eventually was that between an official and a private army. Also, because of the dangers of such unorganized guerilla movements, the Presidential Decree of 1947 united all into the TNI which, because of the 1948 plan for rationalization and reconstruction, had been merged into one organization.

As a result of this step we were not able to provide the division of duties between the regular army and the partisans which is necessary in a war. Only shortly before the second police action and during the time it was taking place did we attempt to institute this difference of duties and organization. The army was organized into battalions: a mobile battalion with a 1:1 weapon ratio for mobile combat forces and a territorial battalion with a 1:3 or 1:5 weapon ratio in each regency (kabupaten) to serve as local sentries. (This distinction failed because of mistakes made in the execution of the re-organization. We were forced to turn the excess into territorial forces because we had set up too many mobile forces.) On the instruction of the Headquarters Java Command in January 1949, a village guerilla troop, as large as one squad and called Pager Desa (Home Guard), was set up in each village. When the underdistrict needed it, the squad sometimes was united with the Sub-District Military Command into platoons. In a short time, such squads developed over the whole of Java and up to the present time they still exist for the anti-guerilla war. In the future, these Home Guards (Pager Desa) are the exact system that we will use for a partisan war in each village and each sub-district. It is possible that in the future, as villages become larger, the sub-districts will be larger so that it may better suit the organization of the Home Guard.

86

The organization of the Pager Desa might be as large as one platoon, that is, one platoon for a large village or sub-district. They should get simple infantry training and their activities include those of a squad or platoon when engaged in such tasks as wiping out a fifth column, aiding the infantry of a paratroop division, guarding important positions and if the region is occupied by the enemy they must conduct partisan warfare. They should be given training several weeks each year. In our own plans it was intended that training should be given by the military district depot which preferably should be attached to an unit located in that area.

The arms from the former KNIL as taken over by the TNI are sufficient equipment, but they will have to be replaced gradually by new purchase. In connection with the actual task of the partisans, a great number of hand grenades are required. The Pager Desa can be attached to army units in executing combat tasks.

Later on, from these Home Guards there can be organized, especially in the cities, artillery troops for anti-aircraft and PBO for the territorial defense against air attacks, along with the infantry-partisan Home Guards in the sub-districts.

In order to fill the ranks of the Pager Desa there are two alternatives open to us. Until now a system of volunteering has been relied upon. In general in the desas there are more candidates than are required, but it may be that economic factors are hereby involved because some candidates hope to become soldiers. Therefore, candidates must come from among those who do not fall under the militia and these will be a sufficient number because of our large population.

A second way is to introduce training duty. All general militia must be divided between army duty and training duty. Those who are liable for training duty are to be incorporated in the Pager Desa. As the group of youths is so large the younger and older ones may be excused from this training. The desa administration obviously can be put in charge of this program.

Special forms of Pager Desa are the various students' militia (TP, TRIP, CM, TGP, CP) and the volunteers among organized students in the cities. Their good results in the past give ample reason to continue them in the future in the cities, organizing them as detachments consisting of companies and platoons. These students' organizations have already proven their worth during the fight for independence. Such volunteers can in the future be called up for training duty.

Whatever the case, it is much better if the partisan war is conducted on a voluntary basis, on a willingness to fight, and urged on by the call of the citizen's conscience.

The sacrifices of the Pager Desa have already been great. Their casualties in the guerilla war were no less than those of the army, and in the anti-guerilla war their losses exceeded those of the army; they fought for months at a time. The country and people must learn to appreciate this. Many among them could make good government employees or police officers. It is the hard luck of fighters everywhere that their services have not been fully appreciated once the war is over and their services are no longer needed. This same lack of recognition occurs in other countries too. Our village administrators who performed services above and beyond their duty during the guerilla time and in the anti-guerilla activities had been neglected and treated very poorly after independence was gained. For the benefit of a future defensive fight we must set up rules to give aid to village administrators whom we know have shown merit in the fight for independence.

All these various aspects, as well as the leadership in the organization and training of the defense forces, must be taken care of by a separate inspectorate, for which we have long strived, that is especially concerned with such important matters. The development of such interests cannot be left to the initiative of just any local authority, but there must be national planning and leadership as in other countries. The present TNI members because of their past experiences have a sound foundation to carry out these duties.

These peace-time preparations must be limited to organizational and training activities and not, as has happened in several places, grown into structures operating on a war time basis. The Pager Desa should continue their civilian capacities in the community life of the village as they would do in time of war. They only shoulder a gun when danger threatens or when they are in training. It is not necessery to set up barracks, but there must be a training centre for the whole kabupaten (regency).

Such "territorial" corps are available to take part in civil defense. Such a civil defense does not imply defense by the people in the cities only, as is usually meant by civil defence in more advanced countries. Indeed this aspect is always needed and is more required in these times of advanced war techniques, which threaten all cities, even those far away from the field of battle. But, mindful of the fact that for the defense of our country our type of guerilla war must be as extensive as possible, civil defense must have as much content as possible, and must always guarantee the continuous ope-ration of the wheels of government, of the community and of national production. It means that in the pockets behind the enemy frontline we must continue to fight to maintain the de facto authority of the Republic with its instruments of power which had been prepared for guerilla warfare. We carry out a total people's war in the fullest sense of the word. Political, psychological and socio-economical forces must uninterruptedly develop themselves and this is only possible with a system of guerilla government or military government that we have formerly been acquainted with. In such a total war, the people must be activated and directed from the beginning according to a systematic method.

The leadership is held by the civil authorities, with the assistance of the "territorial" forces, but in its relationship to war, everything must be brought under the supervision of the military leadership. Such a system has shown its merits in the past. Anything that differs from such a system, such as the defense councils set up during the guerilla war, have proved to be unsuccessful. Their failure can be credited to the fact that the councils could not convene and that party rivalry was too great, turning such councils into political arenas. We had to bypass the councils for the benefit of the struggle.

The relation between the guerilla government leadership and the leadership of the regular forces is that existing between the com-mandant of a base and his troops. It is necessary that such an intimate relationship be created within the framework of an organization and of its laws as we practiced before under the constitution of the "Republic of Jogja".

Every village, every office, every factory and every school is an absolutely necessary part of the organization of civil defense, whether we mean civil defense as long as the area is temporarily occupied by the enemy, or a civil defense within the framework of a guerilla government in an area permanently occupied by the enemy. In the first phase we must maintain the usual system of rules as long as it is possible, but in the second phase, the system must be brought under the guerilla leadership.

There must be a law providing for civil duty and the main outlines of such an organization so that it may serve a guide for peace-time preparations.

After three years of sovereignty our government has not yet started to solve this important problem. There is no inspectorate to arrange such a civil defense, while in the neighbouring countries and even in the neighbouring colonies they are busy training people. There must be a peace-time organization and thus we must also prepare ourselves and be ready for war. As there is a close relationship with the "territorial" corps, their training centres could be jointly used and the "territorial" corps, according to tradition, must specialize in partisan duties and civil defense duties. Local administrative employees and those of the village are excused to be available for the second type of duties. They must, however, also have some similar training.

During the period of anti-guerilla activities such partisan movements and civil defense become of great use, therefore we must pay due attention to them in the future. Such organization (for partisan movement and civil defense) can act as eyes and ears and instruments of anti-guerilla warfare. Every village arranges its own guards and reports all news to the leadership of the operation. A strong Home Guard organization deals the heaviest blow to the guerilla, which must have its base within the people to exist. The people of a village must be urged to carry out its activities, not only by accidental campaigns, but according to a systematic plan which gradually evolves.

7. The guerilla leadership and growth must be indigenous (as the "Wehrkreise").

Because of our country's geographical peculiarity of being a vast area consisting of islands scattered over a wide area, our army, which during the next ten or fifteen years will be simple in structure, must be suited to maintain regional defense. Accordingly, the development must be within each region along similar lines as in the past. Every region, or strictly speaking, every national group, will have its own regiment to provide an infantry for such a simple regular army.

Because the islands are separated by water and because for the next ten or fifteen years our navy will not be strong enough to exercise control properly, every island must organize itself as an individual defense unit. The Dutch had already started such a plan of strategic defense (before 1941) and the Japanese more or less carried on this plan. Our islands, however, can never function as a single unit because of the geography and the lack of communications. For this reason we still require further decentralization. Politically, administratively, and socio-economically each island has not achieved unity. The opening of highways is one step in the direction of such a goal. Plans to build a highway through Sumatra and through Kalimantan therefore should receive all possible assistance from the army. Projects of transmigration from Java to other islands, especially Kalimantan, should be strongly supported and even pioneered by the army.

The present anti-guerilla movement is of a regional nature and its political-psychological and socio-economical connotations must be taken into consideration. The guerilla fighters tend to operate in localized areas because apart from the fact that guerilla troops are geographically separated from each other, they are, because of their very nature, individualistic. The enemy may control the urban centres and the highways so that the area of the guerillas will be divided. A regular war has its base in the cities and at the cross-roads, but a guerilla war has its base in the interior.

A guerilla war is most successful if it defends its own village compounds, defends the family, and moves in the indigenous area. Because the people form a basic factor, the division of the guerilla area must also be based according to the division of the people, and mainly according to the national group. Each area has its own peculiarities, which require a special type of defense, just as each has its own customs and common usages. The mountains of Priangan, the plain of Krawang, and the river area of South Kalimantan, etc., all require special physical and mental conditions.

We must exploit these factors to the fullest, and therefore must not require a rigid uniformity when setting up organizations for the people's defense. This is not because we adhere to the idea of provincialism, but because we must build up our defense in the most efficient way. Our past experiences have strengthened this belief. After the transfer of sovereignty, and especially in recent times, our military development has been very much influenced by factors of provincialism. Each area prefers to be defended or guarded by soldiers from that area, and prefers to have leaders who come from that area. This politico-psychological factor, especially where it concerns the guerilla war, entirely based on the people, cannot be brushed aside, but must be used for constructive reasons. Psychologically, we will feed the provincialist tendencies if we now oppose the existing currents and feelings.

Things can be done much faster by the leaders of a guerilla government if each area has complete autonomy. A future war will be of a decentralized nature; each administrative area must be able to function on its own. Under certain conditions various public offices will not be able to communicate with their ministries, but must depend for decisions on the heads of each state. Therefore, the heads of those offices should, with a minimum of difficulty, be able to form together a sort of "special civil staff" in the guerilla government, presided over by the civil head of the area and under the supervision of the military leadership. The vertical nature of our civil service created many difficulties in the past guerilla war; these difficulties were more pronounced during the first "police" action because we were not properly prepared for it.

Although we boast about our total people's defense we were divided among ourselves within the government, the army, the bureau of national defense, the administration, the police, the lawyers, the economists, etc. Each group only recognized the authority of its own minister, who often could not be reached anymore due to lack of communication and thus our efforts to effect a total people's defense collapsed. The same difficulties were seen in the case of the parties; often they were waiting for instructions from their national committees. It is fortunate that the lurahs (village headmen) at least retained some authority, and we made ample use of this situation.

Thus we see that the preparations for a guerilla war must go hand in hand with a decentralization of the whole administrative system.

When recruiting a "territorial corps" the army must also take into consideration local interests. The territorial officers and the lower-ranking officers should, preferably, be selected from a particular area and should be most suited to the people and land of the area.

It must be emphasized that decentralization of the military leadership is not limited to military operations only, but must pervade all phases of community life. The leadership in a total people's war is usually created by combined total leadership, which has under its jurisdiction political, military, and economic matters at a national level. However, a guerilla war demands that the total leadership be decentralized over the regions that can no longer be governed from the national seat of government. It was for this reason that all military governors of the "Republic of Jogja" were given complete authority over military and civil matters. This is entirely different from what was done during the time of the Dutch East Indies, and which had been continued up to the transfer of sovereignty. This total nature is carried to all levels; even the lowest, the lurahs were given military authority.

8. The guerilla troops are the vanguard of an ideological war, usually a political-ideological war.

The TNI (Indonesian National Army) has been taught many different, and often contradictory, things in the past. Things such as "The army should not engage in politics"; "The army's only policy is the constitution"; "The army must have an ideology"; "This is a revolutionary army"; and, "The army is a tool of the country, an instrument of the government." All these expressions are merely slogans and the person who suggested them utilized them for his own needs. Generally, political figures are of the opinion that the army is an instrument to be used by the government and that the army has no voice in politics as was the case when it was formerly introduced in West Europe. Is this the correct approach?

The character of our war of independence has given a certain function and position to the army within the country and in relation to the people of Indonesia. The conception of a guerilla war as a total people's war should be kept in mind in the future, and in fact has already left a certain pattern of our future military growth in accordance with such a type of defense, the type popular during an ideological war.

It has been pointed out above that not only is it the army that fights but also the people; it is not only a miliary war but also a political, psychological and socio-economic war; in short, a total war. The science of war does not only deal with armed battles, but it has also been extended to include political, psychological and socio-economic matters. The leaders in a war are not military experts only; they must be expert statesmen as well. The activities of these leaders are not limited merely to military operations, but include all the political, psychological and socio-economical phases so that they can activate a total people's war There is no place for narrow-mindedness and limited outlook as has occurred in many past instances. The most important feature of modern war is its total character. We are concerned with strategy which includes all the people's activities.

For this reason, and the fact that the guerilla war is of a decentralized nature, the total leadership is not only founded on a national level, but also on a regional level, such as we carried it out in the past. Also in an anti-guerilla war this is the case; it does not only consist of a military phase, but also is made up of political, ideological and socio-economic phases. It is very wrong

93

to say that the leadership in a guerilla or anti-guerilla war can be free of an ideology, usually a political ideology, and that the leadership in a guerilla or anti-guerilla war should not touch the field of political ideology.

The guerilla fighter, especially the guerilla leader, is an ideological leader and a pioneer, usually of a political ideology. The guerilla carries the banner in a fight for a political ideology, one that takes place in the front lines. He is a guerilla, not because he is ordered to be one by the government, but because of the call of his own conscience and because of an ideological awareness. This is the source of his strength and ability.

For us, who for many years to come must concentrate on guerilla and anti-guerilla warfare in which the army and the people's partisans must cooperate, it is not possible to say that a soldier is a soldier, and politics are politics, and that the soldier must keep away from politics. In the past, people used to preach that the army should have an ideology, but that it must not mix in politics. The facts in our guerilla war for independence have twice proven otherwise because those facts grew out of nature of that struggle, the struggle of the guerilla war for independence. The army as a core of our people's guerilla war has become an important political factor and in the Republic has achieved a certain stature within the country and society. This stature is represented in the position occupied during our fight by our army's Chief of Staff, Sudirman.

With the world politics we do not mean "petty politics" in the sense of parties and groups fighting only for positions in the government, as is usually the case in peace time. It is politics in the wider sense; it is statesmanship; it is fighting and defending a greater policy as is implied in the proclamation and preface of our original Constitution of 1945. Therefore, with such ideas we do not mean to say that the soldier must belong to this or that party, but that he must adhere to the wider political horizons.

The official army and our partisans must in the future be oriented towards the country's ideology in its wider political implications. They must be informed and must discover for themselves about events in our political development and be able to judge them with a deeper awareness. Involvement in the "petty politics" going daily around them in the struggle for position is dangerous, and to avoid them they must be steeped in the proper political ideology.

Within the scope of this analysis, it becomes clear that the moral-psychological problem of the army is more important than the outward officialty of its administration. The TNI soldier is not a mere instrument of government, as for example the KNIL was in the past times a mere apparatus in the hands of the Dutch East Indies Government. Our soldiers, our partisans, are the tools and even the slaves, but they are also the pioneers in the fight for independence of the ideology of our people and our country. Our history itself has demonstrated that the guerilla cannot just be ordered around. He is not merely an instrument of the government — deaf and dumb in politics.

The guerilla should be a revolutionary vanguard; this was our ideal in the past and should be our ideal in the future. He must realize that the revolution has not yet ended. This revolution has forcefully put aside the old laws and introduced new laws which are referred to by the 1945 Proclamation of Indopendence. Indeed, the tactics of compromise assumed by the national fight in 1949 seemed to have reversed the revolution and returned the old laws that the revolution had meant to destroy. The elements that want to oppose the revolution and that oppose the Republic as a spearhead in the revolution more or less utilize the roads opened up by those temporary tactics in order to hit back at the struggle for independence. The first President (appointed) of the RIS (Republik Indonesia Serikat or the Republic of the United States of Indonesia) explained these tactics as follows: ".........we should think along dynamic lines. By the word dynamic I mean, ladies and gentlemen, that we should look at everything as something that flows, something that moves, something that is not solid, not static, as I have pointed out in another speech. You and I must look at all things within the laws of Panta Rei: Everything flows. There is nothing that stands still. Therefore, I see it clearly in my mind as I am now President of the United States of Indonesia that this Republic of the U. S. of Indonesia is not our final aim. According to the law of Panta Rei the Republic of the U. S. of Indonesia is only one part of a big stream in the course of history, which is subject to that law of Panta Rei. We must become a nation that strives to reach a higher level than the one we have now achieved, namely the Republic of the U. S. of Indonesia.

"Therefore I ask all the Indonesian people to continue to work, to continue to strive. Our ideal has not yet been achieved! Our vow, our hearts' desire, which has been burning in our souls will not be achieved in one or two years, but only in a score of years !

"Let us go on. Within the current of Panta Rei, anyone who does not progress will be lost in the turbulent currents of history........."

There is clearly a tendency at this time, for certain elements in the army and the government, and the people in general, to be content with the achievements so far attained. The people are drifting in the direction of the anti-revolutionary elements, who want to make such a temporary tactic into the final aim of the revolution, the aim of our Proclamation of Independence, and the true aim of our struggle.

Our revolution must not stop, and the function of the army in it must not change. The soldier and partisan of the war of independence must continue to be the standard bearer of the revolution. The spirit of revolution should not be allowed to be extinguished by an anti-revolutionary stream and by elements wishing to hold on to institutions and laws that have been revolutionized. This is the right spirit to form a foundation for the development of a regular army as well as partisan troops needed in the future for the country's defense and for the ever-raging anti-guerilla war. With better organization and training it can be rendered even more efficient.

The guerilla soldier and partisan should be a soldier and partisan fighting for an ideology, for a revolution; he must remain its vanguard, its spearhead. He is not merely a tool to be ordered about; he is an ideological fighter, a fighter in a revolution that is far from being over.

Therefore, we must avoid in the development of our army such suggestion as: "The army should not indulge in politics; it must be blind and dumb in politics; the army is only a tool of the government." This is contradictory to the true principles of guerilla warfare and anti-guerilla tactics because it would negate the basic factor of the partisans who are the vanguard of a struggle for a political ideology. Therefore, the soldier and partisan must be taught the country's ideology and policy. He must not be isolated from politics; he must have both feet in the middle of politics. The education of an army must include that of political ideology as well as military technique. The awareness of a political ideology is his conscience and his source of strength.

9. The people's army and the guerilla forces.

Some people have questioned the necessity of a guerilla army existing side by side with a people's army. Theoretically this objection should be correct, but actually it is not always so.

The people's army is an adjunct growing out of the nature of a total people's war, which requires such great numbers of soldiers that they cannot be provided by the permanent army, or what used to be called the professional army. The problem of warfare eventually becomes the problem of producing enough soldiers and equipment in war-time to fulfill the many needs of a modern war. If we go deeper into the question, it is actually the people who fight the war. In principle it is the people who decide on war or peace and it is the people who make the decisions concerning the procurement of manpower and funds. It is the people who fight for freedom, defend their lives and interests against the aggressor, and make preparations to go to war. In short, it is the people who make the necessary sacrifices. It is the people who train themselves in peace-time and recruit their youths in war-time, and then receive them back into society when the war is over. This is the true meaning of a people's army.

The establishment of a people's army cannot be left to circumstance as was the case with the BKR (People's Security Body) and TKR (People's Security Army) in 1945 when independence was proclaimed. It must be carefully planned; there must be a system of giving everyone a training period. The people's army is brought about through the system of a people's militia. Every man has the duty to defend his country. A small part must be called for military duty; a large part for civil duty. Those called for military duty will be used either for army duty in the sense that they will enter the army, serving in certain designated duties, or training duty for special army work. These duties will be assigned in accordance with their age. Thus all age groups will be trained: for example, from as young as 18 years to the age of 35, when they will be exempted from duty. Efficiency in recruiting will be achieved by age classification.

The people's army is a militia army. For a regular army a militia is the most suitable and has been provided for by the Constitution of 1945. For a guerilla army, one must question the correctness of such a militia because the guerilla is a fighter, not because his government forces him to be one, but because his own heart, his ideological awareness urges him to do so. A guerilla can easily join up and detach himself. The rules that ensure discipline in a regular army cannot be made to function in a guerilla army. Fundamentally again, the question is that of awareness of the people, and only later is it a question of whether the system is the right one. The people are prepared to go to war because they want to defend their way of life, or for the sake of their independence. The sons of the people carry guns for those noble interests. The people's army is born in the lap of its own people; they are the children who defend their Motherland. They are different from a permanent army or a professional army whose soldiers carry a gun because they want to earn a bowl of rice and go to war because they are instructed to do so by their master. The people's army is an army which defends the ideology of those people and which is given birth by a people at war to defend their interests. After the war it puts away its uniform and returns to the community.

It is also true that not every one of the people is patriotic. If it is of their benefit, many will try to avoid military duty because they are too attached to personal interests. This we have experienced too well in our struggle for freedom. In 1945 almost everybody was a patriot and after 1950 everybody was again a patriot because the war was over. But between 1945 and 1950, and above all at the peak of suffering during the first and second clashes, more and more people ceased being patriotic; they remained passive as refugees or entered the Dutch occupied areas, or even surrendered and became traitors finding employment as officials or members of Dutch sponsored committees. After Jogja had fallen, the number of patriots decreased steadily, but after sovereignty was transferred even the traitors emerged boasting about their patriotism. That was what happened and we still see them around us and many even have honored and powerful positions, enjoying the fruits of the struggle that they betrayed.

The best thing would be to make army duty and training duty voluntary, considering that the required number of such volunteers would be only a small percentage of the whole, and considering that others would be subject to civil duty anyway, or will be called up to carry a gun when circumstances require a large number. However, it remains to be seen in practice whether enough applicants will volunteer. This will happen if there is a deep ideological conscious-ness and effective propaganda. There must be appreciation and honor for those who volunteer, especially in social, psychological and ideological terms. For a Swiss, for example, it is an honor to be called for active duty. For a partisan, above all, there must be a personal wish to participate in the guerilla force. Important among the preparations are: education in our national heritage, ideological education of the country and the realization that our country is really capable of bringing happiness to the people once independ-ence has been gained.

Whatever the case, we have to introduce a training duty anyway in the villages, cities and schools, even though it be of a limited and selected scope so that an extensive training program may be carried out to reach all the people and so that we shall have as many trained men as possible if war comes. Similarly, army duty must be accelerated because most of the soldiers now in the army were born between 1920 and 1927 and they are becoming old, and the young men between 18 and 25 years have not been required to go into training so that there is a large gap in the supply of those trained to carry weapons.

The speed with which militia can be organized does not depend primarily on whether we have a law providing for it—this could probably be arranged easily if the provisional parliament supported it—but first of all on how quickly we can provide room for it in the TNI's budget. The TNI has become so inflated, with approximately 200,000 APRI; 100,000 civilians; and 350,000 dependents that there is a shortage of funds, dormitories, and equipment. For this reason we cannot accept the few thousand militia that need to be trained every year. Secondly, it depends on how fast we can supply enough able instructors, as are provided by the army under their five-year program of student cadres who become instructors for new student cadres, who in turn become instructors.

Such instructors and a core for the staff and the offices will become the permanent nucleus of the militia army. This nucleus must possess sufficient skill and must consist of a minimum number. In 1951 it was estimated that this permanent nucleus would have to be between thirty thousand and fifty thousand; in addition we would need thirty thousand to fifty thousand permanent forces for domestic security which is approximately in between what we need and what we can afford.

Registration must be done on the administrative village and district level. In the future when the census is taken, the census figures can be taken as a basis for registration for army and training duty. Until we reach this stage we must estimate, as was done in the past with the KNIL militia, with the selection of the PETA and Keibodan during the Japanese occupation in Indonesia and recently with the Pager Desa organization. The desa and district administration could be made responsible for this with the aid of the territorial cadres.

Training duty should be arranged for in each village, and army duty should be done region by region wherever there are infantry regiments in a particular region (or national group).

10. The primary task of the army for the coming years is to restore domestic security.

All preparations for guerilla war in particular and for defense against foreign invasion in general will be worthless if we do not bring domestic confusion under control. This should be made the first duty and the central task of our military preparations.

In the chapter on anti-guerilla tactics we have explained that the anti-guerilla campaign will not meet with any success if we do not have a definite basis from which to work. We must demonstrate political, psychological, social and economic skill in order to win the hopes and faith of the people gradually. First of all, the anti-guerilla war must purposely try to win the hearts of the people so that the guerilla will be cut off from its "base". If we do not succeed in winning the people, all military and police activities, although they may be perfectly executed, will be in vain because such activities strike only the effect not the cause.

During the three years of anti-guerilla war, we have not succeeded in providing a political-psychological and socio-economic basis to put an end to the revolts. It is a fact that the general condition has not improved, but deteriorated. The happy and hopeful atmosphere, prevailing at the transfer of sovereignty, has turned into one of demoralization with crises developing in all fields because the responsible leaders have failed in their duty. They are to be blamed, and not the difficult situation. A good commander can always keep the fire of hope ablaze among his forces even in time of deep distress, when encircled or in retreat, so that there is still faith in the coming victory. A good captain can give his men encouragement when a storm is raging at sea. The main thing is to have good leadership.

We are still waiting for the time to come when the government can give the proper political-psychological and socio-economical basis which means hope for the people and that the end of the anti-guerilla war is in sight. The people have not as yet elected a parliament and government; the inhabitants of the different regions have not been given appreciation for their region; the people cannot yet trust the government apparatus as they should; the people are still complaining about the ever-increasing suffering. We are still awaiting the moment when a hopeful people can become the ally in an anti-guerilla war and spontaneously participate actively in solving its security problems. The answer can only be provided by the political leaders of the country.

The first requirement in this direction is that there will be a parliament and a government of the people, and that there is a full active life in each region. For the execution of a promising program of political-psychological and social-economic development we need leaders who can inspire confidence in the people. The government must be stable, skillful and have authority. The administration must be competent and efficient. After three years of sovereignty there appears to be nothing approaching this goal.

Government is a political question. Administration is the concern of the government. Government employees now number 470,000, in addition to the 100,000 civil employees of the armed forces. Compare these almost 600,000 employees with the approximately 75,000 before the war. Our organization cannot be made efficient yet; for example, in the field of security, duties and rights are all confused and this does not make possible any proper planning or undertaking. Because the workers in the administrative apparatus lack skill and integrity, they fail to radiate the faith and confidence they should; instead, complaints about the administration fill the air everywhere. This can only be overcome by simplifying the administration and placing greater emphasis on such qualities as good character and technical skill. The employees are actually servants of the people and the people demand the best. For the employee, military or civil, to serve the people must be considered a calling and he must possess the skill necessary for his work so that he will have the faith of the people and later the respect of the people. The government must simplify its organization and bring greater efficiency and economy into its organization. The government cannot afford to delay screening and training and improving its employees. The government should not fail to wage an anti-corruption campaign in the broader sense.

We still have a long way to go before we have an administration that could inspire trust and hope in the people and before political-psychological and social-economic conditions have been fulfilled to form a basis for a solution to the anti-guerilla campaign.

It depends mainly on us whether the guerilla movements in West Java and South Sulawesi will become civil war or will abate and become a mere police matter. The guerillas act according to the principles of total guerilla warfare, but we tend to deal with them on an incidental and isolated manner. The military leadership conducts military operations, and the regional council is responsible for political-psychological and social-economic matters; furthermore there is not yet a definition of authority between the central and regional administration, and between the regional head and the administrative offices. There is no one in complete command and in these times when failures occur we like to blame each other. Instead of carrying out a total anti-guerilla war our side is divided and very often accusing each other. That this is not a sound situation is difficult to be denied except by fake propaganda.

If we consider the matter objectively, we must admit that the guerillas have shown progress in South Sulawesi and West Java. Their activities, which in the beginning were carried out underground and were intended to intimidate the people, have reached the stage of guerilla wars; they have been able to stage battles moving along highways and into cities. These are the signs of growth for a guerilla. It means that he is able to move with larger troops and that his "base" in the people has become more solid and thriving. The guerilla "fish" grows bigger in the people's "water" because the "environment" is taken care of politically, psychologically and socio-economically by the guerilla or by the negligence and the mistakes of the anti-guerilla.

The anti-guerilla war is a total war; its political, psychological and socio-economical aspects especially must be given proper consideration, and a solution to it must be sought according to systematic, long-term planning.

The anti-guerilla war does not last one or two years but a much longer time, and a politically unstable, young country like ours needs a special military apparatus designed to guarantee security. This police task for the military is entirely different from its regular task and different from the usual police task; for this it requires a different organization and education. Because our operational methods have demonstrated that they do not bring the results sought, we should set up a special, permanent army for domestic security. Such an army will act principally in platoons, sometimes in companies and at the most in battalions. They should be equipped with 8-cm mortars and 7.7-mm machine guns to aid in difficult operations. Generally, however, it is sufficient to equip them with the usual company weapons. For special duties there must be a few armored units. In order to be sufficiently mobile it must have a motorized part and for duty in the villages they must use bicycles. Some troops on horseback will complete this security army.

On the basis of past experiences we should have a force of 30,000 men making up 25 or 30 infantry battalions. They could be organized from the present TNI infantry. They carry the same duties as the mobile brigade of the National Police. For efficiency's sake the two could be merged. They are both of an infantry nature. In wartime these institutions could be united in units larger than battalions: they could then be used especially for security duty in the home front, for example, to destroy fifth column and parachute invasions. With such an infantry security corps, the police, on the one hand, could concentrate on building its police force and the army, on the other, could concentrate on building a modern regular army, a "territorial" corps, and a Home Guard for guerilla war. The security force must adapt its tactics to its anti-guerilla nature and thus use the same "weapons" as the guerilla, namely: aggressiveness, mobility and flexibility. Essentially, anti-guerilla warfare is a "patrol" warfare which promises victory to the most durable. A passive anti-guerilla campaign doing static sentry duty will fail in its aim and only the active campaign will be successful. The leadership in a chaotic region must be held by those who are in complete charge and in complete power. All instruments of power must reside in their hands and all instructions on military, political, social and economic affairs are given by them; in short they have the overall command in accordance with the total character of true anti-guerilla warfare. They could be of the military or of the civilian; the thing that counts most is their ability to lead such a total campaign. The system and rules must differ from the usual system and rules under normal conditions and must fit the emergency situation.

Their first task is to increase the efficiency of the government apparatus; the second is to win the people and the villages back and to urge them to participate actively in guaranteeing security; and the third is to annihilate the armed bands. Such powers were not found in the Governor or in the General, or in the Head of the Police in the peace-time structure, nor in the rules of the State of War and Siege of the Dutch East Indies, rules which are operating now; such powers are found only in the history of our struggle. The system of military governors of the then "Republic of Jogja" demonstrated its value in the 1948 revolts and the transfer of sovereignty of 1950. After three years of bitter experiences from 1950 to 1953, we should be able to overcome our country's deadlock today: our country has become static and too formal; it has insisted on being legalistic and has become bureaucratic. Only when we break this deadlock will we be able to mobilize again the movements of the country, the dynamic powers and the initiative. These conditions are required if we are to obtain victory. We seem to have lost our guerilla blood, our revolutionary blood.

The execution of this task demands in general a complete and efficient administration, especially an efficiently organized and highly trained security force, which in particular can be trusted. For the coming years this is the foremost task of the army because this is the condition for any other program. A stable condition within the country is the basis for a strong defense and the basis for the development of the country and the nation in general. Our anti-guerilla war today must be considered as a matter of life and death for the Republic which we proclaimed on 17 August 1945.

We hope for the best!

———

III. THE MOST IMPORTANT INSTRUCTIONS TO GUERILLAS (1948—1949)

As chief of the operational staff of Army Headquarters, I was assigned by the Commander-in-Chief to analyse experiences of the first colonial attack in order to draw up more accurate guides against the possibility of aggression for the second time.

This analysis led to a spectfic concept concerning the structure of our defence and military organisation, as well as to new ideas and guiding lines for our troops.

It so happened that before my division evacuated to Central Java, the government (Amir Sjarifuddin Cabinet) had already decided to make changes; preparations were under way and the new regulations were nearly finished, so that the opportunity also existed for introduction of these lessons, though the Government's plans and regulations were only concerned in the main with the composition of the ministry and the top military leadership, while what I brought forward concerned the organisation of the troops and the regions of resistence in relation to a guerilla administration and defence which was composed of pockets.

It is a pity, however, that this matter of the organisation of guerilla troops and regions became negelected through the clash of politics and from the party sentiment which was very fierce at that time. For this reason, only very little was achieved.

The principles I had brought forward concerned two things. Firstly, the need to set up territorial organisattons of pockets stemming from village society where *Pa' Lurah* (the village head) with the aid of the territorial cadres could establish a guerilla administration that could not be swept away by the enemy. These guerilla *Kelurahan* regions were to be gathered under one military sub-district pocket led by the Military Sub district Command together with the *Tjamat,* the sub-district Head. Further, the Military Region Commands were to be set up for the "*Kabupaten*", the Military Sub-territorium Command — later on, the Military District Commands for the Residency, and a Commander for each province — together all making a complete leadership, in the sense of leadership for battle as well as for guerilla administration.

Secondly, it was necessary to devide the troops into two types, in connection with there being local defence and mobile defence duties. Thus it was necessary to compose territorial battalions from existing troops; their armament ratio would be 1 : 3 to 5, so that every Military District Comamnd would obtain 1 battalion or 1 company for guerilla resistance in miktary sub-districts. Furthermore it was necessary to establish fastmoving fighting battalions with an armament ratio of 1 : 1, among which must be included trajectory guns for offensives, of which there should be 1 or more in each sub-territorium (Residency), so that the Military Sub-torritorium Commands could make guerilla attacks wherever tactical and/or politico-psychological conditions required measures of attack.

The plan failed over this, because the commanders tried to make up as many mobile (fighting) battalions as possible, in order to obtain as many brigades as possible. In consequence, it was necessary to make a great many people inactive and there were too few territorial battalions, which moreover, were regarded as being "low rate" in the beginning. Besides, such a breaking-up of units was too often provoked as a means of destroying our military unity and in preparation for the federal army of General Spoor, even though our plans were a lesson drawn objectively from past experiences; the political and psychological problems of that time were fast intertwined with all other kinds of problems.

With the occurrence of the Madiun Affair, the government dared and was compelled to act severely and decidedly, so that only then were we able to reorganise more smoothly. Besides this, the illness of the Commander-in-Chief caused him to give me full authority to take the steps required. Nevertheless, it was already far too late, for in the middle of September war started amongst ourselves and it took two months to break the well-orginased resistance of the rebels; and on 19 December the second colonial attack began. However, we were yet able to draw up the Commander-in-Chief's Instruction of 9 November and to hold a meeting with all the territorial commanders, governors and residents on 11 November to hand them the implementating regulations of that Instruction, which regulated scorched earth activities, evacuation, resistance and the guerilal administration in the pockets.

However, the reorganisation of the troops could no longer be effected and in consequence of the non-formation of the two types of troops, at the moment that guerilla warfare began, all the "mobile" battalions had to be "territorialized" and several existing "territorial"troops had to be made "mobile" in order to create one type of troop. Such things caused our scheme to fail to carry out tactical measures of attack on a sufficiently large scale, which would be capable of the tactic of destroying convoys, isolated posts, and the like.

106

The instructions and announcements which follow are:

A. My explanation of what our guerilla warfare should have been (before the second Dutch aggression began).

B. Instructions for the guerilla administrations enable them to regulate the total people's resistance, immediately after the outbreak of the second colonial attack.

C. Instructions for the conduct of guerilla fighting.

D. Instructions from other leaders (the staff of the Headquarters of the Sumatra Command, the stall of Division I and from late Lt. Col. Slamet Rijadi).

E. Instructions on the guerilla code of justice composed by Prosecutor General Tirtawinata.

F. Important sections from the instruction book for the guerilla administration of the Military Sub-district Commands/Ketjamatan.

A. EXECUTING TOTAL PEOPLE'S RESISTANCE

We fighters ought in fact to prepare ourselves to face a second Dutch aggression. True, the "Renville Agreement" is there and with it the armistice. True, a political solution is being sought. True, there is the President's counsel: "From the bullet to the ballot". But to us it is patently clear that the strategical position of our Republic is merely one of siege, being only one-third in area of what it was originally, and surrounded by federal territories. The heart of our Republic is no longer far from the Dutch positions.

While we are faced by the possibility of a second attack, we are attacked from within by a war of ideas, seeking to overthrow us from within. It is very hard to point to the persons who set that war of ideas into motion. But what is evident is that those doing so are certainly enemies of the Republic, and that in fact we are very easily afflicted by that war of ideas. Breaches between right and left wings become more profound; leaders accuse one another in public; the influence of this war of ideas grows deeper, even affecting the armed forces.

However we do it, we must prepare ourselves for the possibility of a second Dutch attack, for they are certain to make one, if they can not obtain their ends by means of negotiation. Their military position vis-a-vis ourselves is already very strong.

Their first attack has provided us with a great deal of experience, especially in localities where we ought to have pockets. We can not face the enemy's strength, well-equipped and modern in every way as it is, in an ordinary war, in the lines of battle our troops used to study. We do not have the equipment to stand against our enemy in open warfare; the enemy would be able to break through everywhere, to take possession of all the towns and to control all lines of communication. But we have had our lesson already. At the very least, the enemy is unable to destroy us. See how 35,000 of our men came out from the pockets in Dutch occupied territories ! We can surround and we can harass the enemy. We can make the enemy's position into pockets in the territories we control. We can keep our instruments of government intact in our territories. When the enemy attacks again, he will start by occupying the towns, by controlling the main roads and then by occupying the economically important regions. His strength in Java is only there to four divisions. In order to occupy Java down to the sub-distrcts, he would need more than ten divisions, and it is certain that he is unable to form as many as that. He is able to maintain occupation of only a small part of the territorial regions. The remainder he tries only to patrol or may even never go there at all.

Therefore, he will try to break our strength gradually by political, social of our psychological means, to win the hearts of our people and of some of our civil servants. He will distribute clothes, medicines, food etc. He will make wide-spread propaganda campaigns. The members of the population following him will be protected, will be given all their daily necessities. The people who will have none of him will be terrorized by banditism, by arson, by kidnapping and so forth, in such a way that they will always feel unsafe, afraid, and thus eventualy they will lose hope and become tired of the struggle. They will become the people colonized by the Dutch. Amongst the leaders and the educated who are not used to suffering, there will be many who go right away to Dutch occupied towns, for it is safer there and because there are enough necessaries of life there. They will begin by returning to occupied towns, and gradually they will collaborate with the enemy. Gradually they will be prepared to become NICA-employees, *) to build up councils of people's representatives and finally to become puppet states. They are the traitors of our struggle for independence, the greatest and most dangerous traitors.

That is why it is necessary from the beginning to organise a territorial structure taking the form of military dictricts commands, military sub-district commands and cadres of village territories. These bodies are charged with preparing measures in the civil field. When the enemy attacks, it is necessary to evacuate the people in an organised way to scattered places already prepared, in oder that they shall not be used by the enemy, who thirst for people to command. It is very important to evacuate government officials and leaders, for they are greatly needed by the enemy as mediators for exercising enemy control over the people. All the equipment important for continuing the struggle should also be evacuated; nothing may be left behind of such a kind that it might be of benefit to the enemy.

After the enemy has occupied a given place, he will gradually patrol its surroundings, in the beginning to clear it of our troops, but eventually to restore an ordinary atmosphere of peace. He will try to appoint a new civil service and a new village adminis-

*) NICA: Netherlands Indies Civil Administration.

tration if the old personnel are not willing to work with him. He will try to open offices, markets, schools, shops, etc. The people's hunger for imported goods in consequence of the blockade up to now, will be used to attract the people back to the towns. Pensioners who have not been paid since the Japanese time, will have their rights guaranteed once more. Through the elderly people who have been lured into town, the enemy will try to attract their children back who are still fighting in the mountains. There are many devices and stratagems which the enemy can use.

Because of this a permanent military administration is needed which the people will always know is there. This military administration will be in the hands of the army's territorial officers. The civil administration will be included within this structure. In this way it can be arranged that the Republic of Indonesia's de facto authority continues firmly over the people. The apparatus of state remains intact, for it is evacuated if an enemy patrol comes. Officials will be taught to play "hide-and-seek" with the enemy patrols. They ought to be permanently mobile in their territory, so that the people will come across them everywhere. They will always be able to lead their people and they will always be able to punish those betraying the state's cause. They can continue to make information campaigns and the collection of taxes and the like can be dealt with in ways to suit the emergency. Efforts to keep trade flowing via the ever-moving markets must be made constantly. Republican currency should be the only money in circulation; Dutch money must be destroyed. With the help of the territorial cadres the guerilla administration can operate in the pockets by "hide-and-seek" methods. The basic aim is that the NICA administration cannot become established, so that the people recognize only the government of the Republic of Indonesia alone. This means that the people refuse to be colonized again.

In conducting an administration of state such as this, the regional unit which is compact and which can be guided directly is the village. That is why the village leaders, the Lurah, are the core of the maintenance of the Republic's government. The Lurah are the only leaders amidst the people who are still obeyed by the people. And these Lurah are indeed the choice of the people themselves, whom the people know closely, and who know the ins and outs of the village. The Lurah must be protected and respected. Members of the armed forces put at the disposal of the village, such as territorial cadres, must come fully under the authority of Pa' Lurah. The Lurah himself must hold the authority of the military administration.

Higher than the Lurah, the Tjamat is the only level of official who can permanently control his region intact. A sub-district should be maintained as an integral part of the administration. For this purpose, it is necessary that the Military Sub-district Command hold the military administration. Higher levels will no longer be able to exercise full administration, so that they become intermediates, inspectors and plan-makers. The Military Sub-district Command together with the Tjamat ought to guide and to co-ordinate the activities of the Lurah, because the Sub-district are pockets of our administration. The Military Sub-district Command, the Tjamat, the Lurah and the village officers and cadres are able to play hide-and-seek with the enemy, should he come on patrols. As soon as the enemy has gone, the administration is carried on again.

In order to bring de facto pockets into existence, military tactics must be so arranged that operation of the administration is guaranteed. The troops are stationed in the pockets. The army must spread throughout the whole of the island from Banten to Besuki. In every Sub-District a Republican pocket must be established with instruments of authority of the Republic of Indonesia. If necessary, new officials should be appointed to complete those instrumenst of authority. As the troops spread, "Wingate" fashion, to the West, to the North and to the East, an evenly-spread guerilla defence will be accomplished throughout the island.

Two kinds of troops are needed, namely those with a territorial duty and those who are mobile. For each Military District Command Kabupaten we should try to have a strength of between a company and a battalion. Their task is to protect the Republic's pockets by guerilla means, both against attack from within as well as from without. These units, together with the people, guarantee the presence of permanent resistance in each outlying district. The units must know the region and the people thoroughly. We are now organizing these territorial battalions under the command of sub-territorium commanders. It is intended that in the future these territorial battalions will become training-centers for the youth of every Kabupaten, in order to train them for sentinal and guerilla duties in each sub-district and Kelurahan. In this way the people's military units will be obtained for the total people's resistance.

These territorial battalions do not need to be fully armed. Up to the present it is adequate if we take as guide a ratio of armaments in the proportion of about 1:3, in accord with the regulations in force for the people's defence tactics of former times. Many people mistakenly take these territorial battalions to be the formation of a second army, or as places to put people who have been rationalized, or as the fractionalizing of our Indonesian National Army. Naturally, the plan could be implemented for such purposes, if the need for territorial duty is not understood; if there is no understanding, there will be many difficulties in its implementation. During the Japanese occupation there already were two types of duty. The territorial duty, area by area, was entrusted to the PETA daidans *). The mobile duty of fighting was given to the Japanese army itself. In this way it was ensured that the Japanese Army was not scattered everywhere, so that it was a force sufficiently compact and quick on the move to fight wherever if was needed.

The Ministry of Defence has already decided that there shall be mobile battalions side-by-side with territorial battalions. There battalions need to be armed in the ratio of 1 : 1. Their task is not territorial but mobile, that is, they must be able to attack the positions, the isolated units, and the communication systems of the enemy. Their task is to be on the offensive, to attack. The territorial battalions have a defensive task, to make the defence. In fact, it is not necessary to form large numbers of these mobile units. If there is one battalion mobile in each sub-territorium, it is more than enough. Whereas territorial units and people's resistance troops tie down and harass the enemy sub-district by sub-district, so that the enemy's strength is nailed to wherever it happens to be scattered as guard detachments, as police detachments and as small patrols, the mobile units obtain an opportunity to fight and to destroy the isolated enemy detachment, his small patrols, and his communications. With these units we can make "Wingate" raids against the regions pacified by the enemy. Behind the mobile units come the territorial cadres and then the Republic's civil service and the village officers can be organized again, so that the federal regions will be gradually recaptured, and federal authority will, as far as possible, be driven back into the large towns.

Thus, each Kelurahan, each sub-district, in short every conrner of the whole island becomes the battle-ground of a guerilla war, which can never be extinguished, which harasses and ties down the strength of thousands of enemy detachments, which interminably wears away and exhausts the strength of the enemy. Meanwhile, our mobile battalions gradually strengthen themselves and attack an enemy ever more out of breath, while our civil and ter-

---

*) PETA daidans: the regional organisations of PETA, the Home Defence troops of the Japanese time.

ritorial instruments stabilize the pockets and attack the enemy politically, socially, economically, and psychologically.

At last the enemy will have only two paths open, namely, to keep on sending out troops for his own defence, and it is obvious that he has neither men nor money enough for this, or to vacate parts of the regions he has occupied. He could vacate some regions altogether or he could concentrate his forces in the towns. But this would mean that he degenerates in strategy, even though in tactics he still attacks every now and then, as his equipment is more perfect and in every way is adequate. This implies that he is no longer able to advance in the military sense. The only thing left to him to do is to try political and economic paths.

That is why the territorial and civil organisations in the pockets are of the utmost importance for they provide no room nor time for the enemy's political and economic strategies.

The people must evacuate from the enemy's centres of occupation they ought to play hide-and-seek in the pockets of the Kelurahan and sub-districts. Every economic endeavour the enemy makes must be brought to nothing; his markets must be destroyed, his money must be forbidden, his economic centres must be constantly harassed, his transport must be constantly interfered with until it is broken. Civil servants and influential leaders of the people should be guarded, not left in the towns or allowed to return to the towns, for they would be captured or made use of, so that basically they would betray the strategy of the people's total struggle. Therefore territorial cadres must guard and support them so that they do not go over to the enemy. Once the war for freedom has begun as the total people's resistance, no compromise whatsoever is possible, as has been counselled by our Commander-in-Chief.

Hence our commanders should fully realise that territorial work is not of second rank and is not less important. It is even the case that during the first Dutch attack we had sufficient experience showing that territorial work is the basic task, whilst the work of the fighting units is only as an instrument of the territorial task. The fighting units were the pioneers and protectors, so that the territorial cadres would be able to work succesfully. Up to now there are still many misunderstandings about what is called territorial and what is mobile. For the success of the coming struggle we ought to clear up those misunderstandings.

A sector of warfare which is of the utmost importance is psychological war, the war of ideas and the war of nerves. In general, we are prone to fall victim to it. We too easily affected by provocation, too easily subject to misunderstandings, because of our lack of general education etc. We are too much split up and affected by rumours. In this matter the enemy obviously has a better organisation and strategy. Through psychological warfare one leader can be set against another, one division against another, the army against the people's defence, one party against another, one group against another, so that state and army collapse from within or at least continue to split apart and to quarrel, so that the enemy can easily defeat us. One way of overcoming this is not to trust anything too quickly, to ensure that information from above is given constantly via organisations, and that there is contact all the time. If anything is felt to be out of the ordinary, seek contact directly, ask questions and discuss the matter. This will be all the more necessary, when we are in the guerilla pockets in the future, for provocation and rumour will increase and grow stronger, so that A will take B for a NICA agent and vice-versa. In such a situation each person suspects the other, or each will think that he alone is fighting, and so will gradually lose hope, because he feels left alone in the midst of all kinds of suffering. How strong will his spirit be, if he knows that everywhere the struggle grows in intensity, and if there is a mutual confidence! And now it can be seen how important it is to organise a method of communication and information which is orderly, eventhough in the form of relay runners.

Each command needs to establish communication posts covering the whole region like a net. Those posts must be able to conceal themselves from the enemy, and by "hide-and-seek" escape his patrols and raids. The posts must be in constant contact with the military and civil authorities. Couriers or a roving leader must always keep contact between posts. Later on, our information section can pass on news of the struggle and give counsel through these posts to the Kelurahan and the sub-districts, to be made public on information bords, at meetings, or as guerilla news-sheets. Such contact and information are necessary to ensure the integrity and completeness of both state and army.

It is not the place here to explain the techniques of communication, transport, supply, equipments, expenses, health, information etc. But it is necessary first to keep in mind that present methods are no longer suitable and must be adjusted to the methods of working in pockets and by "hide-and-seek", and to the methods under which each region from the Kelurahan upwards does everything possible by its own power with its own resources. The autonomy of Kelurahan and military sub-districts must become facts. The Lurah and the Tjamat are the foundations of our state; they will be the leaders and the men who activate our people in the guerilla war which we will shortly face.

114

Mobilize all influential powers in a single body — no matter what — in order to strengthen and to support the pillars of the state, especially in the time of people's struggle which is now ahead.

Jogjakarta, August 1948.
Headquarters of the Armed Forces
of the Republic of Indonesia
Operational Chief-of-Staff,

Col. A. H. NASUTION.

B. BASIC INSTRUCTIONS CONCERNING THE GUERILLA ADMINISTRATION AND THE PEOPLE'S RESISTANCE IN JAVA

The Republic was the basic capital in the struggle for the independence of the whole of Indonesia. Java was the basic political issue in the struggle of that time. Therefore, the Dutch aim with their second aggression was to do away with the Republic and its Indonesian National Army. Several days beforehand, the Dutch had stated officially that it was no longer necessary to negotiate with the Republic, and on the night of 18th December L. J. M. Beel announced that the Netherlands had set aside the Renville Agreement; several hours afterwards, their army invaded the Republic which had already been pressed back in to a small territory on the island of Java.

Their first objective was to do away with the leadership of the state and army. Thus their sudden air attacks upon the capital, which fell upon us all at once both tactically and strategically, while we were entirely powerless to protect ourselves against air attack, for we had no planes, no artillery defence, and no anti-aircraft guns. Militarily, this operation was indeed a success for the greater part. Sukarno, Hatta and other leaders gave themselves up, but the most important National Army leaders managed to save themselves together with their units for the organisation of a guerilla offensive. It is true that it was never intended to defend the capital; what had priority was to save and to evacuate manpower and leadership, as had been arranged by the Commander-in-Chief of 9th November with the approval of cabinet. The first phase for us meant preventing the destruction of the troop formations and carrying out the scorched earth policy.

In line with this attack upon Jogjakarta, the enemy's A-division penetrated into Republican East Java in the direction of Malang-Kediri, Sourabaya-Ngandjuk and Glondong-Madiun; the B-division into Republican Central Java in the direction of Semarang-Jogja, Semarang-Solo, Semarang-Magelang and Purwokerto-Magelang, while the C-division entered Banten in the direction of Tanggerang-Serang and Bogor-Rangkasbitung. Through these movements, the Dutch aimed at immediate control of all centres and main roads in order to pursue and destroy Indonesian National Army units, which by these means, to use the usual term, would be split up without an organisation any longer, so that would only be necessary to make cleaning actions against the "remainder".

In this way, the destruction and the occupation of the Republic "was finished", without any further fear of U.N.O. intervention, and likewise immediately the destruction of the T.N.I. would be "completed", so that guerilla warfare would be prevented. That the Dutch held misgivings about a guerilla war is shown in what Van Poll of the Commission-General wrote:

"Not only guerillas, but also a scorched earth policy and the inevitability of contra-terror against terror, were part of the forseeable consequences of an attempt by violence to restore the Netherlands authority.

As for the guerillas: the Commission General knew with absolute certainty — how knowledge was obtained cannot be openly stated at present or for the time being — that the Republican troops, in the event of military action from our side, would not venture an open battle, but would do everything to maintain a constant attack upon our communication lines. This implied a method of waging war in which especially our Netherlands troops would not rise to the occasion, and the small daily losses would mount to heavy losses in the long run. Later on, the facts confirmed that the prophecy of the Commission General was right.

"Next to the certainty of a long guerilla war and unceasing attacks on our lines of communication, the Commission General had the absolute certainty that scorched earth policy would be relentlessly applied. This too has been confirmed by the facts, even though the extraordinarily quick march or the Netherlands troops in the police action was able to save a number of things, the destruction of which had been intended. Had there been more time in Central Java, there would have been more destroyed than actually was the case".

At that stage it was thought there would be enough political and military leaders of the Republic prepared to join an interim government, and indeed, many did go over to the Dutch, or were at least prepared to be evacuated to the federal towns or who had already asked protection or had been writing letters to the Dutch.

Therefore at that stage Beel thought fit to set up an interim government together with the B.F.O. (the deliberative organisation of the Dutch sponsored "Federal State"), based on the Dutch regulation for the "Indonesian Administration in Time of Transition", the initiative for which had been taken by the "federal" conference in Bandung and which had been approved by the Dutch parliament. It was hoped the Republican leaders would be quickly invited to join it, as happened with the B.F.O. invitation later on to Sukarno-Hatta and others like them.

We have witnessed the failure of that Dutch scheme, because they did not appreciate sufficiently the firmness of our resistance. However, the blows they rained upon us in the first moments were very heavy, and needed quick and appropriate measures protect our front from within and without.

Within, the atmosphere became extremely critical. The ordinary people received Dutch pamphlets with pictures showing the surrender of Sukarno-Hatta, thus the surrender of the government. The people did not know about the mandate to Sjafruddin, about the Emergency Government of the Republic in Sumatra, about the Security Council, and so forth. At that time what they knew was only that there was no government. And at the very same time in the regions of Central Java, where there had recently been revolts, the rumours spread widely about there being no administration any longer. In East Java (Kediri) there also occurred a movement which expatiated upon the government vacuum and proposed a new leadership, and which took the name of "Markas Murba Terpendam" (the Hidden Centre of the Proletariat). In West Java there appeared announcements from Kartosuwirjo who obviously no longer recognized the Republic and the National Army.

During these days our authorities and our troops were split up, and many doubted whether the struggle would continue as that of an organized state, for they did not know the situation outside their restricted environs.

Hence our first steps were in the political and psychological field in order to overcome the Dutch policy and the upheaval and confusion within: the State and the Nasional Army stand firm still and continue an orderly struggle under leadership. Preparations for the People's over-all struggle were made, based upon our experinces during the first attack.

It is in this connection that the issue of the very first announcements and instructions of the Headquarters Java Command should be seen, which, through having in readiness a number of liaison officers at headquarters, were soon disturbed in all regions. Groups went on foot in all directions, and radio broadcasts from Mount Lawu (Major Maladi) also spread news abroad immediately.

The political and psychological shock was in general overcome, the guerilla administration was established, the lines of struggle from then onwards were united and harmonised, the organisations

118

of the state's authority were kept whole vis-a-vis the seizure of power from within and without, the discipline of the struggle was firmly maintained with sanctions under military guerilla law.

To these ends the following documents were issued:

1. Decree of the Military Administration.
2. Instruction from Headquarters Java Command No. 1, concerning the methods to be used in guerilla administration.
3. Instruction for establishing means of guerilla communications.
4. Instruction concerning methods of supply for guerilla war.
5. Instruction about non-co-operation.
6. Instruction on how to overcome false news.
7. Instruction on no contact with the outside.
8. Decree on the continued functioning of the State of the Republic of Indonesia.
9. Order of the Day, 17th February 1949, concerning the stage of the struggle.
10. Decree for prevention of agitation and disorder.
11. Instruction to defend the existing apparatus of the State.
12. Decree concerning officials who have not brought themselves under the organization of the guerilla administration.
13. Instruction concerning "Pager Desa" (Village Home Guard).
14. Elucidation of the relative powers within the guerilla administration.

As soon as the Command Post of the Headquarters Java Command was set up at Prambanan, the following decree was issued:

HEADQUARTERS JAVA COMMAND
No. 2/M.B.K.D.

ANNOUNCEMENT.

In connection with the state of the War and based upon Government Regulation nos. 30 and 70, we herewith decree a Military Administration in force for the whole of the island of Java.

Issued from: The Seat of Command.
Hour : 08.00.
Date : 22nd December 1948.

COMMANDER OF THE ARMY AND JAVA TERRITORIUM,
Sgd. COL. A. H. NASUTION.

Copies to:

1. *All divisions.*
2. *All brigades.*
3. *All Sub-territorium Commands.*

Explanation:
To be conveyed to their sub-ordinates.

This was followed immediately by the decree of a Military Administration, as follows:

HEADQUARTERS JAVA COMMAND
No. 1/M.B.K.D./48

WORKING INSTRUCTION
MILITARY ADMINISTRATION THROUGHOUT JAVA

I. INTRODUCTION

1. With the outbreak of this second colonial attack, the State of the Republic of Indonesia is no longer bound by the existing agreements of the State with the Dutch, and the State of the Republic of Indonesia returns completely to defending the Proclamation of August 17th, 1945.

2. The State of the Republic of Indonesia which has been proclaimed already is an organisation of the State as an instrument of the entire people of Indonesia for achieving their ideals. Therefore we must fight as a state which has been set up and which has its own laws already; if our struggle as a State is smashed, we shall degenerate to struggle as a movement. *The army has sworn: We stand or fall together with the State of the Republic of Indonesia.* The Order of the Day from the Commander-in-chief of the Armed Forces dated 15th September 1948 is stronger.

3. To make it possible to execute this duty, Instruction and Regulations have been issued. The Commander-in-chief of the Armed Forces issued Order No. 1/Sombap/48 for the defence, and for the administration there have been issued:

    a. Government Regulation No. 30, Directive of the Military Government; all instruments of the authority of the State are under the military, all important bodies and departments are militarized, and military law is in force.

b. Regulation No. 70 annuls the Regional Defence Council and people's defence bodies, which are not in keeping with the Armed Forces Commander-in-chief's Instruction of November 9th, determines the responsibility of military commanders over all regional heads of the same standing and of orders from regional heads (Residents, Bupati, Tjamat, Lurah) over all civil bodies in their regions.

c. The Armed Forces Commander-in-chief's Instruction of November 9th regulates the execution of the military and civil "Wehrkreise" *) and their duties. Thus on the island of Java *a total military government* is organised. And it brings with it a tactic of *civil administration which is also characterised by totality*. All of this is an absolute condition for defending the Republican State in war.

The military government authorities are: Commander-in-chief of the Armed Forces, Commander of the Army and Java Territorium, Military Governor, Military Regional Commands (Sub-territorial Commands), Military District Commands, Military Sub-district Commands, Village Cadres, and Hamlet Cadres.

The civil authorities in Java are: Resident, Bupati, Tjamat and Lurah.

NOTES

1. During a cabinet sitting it was arranged between the Headquarters of the Armed Forces and the Ministry of Internal Affairs to do away with civil governors in time of war and make them advisors to the Miiltary Governor; this was not announced probably due to the sudden crisis of 19th December 1948.

2. The Central Government was transferred to Sumatra by Vice Presidential Order of the Day dated 19th December 1948. Orders and authority were given to the Armed Forces and to all state bodies to continue the struggle.

The Vice President's Order of the Day dated 19th December 1948 addressed to all of the Armed Forces and to all government bodies is as follows:

"It is likely that the Government of the Republic of Indonesia in Jogja will be surrounded and be unable to carry out

---

*) Werhkreise: an area in wartime with fixed boundaries beyond which the competence and/or authority of bodies within it do not extend.

its duties and obligations, but preparations have been made
to continue the Government of the Republic of Indonesia in
Sumatra. Whatever befalls individual Government officials in
Jogja, the struggle will be continued.

VICE PRESIDENT OF THE REPUBLIC OF INDONESIA
DEFENCE MINISTER OF THE REPUBLIC OF INDONESIA

Sgd. MOHAMMAD HATTA.

And so the territorial organisation in Java was empowered to
become a completely military government in order to save the
Republic of Indonesia.

II. MILITARY AND POLITICAL DEVELOPMENTS

1. In the military sense, the Dutch will occupy the towns and their
   surroundings. These will be the pockets in the midst of country
   which continues to be controlled by the National Army. Through
   the preparation of our territorial organisation, our regional
   organisation can be mobilised for the sake of district order.
   Through the use of "Wingate" action, our military government
   has been established from Banten to Besuki, covering the whole
   island.

   From these districts we will gradually decrease the Dutch
   occupied regions until no more are left. The maximum strength
   of the Dutch in Java is 4 divisions, which means that approximately 2 battalions can be used for the occupation of each Residency, and these can not possibly control more than several towns,
   so that they are forced to be mobile. Therefore the destruction
   of roads will lessen the enemy's control.

   Our mobile troops will protect and extend the regions under
   authority of the military government, and will create disturbances in or will surround the towns, especially harbours, and will
   annihilate the enemy's flow of transport.

   The enemy's strength will steadily decrease, because in this very
   year his troops must be replaced by new troops with no
   experience,and because his funds for expenditure will fall in
   consequence of the boycot by many countries and the exclusion
   of the Netherlands from the Marshall Plan. It is evident that at a
   certain moment our military strength will surpass the enemy's
   so that he can be driven out of the country entirely.

   a. Military targets: such as convoys, camps, harbours and
   aerodromes.

b. Targets of society: disturbances in the towns at moments of political importance, such as when there are conferences to discuss Indonesia or regions of Indonesia, the formation of puppet-states, etc.

c. Targets of the military government:

to extend the military areas and to protect them.

d. Targets of society: to create disturbances in the areas occupied by the enemy.

2. Political developments.

a. The aim of the Dutch is to form immediately an intern government with some important persons from the Republic who have become traitors, then to install the United States of Indonesia; eventually authority and responsibility will be transferred to these puppets.

It is clear that such a government can only control Dutch occupied towns and will fall of itself if the Dutch strength decreases, so that finally they must surrender to us, because a government which is not supported by the people but only a foreign state must fall at a certain time.

Therefore the districts which are still under our control must be regulated in firm and orderly fashion to be able to compete with and then to overthrow the puppet government in the towns.

b. It is also possible that, our strength exceeding theirs in consequence of the *Wingate* actions and revolts in the occupied areas, the Dutch will not be able to endure for very long and will leave our state in a chaotic conditions (Adil and his group and Agung with his friends having resigned), with troops moving in all directions. It is only a strong and orderly military government which has the backing of the army which can overcome such chaos and restore order in our State because of the dislocation and disorganisation in all fields.

c. Intervention by the United Nations Organisation or some foreign state is also possible because of the former request by the government of the Republic of Indonesia for arbitration by the United Nations. But such intervention can no longer reach us who have left the towns, so that the districts throughout the whole of Java will continue in revolt until our objective has been reached.

The Emergency Government of the Republic of Indonesia in Sumatra has demanded as the first phase the withdrawal of the

123

Dutch army from Java and Sumatra first and then the liberating of the other islands in accordance with the wishes of their own people. Our capital for facing all possibilities is only a strong and orderly military government in the areas which we still control.

From the outline above of the possibilities mentioned under points a. b. and c. it is obvious that for the island of Java our military government is at present the one and only basic organisation for regulating our national potential for the victory of the Republic of Indonesia through its protection by a mobile army. The organisation of this military government penetrates to the village and takes benefit from every citizen of the Republic of Indonesia in the national struggle which is conducted in total and under military discipline, and which for all time bring discipline, education and war experiences to our people, so that we rise as a militant nation in keeping with our strategic position in seeking world peace.

d. In discussing domestic political developments, it must first be understood that experience has shown that groups still exist who fish in troubled waters. They attempt to seize authority in the state by setting themselves up besides the lawful organs of the state. The Order of the Day issued by the Commander-in-Chief of the Armed Forces on 15 September 1948 especially explains the duty of the Armed Forces of the Republic of Indonesian to protect the organs of the state.

New bodies and committees are also appearing which carry out the obligations of the state and which at times are set up by military agencies. The setting up of bodies which do not conform to the structure of the State of the Republic of Indonesia will facilitate anarchy. Regulations by the government are adequate for overcoming any forthcoming difficulties so that it is quite unnecessary to set up more new bodies. What is important is to ensure that the State of the Republic of Indonesia stands firm, that is, to see to it that army and people uphold and respect the agencies of the States and the laws of the State. Once these are neglected the state will be increasingly neglected. The *Lurah*, the *Tjamat*, the *Bupati* and so forth, and the Military Sub-district Commands, the Military District Commands, the Military Region Commands, the Military Governors and so forth must be obeyed, upheld and respected. This is the reason for the military administration which protects and ensures the safety of the organs of the State. For this purpose, it continues to stand above all political parties and all groups.

III. THE STRUCTURE AND TASKS OF THE MILITARY GOVERNMENT

Order No I above has given instruction regarding the structure of the Headquarters of the Java Command, the Military Governors, the Militay Region Commands (Sub-territorium Commands), Military District Commands, Military Sub-district Commands and the Village Cadres. What is now needed is to round out those bodies so that they become a total military government. In the very fisrt it is necessary immediately to build up Village Cadres and Hamlet Cadres, respectively to stand beside the *Lurah* and Hamlet Heads as members of the lowest level of military government. Local government civil servants must also be made to understand the form and content of the military government. Military Sub-district Commands which are not very suitable should be replaced. In every military area there should be a group on tour in order to round out the organisation of the Military Sub-district. By these means the Staffs of each Military Governor, Military Region Command, Military District Command and Military Sub-district Command can be composed of the following sections:

a. General Affairs
b. Economic Affairs
c. Community Affairs
d. Defence.

The existing composition of the Sub-territorium Command and the Military Region Commands are peace-time structures and are organisationally part of the Indonesian National Army. The composition referred to above is a war-time structure to enable the Military Government to perform its duties, which are total in character. But it must always be kept to the forefront of our minds that the new Staff does not do away with existing civil and military service and departments; on the contrary, it coordinates and mobilises them in conformity with the total character of the struggle and via the authority of the Military Governors, Military Region Commands. Neither is it necessary that all personnel are military; what is needed is capacity and the ability to do a certain job well. All personnel are under military law.

a. GENERAL AFFAIRS SECTION

This section sees to:

1. Organisation
2. Justice, Order
3. Communications.

EXPLANATION

1. As is outlined above, it is necessary to keep on equipping and rounding out the military government and its personnel which is to be done in part by going on tour.
2. The people will continue to feel the presence of the Republic so long as there is public order, so long as there are police taking action and judges bringing cases to justice.

Police organisations have been automatically militarised with present war conditions, so that the Military Police Corps, the State Police, Local Government Civil Servants and the Village Police can be organised as a single body guarding security and set up with an over-all character in every Village, *Ketjamatan* and Military District.

For bringing cases to justice, there are:
* District judges (*Tjamat* or *Wedana*).
* Military courts of lower-level regions in every Military District, in which the Military District Commander is the president who holds the power of summary judgement.
* Courts martial in which under battle conditions the Battalion Commander is the president and holds the power of summary judgement.
* Formalities should be preserved such as there being a prosecutor, a defence counsel and clerk (records keeper).

In general sentences are fines in the form of goods or, for serious offences, a sentence of death. There are no appeals to higher courts.
3. Communications must continue between superiors and subordinates, between neighbours such as Military Sub-district and Military Sub-district, Military District and Military District and the like Communications are the soul of the commands. Orderly regulations, co-ordination of work and the like will be ensured through permanent communications. For this work, couriers must set out periodically to bring one group into contact with the others.

b. ECONOMIC TASKS

Attending to the military's need for supplies and also to the needs of the people in general.

1. For military supplies, it has already been laid down in the Army H.Q.'s Instruction of 9th November 1948 that each Ketjamatan should have ready stock for 1 section (50 men). This requirement must be separated from all the other needs. In order to lighten the supply situation, troops on furlough should be billeted with village families, and should deepen their contact with the people.

126

2. To be able to go on paying the expenses of the most important apparatus of state, it is necessary to regulate the abolition of the various kinds of taxes and to establish funds in their stead for defence of the struggle these finds are to be field by gifts from the people in ways subject to local regulation, and are to take the form of goods. From this time on, the civil service, the police, education etc., and also the necessities of the army can be paid from these funds. Implementation of this effort is to be arranged together with the civil bodies in the usual way, and in accordance with the capacities of the Kabupaten. The total character of the military government will materialise out of this "gotong royong" (mutual assistance) procedure.

3. In order to meet the needs of the people and army, and for the sake of security, it is necessary that trade is conducted in toto, by means of village, hamlet, and other cooperatives, so that effective exchange takes place between the Military Sub-districts, and also for the sake of being able to conduct effective trade with the occupied towns to obtain the necessities which can be obtained only from towns, such as clothes, salt etc. In this way too financial or material contributions can be made to the funds for defence of the struggle. The supply sections of the Military Region Commands should build up trade organisations in the districts.

4. The value of Republican currency must be maintained. NICA money must be confiscated. If paragraph 3 above is implemented with success, then the value of Republican currency will rise constantly.

5. The Chinese living outside the towns should be sent to the towns to facilitate economic affairs and the guarding of security.

C. THE AFFAIRS OF THE COMMUNITY

Regulating the efforts for the welfare of society.

1. Information should be given in an orderly fashion to avoid provocation, psychological warfare, infiltration, etc. Each Military Sub-district Command, Military District Command and higher authorities should issue "Military News" bulletins periodically through the village meeting hall, the *langgar* (small local mosques) etc. And through the civil and military bodies the bulletins should be passed on to the people. In this "Military News" there should be included home and foreign news and news from the front. The news can be obtained from the jungle radio etc.

2. Education is to be arranged with two levels of elementary schools where the children continue to learn to write and so forth in the ways customary in the *langgar*. Teachers should be paid in kind. From time to time courses on the struggle, especially on military matters, should be given to the youth and pupils of secondary schools: not speeches, but lessons, such as the use of weapons, technical matters, the tactics of the military government, how to conduct the scorched earth policy, and the like.
3. The care of health must become ever more the concern of the people through the presence of a nurse or a doctor touring the villages and distributing medicines made with materials from the villages.
4. As far as possible, evacuees should be given into the care of families. If they cannot stand the economic pressure any longer, they may be allowed to return to town having sworn that they will not work for the enemy. They should not go away as enemies, but as constant friends, as citizens of the Republic.

d. DEFENCE

Defence here refers to that in the compass of the Military Region, the Military Sub-district and the Village.

1. Every Lurah, every inhabitant, every person or family must know how to behave if they are taken prisoner, how to save valuable goods, domestic animals, paddy etc. Every village must have it news gatherer in the surrounding villages, so that it always knows all the news. Between villages news of danger must be passed on by means of the "tong-tong" drum should an enemy patrol approach.
2. The village youth should not be ordered to fight with bamboo spears against machine guns, but should be directed to turn their attentions to factories, telephones, electricity; village roads must be narrowed into pathways.

NOTE: Should the enemy come to villages by truck, he will certainly often take away paddy, domestic animals, workers (forced labour) etc.

EXPLANATION

1. The villagers must fully realize that the enemy cannot occupy the villages. Therefore he patrols the villages only from time to time. Thus village life need not be disturbed, if only the people have prepared a tactic of hiding themselves. The people must understand the importance of estates and factories to the enemy as a source of financing his war costs.

2. The breaking up of railway tracks should be made in such a way that the iron and timbers cannot easily be found again.

IV. WARNING

1. The Military government is to be formed and conducted in the same way throughout Java in order to obtain the greatest possible potential. Individual measures will damage the struggle in its totality.
2. Everybody of the military government must take its own initiative for work. Do not wait for instructions to come, so that there will be no vacuum. Every vacuum is dangerous because it will be filled by infiltration.
3. Units of the Military Region Command should respect and appreciate the regulations of the military government and make of themselves an example to others.
4. It should be kept in mind that the village and the Ketjamatan (the Military Sub-district) are the foundation of the *Wehrkreise* and of the military government.
5. Keep on caring for the military hierarchy.

Issued from: The seat of Command.
Date   :   25th December 1948.

COMMANDER OF THE ARMY AND JAVA TERRITORIUM,
Sgd.   COL. A. H. NASUTION.

When making the above, there were no archives available any longer, so that everything was merely based on memory. Fortunately, when I had been in the capital, I had an active part in all these matters, so that I knew a great deal about them and still remembered them.

And so it came about that, among other things, the introductory section mentions Government Regulation No. 30, whereas it should have been No. 33, namely the Government Regulation at the time of the Madiun Affair which regulated the special military regions and military governors, based on full authority in the hands of the President, which had been granted by Parliament in order to overcome the danger to the State. Right through the guerilla period it was always referred to as No. 30 and no one danied it. Only after returning to the capital seven months later, was it felt that a mistake had been made, and only then did political groups doubt the validity of the military government, doubt the validity of the

129

organisations and the structure which had been determined upon throughout the guerilla period, because their legal basis was lacking. The regulation which had always been referred to turned out to concern the granting of allowances to former civil servants and their widows and children (orphans); this matter had become urgent in connection with the great number of casualties consequent upon the Communist Party revolt of that time. The regulation dealing with the special military regions was Number 33.

It is true that in the conditions of that time there were no archives, no legal experts, and due to the pressure from circumstances to take immediate action, shortcomings are to be found in our work.

Another similar case concerns the State and Regional Defence Councils and their regulations which were still officially in force. And one of the Government's announcements in that crisis of 19th December mentions these Councils again. As these Councils had failed during the first clash, their abolition had already been sought for a long time. However, the procedure was extremely complicated and when the second clash began, the work was not finalised. Therefore I took action which, according to law, was certainly not valid, but was forced by circumstances. Before this I had determined upon a code: "D.P.D. dirobah" (Regional Defence Councils are altered) as a signal of warning about fresh agression, and "D.P.D. hapus" (Regional Defence Councils are abolished) as a signal that the second Dutch aggresion had begun. And so these messages which were sent out beyond our own circle were also taken in the literal sense of the words.

At variance from the regulation governing commando groups in the "x-posts", which were sent in the second week to their respective places of duty, the afore-mentioned announcements and instructions were sent out both through the hierarchy and by relay runners to all military and civil officials. Under conditions where one group was cut off from the others, amidst attacks and mopping up actions by the Dutch, who still had the initiative everywhere, even this distribution was able to contribute to the restoration and the improvement of morale. Military and civil officials who saw their addresses listed, as with all Residents from Besuki to Banten, all Brigade Commanders from one till twenty-two, and other such persons were also effected. Many of them had already assumed or believed that our struggle had broken into pieces, that the Dutch had won everywhere, each person thinking that he was left on his own. So that when the instruction came and they saw the hierarchy and structure of the state, it helped them to understand and to feel

130

that the Republic and the National Army were still intact and still bearing up. Indeed, I urged all my messengers leaving for all directions to act also as information officers.

Meantime a report was received from Division II that my messenger had arrived, and had also met the Republic's Ministers who on that 19 December happened to be in the Solo area. They had retreated to Mt. Lawu together with the commander of Division II, Colonel Gatot Subroto. They had known nothing about the decrees from the government in Jogja, and had formed an emergency government under leadership of Minister Sukiman. From him as its head I received a letter in his own handwriting, saying that the government approved of my proclamation and the directive instructing formation of a military government, with the possession of this, there appear to be sufficient legal bases for the later measures.

I was of the opinion that the commanding post of the H.Q. Java Command should remain close to the capital, within a distance of several hours' walk. I planned a temporary place while I was still finalising the basic instructions at the boundaries of Jogja and Solo, which was known as "boundary plain V and T brigade". If the T region was being patrolled then we retreated to region V, and vice versa.

Connection with the capital was necessary in order to obtain news, and for the liaison men for communication with Semarang, Djakarta, Bandung and Surabaya through the enemy occupied regions.

It had been calculated that our couriers would reach the provincial capitals quicker, going from there to the command posts in the mountains, if they used enemy's transport system. Besides, there were still many matters in the capital which had to be seen to from outside.

Only for me and my friends who had faithfully carried out the government orders in putting down the past revolt, it was very dangerous in the regions around Solo, because the rebels' influence was very strong in the villages. Their cells were still everywhere. Several attempts, fortunately averted, were made to kill us, and similarly also with our families. Two middleranking officers of my group were murdered.

As in the first clash, so also in the second, the enemy were never able to imagine where our commanding post had been sited. Once they thought it was in East Java, later in South Jogja, in connection with the fact that psychologically this was a great possibility for the retreat had gone to the South with the enemy coming from the North.

For the conduct of guerilla warfare, communications are difficult in the extreme, far more difficult than in an ordinary war. In an ordinary war, the troops are compact units and the command is central. In a guerilla war the command is de-central. The troops are spread evenly in all directions; generally, the largest moving unit is the fighting battalion team and usually units are far smaller; and those troops are very mobile and move from place to place. A modern guerilla army can of course make use of radio sets which can be carried along by the guerillas. For us, the radio was restricted to communication between Java and Sumatra, and between the H.Q. Java Command and the divisions alone. These radios were only stationary ones. Of course, the enemy reconnoitred and looked for them, and therefore they also were removed from time to time. For ordinary communications we were forced to use couriers by relay methods. With the aid of the Military Sub-district Commands a courier service was opened covering the whole territory, in the place of the Postal Service. Each village had a section for the forwarding of letters. The special communication via the system of the well-known "x-posts" was used by the H.Q. for important letters. In similar fashion every division and brigade set up a special communication system for the needs of their own command.

In guerilla warfare, it is truly felt that communication is the soul of military unity and the soul of the state's unity. It should be the unceasing effort of each commander to care for and to maintain communications. In the beginning many commanders neglected this absolute condition for guerilla warfare. They were constantly on the move going everywhere, so that they were indeed able to reach their subordinates in accordance with their plans, but on the other hand their subordinates could not reach their commanders if there was some need. Communication should be possible at the time from both parties even though the enemy is continously pursuing us in mopping up operation, and notwithstanding the fact that our sectors are separated by enemy-occupied areas and the regions he patrols. It must be possible to overcome all obstacles, if necessary during the night.

On 7th January 1949, the H.Q. Java Command was able to issue a first working instruction for regulating and spreading communication. For the needs of the H.Q. Java Command itself a net of "x-posts" had been begun beforehand, so that it could quickly forward instructions and news to those under it, and was able to receive reports and requests from each region. For this reason, those under this Headquarters were able to feel from the beginning the presence of leadership, of the fact that organisation of state and army were intact.

That instruction was as follows:

HEADQUARTERS JAVA COMMAND
No. 7/M.B.K.D./49

INSTRUCTION ON COMMUNICATION (RENRAKU)
INTRODUCTION

In guerilla activities (that is, with small units of troops) conducted by means of *Wehrkreise* (that is, each small region, such as a Military District or Sub-district, acting separately upon its own initiative), communication is very difficult. Thus it often happens that regions or units pay insufficient attention to the hierarchy, and on the other hand higher commands often let their subordinates go on their own. In this way the danger is great that the absolute condition for every army can no longer be met, namely, unity of command, army (organisational) unity, unity of strategy, and so on. Let alone the presence of great danger also for conducting total defence — the mobilization of power in toto and activity in toto. Guerilla and *Wehrkreise* methods bring the splitting up of units, of activities and of regions, but the nature of total struggle on the contrary requires the utmost unity possible. As long as there are still telephones, radios and transport, this is easy enough, but in the present difficult situation, how is it to be organised?

The State will continue as a state so long as it is a complete organisation with a leadership; the same is also true of its army. This means that everybody of leadership continues to give orders, instructions, information and the like to those under it, and on the other hand each subordinate body continues to give reports, ask for information, make proposals and the like to those above. And this is possible only if there are communications. Communications are the soul of the army's unity. If a higher body is cut off from those under it and it no longer gives leadership, or if a subordinate body no longer makes reports anymore and so forth to those above it, then, in principle, elements have been born which will cause the army to collapse, which will bring about the downfall of the over-all, total, movement.

Therefore, every superior body has the obligation of maintaining constant communication with those under it by any means whatever, and on the other hand every subordinate body must keep constantly

133

in touch by any means with those above it, and two neighbouring regions (units) must maintain reciprocal communication all the time.

METHODS OF COMMUNICATION IN THE WEHRKREISE

Communication must be constantly maintained between the battalion of the Military Region Command and those units under it everywhere, and vice versa. This must also be the case with communication between the Military Sub-district Command and the village cadres. It is especially important to regulate communications between the H..Q Java Command-Division-Brigade-Battalion, or the H..Q Java Command-Military Governors-Military Region Command-Military District Command.

For example, let us take Division/Special Military District II, where there are two brigades, several battalions standing on their own and four Military Region Commands (Sub-Territorium Command — Divisions/Military Governors) for instance, set up the following divisional posts:

a) Post a.I in the environs of Mount Merapi, which is close to brigade 5, Military District Command of Semarang, and others in the same region. Post a.II in the region of West Lawu which is close to the Military District Command of Solo, and other units. Post a.III in the region of East Lawu which is close to the Military District Command of Madiun and Division I. Post a.IV in the Purwodadi region which is close to units around there. Post a.V which is close to the Military District Command of Pati.

b) Mobile Post a.12 etc. between a.I and a.II, mobile post a.23 between a.II and a.III and so forth. At each post several officers and assistants are stationed, whose tasks are:

   1. To pass on instructions and letters from the Commander/ Military Governor and to collect reports etc. for the Commander/Military Governor.
   NOTE: For this purpose, post a. makes communication with the Military Region Command, Military District Command, Military Sub-district Command, the nearest Battalion Commands, and continues to look for its own communication. The officers of the post must know and must be throughly versed in the matters concerned in the instructions of the Commander/Military Governor.

   2. To control execution of the instructions and to act where necessary in the name of the Commander/Military Governor, in matters which do not involve principle (daily routine, advice, etc.).

134

3. To give information to the nearby brigades of Regional and District Military Commands etc.

4. To make weekly and monthly reports to be sent all posts and to the Commander/Military Governor. The mobile posts constantly move between two posts to maintain contact and to nuture the compact nature of the Division/Special Military District, and while on the move also carry out the tasks of points 1, 2, 3, and 4 above in the units, Military Sub-district Commands and others which they pass. Each post has 3 or 4 couriers who are officers (or reserve officers from the students), and who carry letters etc. to neighbouring posts every week. If the distance between two posts is far, for example 8 days' walk, then sub-posts are to be set up by the mobile post concerned, so that by relay letters will be delivered more quickly.

NOTE:

The men of brigade 17 are charged with post or courier duties. Communications men should also become adjusted to this task and the communications commander should continue to try to perfect this chain of posts.

Commanders/Military Governors must at all times be in communication with all posts and in this way in communication with all subordinates. Although these officers are mobile, they continue to be in contact with their bodies.

SECURITY OF COMMUNICATIONS

1. *The post is not an ordinary quarter*, but a post kept secret from the public. The post moves around at its own initiative in its "rayon" (area) in accordance with the situation of battle, but should always be in touch with other posts and units or bodies which are close to it. Usually a post will consist of several scattered houses, a place to receive visitors, a place in which to work, a place for sleeping, a place in reserve. Besides this there are also reserve posts in readiness to North, South, West and East, should it be necessary to move later on. Personnel of the posts disguise themselves as ordinary people.

2. *Ordinary letters* should be burnt after their contents have been thoroughly understood, and should be registered in code in a book kept by the head of the post. Only important letters, such as basic instructions, etc. and letters to be forwarded, must remain in the post, and these also must be kept secretly. Commanders should endeavour to reduce correspondence and to

convey news and orders orally by officers. But for document-ation, the post should have a book such as is referred to above, in which all important matters are registered in separate codes by the head of the post, so that he can later draw up a complete report when the war is over. It will be proved in the future how important is this documentation of our struggle.

3. *Couriers:* These posts, and the commanders too, have their own couriers whom they have trained themselves for the weekly contact between posts, quite apart from the courier service conducted by officers (students).

4. *Speed:* Continuing efforst must be made to speed up communi-cations, for the absolute condition for all communication is speed and accuracy. By improving the methods of getting from one place to another, the time for the journey can be decreased.

5. *Prepared at all times.* Each post must be always prepared to face the possibility of mopping-up actions, if necessary it must be prepared to remove immediately. Clothes, goods and letters must always be in readiness to be hidden or to be removed.

6. *Code.* The members of the post and the couriers must use other names and a code on their journeys which is to be arranged by the head of the post for his subordinates.

7. *Disguise.* Adjust yourselves to conditions in the village, this is the best method of disguise.

WARNING:

During the continuation of this guerilla war, each Military Sub-district Command will face enemy mopping-up actions one or more times, but through using the methods mentioned above, it will not be possible to sweep us away.

> *Issued from:* The seat of Command.
> *Date* : 7th January 1949.
> *Hour* : 11.00.

COMMANDER OF THE ARMY AND JAVA TERRITORIUM, *Sgd.* COLONEL A. H. NASUTION.

To:

1. *All Divisions, Brigades, Battalions, Companies.*
2. *All Commanders Military Districts, Commanders Military Sub-districts, Posts of Java Command Headquarters.*

Copies to: The Commander in Chief of the Armed Forces/Chief of Staff of the Armed Forces.

*
* *

It was necessary to issue a general instruction concerning supplies for the guerilla war.

Due to the extremely narrow opportunity previous preparations had been limited. What was available was only the result of personal initiative or unorganised efforts. The Central Government had stocks of opium both in Java and Sumatra, which were intended to be as a source of foreign exchange. The price was high and transport easy. In Java opium was kept in the Gunung Kidul region, and there were still small amounts left in the cities. What was in the cities was traded, as far as possible, by our Supply Office. What was in Gunung Kidul was taken away and used by the Intelligence Branch without my knowledge.

The stock of money printed shortly before in Madiun was used for the greater part by organisations close by, because distribution was not properly planned beforehand. Because of the over-all nature of the Commands, it often happened that steps were taken which arbitrarily assumed the authority and rights of the Central Government. In the capital there was also a small stock of gold left there by the Government. The Central Supply Office had earlier distributed lenghts of batik to commanders, also intended for use in exchange. Meanwhile, it had become customary for each unit for troops to have its own goods for exchange obtained by its own efforts, and consisting of all kinds of materials and commodities. In this way, those troops were able to stand on their own. That is why it was common to say that some battalions are rich and some are poor.

It had been clear to me from the beginning that these incidental and individual stocks would be zuickly used up. Also, that this unorganised and individual action would disorganised the people's economy and that of the State.

And if troops become used to acting on their own at trading and confiscating, then, as we had often experienced it already, they will tend to give priority to trade and to their own undertakings above the real struggle. Trading troops had become a saddening disease in the National Army. There were numerous commanders from the lowest to the highest who indulged in trading transactions, some of them on a large scale, with their companies and corporations. In such cases very great exesses occurred. A great deal of the people's stocks and those of the Government, such as sugar, coffee, tea, quinine, etc, in this way passed out of the hands of the people and the government. Of course, it was often just a small group of people who profited from this, who themselves conducted these individual endeavours. Officers who collect gold, stors opium, etc. are of course usually suspected of being corrupt by the troops.

It was certain that gradually, the village people, who at the beginning enthusiastically collected supplies for the army, the civil servants and evacuees, would make complaints. Eventually they would not be able to continue endlessly looking after the numerous guests at their own expense, and so, gradually they would come to hate these guests.

In the field of supplies munitions are the greatest difficulty.

As has been explained before, of stocks were no more than sufficient for one year. A great deal of the stock vanished during the Madiun action. A large stock in Gunung Kidul was captured by the enemy. Our arms were of a variety of types so that the supply of bullets was most difficult. Automatically, the soldiers come to appreciate more and more profoundly what a single bullet means Guns and bullets are the soul of a soldier.

In this connection, I issued a general instruction about supply, to be used as a guide for measures by responsible commanders in carrying out their task. Especially for organs of the Military Government it was very important that there should be a single guide, which had been properly prepared.

This instruction reads as follows:

JAVA COMMAND HEADQUARTERS
No. 4/M.B.K.D./1949

WORKING INSTRUCTION FOR SUPPLY
INTRODUCTORY

With the adoption of the "*Wehrkreise*" system, it is obvious that supply should also be obtained by "*Wehrkreise' 'methods*.

Formerly, the units received a monthly budget from the centre to meet expenses. The regions, too, had their own undertakings using the state's resources to be found in their areas. But now, the budget from the centre has stopped and the self-organised undertakings with activities centring around the cities (enterprises, factories and transport vehicles) have also ceased. Therefore, the supply is now seen to in its entirety through regional recources.

Before the war, the Central Government gave:

a. authority to Commanders of Military Districts/Sub-territorium Commanders to borrow in the name of the State.

b. authority to make use of all goods which are state property.

c. a supply of money and goods from the Army Service Corps.

Thus the army has received a modicum of supplies for several months, while supply is being organised in keeping with the *Wehrkreise* system.

Both calculation and experience show that supply can be organised according to the *Wehrkreise* system using the resources of the region. All that is needed is organisation, effort, activity and honesty. This is all the easier to arrange as the authority of the District Military Commanders is now total in character for their respective regions. However, on the other hand, it is necessary that all army men, from the top leaders down to the soldiers, should carry out their tasks carefully and thoroughly in the field of supply in order to gain results. This means economizing down to the smallest items, carrying out all undertakings possible in the regions and the best relations with the population.

Waste on the part a battalion commander can rupture the supply of the whole region, unsuitable behaviour by a few soldiers can cause the disaffection of the entire population, and so on.

It should also be borne in mind that soldier should receive some money every month so that he can feel clearly that he is being looked after. What is most important is food for everyone, and after that, wages. Food and wages should be divided equally among private and officer irrespective of rank. Officers and privates ought even to eat and sleep together. Remember that with the Vice-Presidential Order of the Day of 19 December 1948, our struggle as a state is now no longer committed to earlier agreements, and that now compromise is completely ruled out, which means a long struggle. It will be he who endures longest who will win.

SUPPLY GOODS.

(1) Supply goods may be obtained only by the following methods:

a. Collection from the people by the military government (rice, taxes, fines, goods from scorched earth actions, confiscation of enemy property).

b. What is captured as a result of fighting (convoys, attacks, on towns illegal activities in towns).

c. Trade (village co-operatives, trade with towns) and modest businesses (market gardens, guerilla factories, or factories in towns using set illegal means).

d. The greatest economizing in the use of money and material. Primarily, those who must work are:

   (a) The economic branch of the military government which regulates as a totality the efforts mentioned above.

   (b) Supply officers who as special army men arrange things for the units.

   (c) Commanders of units, who economize and arrange a strategy of fighting to obtain supplies.

     Officers of the Supply Office, the Financial Office and the Arms Supply can no longer from the central government, Arms Supply can no longer work as they used to (that is, with material and capital from the central government, which they distributed) but must now be put to work by the respective Military Governors/Commanders of Military Regions in the economic branches of the Military government, or in the supply sections of units.

Commanders of battalions should organise a supply section in each company's staff. This section in to be an armed unit composed of members who understand and are capable of supply work in the villages, and who, using all kinds of capital and the army's authoritative influence, are specially charged with making preparations (searching for, collecting, putting in readiness and distributing). They make lodging ready, arrange quartering, and so forth. When this supply section has gained considerable experience the battalion commanders will be relieved of supply difficulties. This section must, of course, maintain relations with the Military Sub-districts and the village cadres.

Supply Officers of brigades and divisions give points and guidance to supply sections and regulate co-ordination and control.

   (2) Most important suplly materials:

(a) Food.
(b) Ammunition
(c) Clothing
(d) Money
(e) Goods for exchange.

   a. *Food.*

Food is received from Military Sub-district stock, that is each Military Sub-district should be capable of sustaining at least one section permanently. The Military Sub-districts get supplies from the village, such as village cash reserves, collections from the people, fines from punished persons, and from their own efforts.

Estate lands should be dividend up among the people, planted with food crops of which a part is paid to the Military Sub-district Command.

Persons who are sentenced by the district court or Military District Command/Military Sub-district Command should pay their fines in rice or domestic animals. At each harvest there should be a special collection for funds paying for our struggle. Land tax should be paid in rice. The *Ketjamatan* as a *Wehrkreise* (Government Regulation No. 70) has the right to regulate this.

On the other hand, the Military Sub-district Commander should see to it that the village people are not spoiled, for instance by giving food to persons who guard the village every day, etc. Village people on guard in their village should eat at home and are given merely some simple refreshments .... 7) Rice from the village treasury (the product of an area measuring about 10 *bahu*) should be used economically for the army, and a part set aside for special needs.

With the system explained above, every commander of a Military Sub-district should understand that he is the most important guarantee of supplies in a Wehrkreise. The safety of the army greatly depends on Commanders of Military Sub-districts.

The Commanders of Military Districts arrange the transport of rice from a Military Sub-district which is a surplus area to another which is a minus area. He also arranges storage of rice in Military Sub-districts lying far from main roads. Rice should be stored by leaving it in someone's core at scattered places, so that it can not be seized by the enemy. Further, the menu be compiled economically, that is it should contain large quantities of vegetables while at breakfast or other meals cassava, sweat potatoes etc. should be the main dish.

Unit commanders must assist in seeing to this.

(b) *Ammunitions.*

In a long war, the stock of munitions decides the ultimate victory. Arms without munition are useless. Therefore the use of ammunition should be as economical as possible.

In the *Wehrkreise* we do not make munitions, thus we posses only the initial stocks. Each commander should calculate that his stock is for one year's requirements, and arrange its use in such a way that the stock is sufficient for one year.

Explosives and hand-granades can for the time being still be made by the guerilla factories set up by the Arms Service Corps in a number of Subterritorium Commands. Furthermore, it should be possible to produce them illegally in occupied cities. Experience so far shows that we obtain supplies from weapons to other necessities, in considerable quantities from the occupied towns, where we have helpers to make purchases or to seize them. As is the case in West Java, we can also get ammunition from enemy factories via our agents working there (the Dutch themselves are of course in their guard and frequently make raids). For the rest, it must be left to the strategic skill of brigade and battalion commanders to launch periodic actions to capture weapons and ammunition, such as attacking convoys, ambushing patrols, attacking small camps, and so on.

NOTE:

Experience proves will enough that we can obtain quantities of munitions from occupied towns, so long as active attempts are made. Indeed, guerilla troops must eventually be able to capture their supplies from the enemy. From now on, every commander should see to it that weapons are properly maintained.

(c) *Clothing.*

The Central Government has no stock of clothing. From now on clothing should be acquired by the regions's own endeavours.

Commanders must arrange guerilla attacks on towns to capture clothes and other important materials. There are many methods for doing this.

Trade with towns by the Military Sub-district and Military Districts must produce clothes (and other important materials).

„Basket tax" on women vendors, marketing taxes, fines by Military Sub-district Command/Military District Command can from time to time be paid in clothing. If there are cash surplus in the Military District Command, it can be used from time to time to pay for clothing, for later contribution to the battalions.

Every officer should give priority to the clothing of this men.

Experiences from the first colonial attack has shown, that organisation and energy can produce a moderately sufficient supply of clothes for the troops, if only we think of many schemes and make many attempts.

(d) *Money.*

Money also should be a matter for the regions from now on.

As far as possible, equal amounts of monthly pocket money should be paid to private and officer. Money can be obtained in the following means:

By authority of the President, the Commanders of Sub-territor
ium Commands can contract loans in the name of the state, to be
paid back when the war is over. Each Military Region Commander
already has a moderate amount from the Army Service Corps or
from state resources in that region. Each regional commander
should put this to use as capital to obtain the funds necessary to
buy the army's needs (sugar, salt, oil, coffee, tea, etc. that can be
saved are the capital for supplies).

Materials from buildings to be subjected to scorched earth action
should be sold as far as possible or exchanged (tiles, wood, zinc, etc.).
NICA-money must be prohibited from circulation and exchanged
against the official rate fixed by the commander. This forbidden
money is for use in paying for goods in occupied towns. If the
military government is successful in the district, Republican
currency will ultimately gain in value once more; the value of
Republican currency is dependent on the success or failure of the
military government is performing its obligations.

Taxes must be re-arranged by the Military Sub-district Commands,
in order to be able to pay for the struggle. The *Ketjamatan* as being
a *Wehrkreise*, is authorized to make its own regulations for administrative autonomy, in accordance with Government Regulation No. 70.
Taxes should be paid as far as possible in kind, while both the
name and nature of taxes is to be altered to "Funds to pay for the
Struggle". Land taxes, marketing tax, "basket tax", "fitrah", "zakat"
(religions charitable contributions), etc. to be found in the villages
must be gathered into one fund and put in charge of the village
authorities under the responsibility of the military government.
The collection of funds except by the government should be forbidden, to guard against the people being victimised.

Fines to be paid by punished persons should also be paid into
this fund. The fullest assistance of the people, and also contributions, will be great, if the military government in turn gives to
the people. If basic schooling can continue to be provided the
people will appreciate it. If the eradication of illiteracy goes on
without interruption the result will be favourable. This will be
the more true if the army can bring health with it. The system of
treating the people through a mobile polyclinic with a doctor (nurse)
has already been practised in several pockets. Medicine in the army's
possession can be used partly for the people; many of the efforts
of the Indonesian Red Cross to obtain medicines from the towns
have been successful. The army can also make simple medicines from
materials available in the villages (instructions will be sent). For
a long time the people have been without adequate medical care,

143

and the army can now improve the people's health. For such reasons the people wil always be grateful to the military government of the Republic of Indonesia.

The supply and security of the army will be facilitated if the people benefit from the medical help of the army.

For the time being there are still recources of the state that can be exploited, such as the forests, pawn shops, post offices etc. These should all be mobilized in totality by the military government. Lands which were formerly estates, conversion land and the like should be returned to the government and divided amongst the people, with payment of part of the crops to the military government. Salt manufacturing can be orginised in several places. The sale of salt, oil, salt fish, etc. can be regulated so that profits come into the military government's treasury. Even though the notes are some what torn, Republican currency must be accepted by the people.

(e) *Goods for exchange.*

It stands to reason that the army should endeavour to acquire all sorts of goods which the people like to accept as exchange, such as clothing, salt, oil, etc. These articles constitue capital for the military government side by side with capital in the form of money.

Economizing.

Realistic economizing by Military Sub-districts and unit Commanders is necessary to be practised, as follows:

(a) The Military Sub-district Commands should prevent waste of what belongs to village and military government funds, as frequently happens when as many as 10 to 20 people from the village do guard duty in a day, and are all given food whereas they are part of the population of that same village. Officers passing through villages in small groups should stay with well-to-do families and not become a burden upon the village treasury.

(b) Unit commanders should arrange for supplies of troops as far as possible in keeping with the prosperity of the region (within the bounds possible for strategy). If the troops are not on duty (and usually the period of rest is longer than the period of fighting) they should be quartered in small groups with families who can afford them as guests, and not become a burden upon village treasury.

It should also be seen to it that the soldiers behave themselves well do not offend the people but win their hearts. It often happens that an officer or soldier enforces compliance with his requests, asking that a fowl be killed for dinner, that the dishonours women, behaves like a "master", etc. We must adjust ourselves to the way of life of the village. We help the village people to care for their health, we help their work in the rice-fields, to repair their houses, with irrigation, etc. We guarantee their security of their village against thieves, robbers etc.

Warning. It often happens near front lines or battle are as that new troops appear (usually people evacuated from the towns), who call themselves guerilla troops, and then demand that the people support them, — they want food, goats, etc. Such incidents have often turned into a terror, and have lowered the name "struggle" During these three years, especially in the environments of demarcation line and in the pockets where there is a vacuum, there have been many such terrors, and often they are staged by the enemy.

Therefore, unit commanders and Military Sub-districts should be on the alert and take appropriate actions against such terror disguised as struggle.

Certainly, in the course of this war a process of selection will go on and those whose struggle is not clean will be cleaned up by conditions. Remember that our capital is the people, that our capital is the village. Adjust and unite yourself with the village people. In the reverse direction we see how the enemy seizes rice, domestic animals etc. from the people by force. Show the big difference between the National Army and the colonial (foreign) army!

FAMILIES.

Guerilla war automatically necessitates separation of soldiers from their families, but the soldiers will surely go on leave from time to time and visit their families. Officers should set an example to their subordinates by living apart from their families.

Members of families who can work in the defence effort, for instance in public kitchens, the Indonesian Red Cross etc. automatically accompany the units or command posts.

In general, members of families should be entrusted to relatives in the villages and towns, to lighten the supply position and facilitate the movement of units. Contributions to the support of these families can not possibly be ensured in this guerilla war. So long as these people cannot return to their relatives they should be scattered amongst the villages, and if possible put to work in the villages, for instance is market gardening, in small shops, in the polyclinic (with medicine made by the army) etc.

145

Territorial Cadres in Pockets of Mount Sanggabuana did not forget to do excercises.

It should also seen to that the people do not see groups of families of army men living an idle life. The people must see that the members of those families work at such things as market gardening, eradicating illiteracy, polyclinics for the people, public kitchen, etc. Families of army personnel should associate in unity with the village people and make themselves useful. It is not possible to make a general rule; each member of the army should co-operate in lightening the drain on war supply goods by making their families independent of the unit as far as possible.

All military sub-districts and village cadres are obliged to help soldier's families living in their respective regions.

NOTE: The care of families of Indonesian Communist Party troops in earlier times and now of the Siliwangi-troops returning to West Java, demonstrates clearly how much it handicaps the movements of units.

With the existence of war, a selection and or cutting down of personnel has also taken place. Staff members of the Java Military Commands and the Ministry of Defence have been reduced, and purely administrative personnel have returned to the community. Members of other staff have also, of course, been treated likewise.

There are also members of units who cannot bear the present difficulties, and leave their units. Commanders of units and chiefs of staffs should ensure that this "natural selection" is properly done. Members of the army who do not report at roll-call during one month without proper reason should be automatically considered to have left. Meanwhile, it is necessary to transfer capable persons to the staff of the military district and sub-district commanders from other staffs, because the war increases the tasks of the military government and makes them more difficult too.

In the meantime, new organisations arise, such as guerilla troops, army troop centres, etc. outside the official units (mobile battalions and territorial battalions), and the existing staffs. Basically, all citizens have the right and the duty of fight for their country, but the army has the duty of leading them (within the defence system and military government), and therefore, the army has the obligation of regulating and forming them. New units should be included within mobile or territorial units, carefully and tactfully but also decisively, and new troop centres should be abolished. The formasion of Battalion, Brigade, Division and also of Military Governor, Military Region Commander, Military District Command, Military Sub-district Command, and Village Cadres with territorial battalions (military district or sub-district units) are quite sufficient.

MANY KINDS OF FORMATIONS WILL CREAT CONFUSION.

It must also be recalled that there is the possibility of terror or action by enemy spies if there are formations not included in the structure of army or military government.

Also in the villages there have arisen people's guerilla units, usually without arms, who are then put into hostels. Usually they only become a burden for the village. Village troops cannot be put into hostels. In executing strategy it even happens very often that people only think about attacking the enemy army, but completely forget targets as destruction of roads, railways, bridges, buildings etc. which are not battles (with arms and bullets) but are of no less importance in causing losses to the enemy. Also, youths who are not armed, let alone with no training, should not be ordered to face machine-guns and mortars.

(b) Civil personnel is placed in totality under the authority of the Resident, *Bupati* (Head of a Regency), *Tjamat* (District Head) and *Lurah* (Village Head) in accordance with the Instruction of Armed Forces Headquarters, dated 9th November 1948. Here too there should also be a selection of personnel and adjustment of these persons to the struggle. They should be attached to the *Lurah*, etc. It should also be ensured that the civil departments do not become social bodies on their own while using the resources of their departments as capital.

WARNING.

Because the State of the Republic of Indonesia is no longer bound by the agreements with the Dutch, and is now fighting to the utmost on the basis of the Proclamation of Independence for the whole of Indonesia, it is obvious that the struggle will be a long one, and therefore the problem of supply is even more important than in earlier times. Failure of supply will mean failure of the struggle.

But calculation and experience give sufficient proof that with the *Wehrkreise* system we will continue to be able to organise supply, if we only work energetically and continue to develop much initiative.

Because of the over-all, total, nature of the struggle, the success of execution depends much upon the commanders of units, especially Commanders of Battalions, the Regional Commanders, and more particularly the Commanders of Military Sub-districts.

Issued from: The Seat of Command.
Date : 1 January 1949.
Hour : 10.00.

COMMANDER OF THE ARMY AND JAVA TERRITORIUM,
Sgd. COL. A. H. NASUTION.

To:

All MilitaryGovernors/Territorial Commanders,

Brigade Commanders (to be forwarded to their respective Battalion Commanders),

Commanders Military Territories (Sub Territorial Commanders) to be forwarded to Commanders of Military Districts, Commanders of Military Sub-districts, Residents and Regents (Bupatis). Commando Groups.

The basis for psychological war indeed need to be organised immediately, because we had first to surmount the strong psychological attack by the enemy combined with a lightning strategic and tactical attack upon us. We also had to fill the vacuum in people's minds about having a state because of the capture of Sukarno-Hatta, and surmount the intensity of measures taken by extreme leftist and rightist elements who made use of the confusion to fill in this vacuum, all the more so in conditions still bad because of the Madiun rebellion. In West Java Kartosuwirjo had already taken action, giving orders and making decrees, for fighting the "remnants" of the Republic. Just read the following announcements:

COPY

ORDER AND DECREE OF THE INDONESIAN ISLAMIC STATE.

Gentlemen and friends, as you all know, after the attack by the Dutch on territories of the Republic of Indonesia, group after group of the Army ran away from Jogja, especially those of the Siliwangi Army; they came here to become irregular troops creating chaos in the territories of the Indonesian Islamic State. In no way at all do they appreciate or obey the leadership of the Indonesian Islamic State, and therefore we issue an order with regard to all troops who come from Jogja to the Indonesian Islamic State, that the Islamic Army (Armed Forces of the Indonesian Islamic State) should be at the ready for action to destroy those irregular troops.

149

We must not waver and pretend not to know the orders, we only have the Islamic State of Indonesia. The Republic has been wiped out and no longer has any authority or power. Therefore we must destroy all its authority and power, and in the first place its Armed Forces; give them no mercy any longer, especially not the Siliwangi Army which has become those irregular troops.

Destroy their power, disarm them as far as possible. This order is directed to the Armed Forces of the Indonesian Islamic State, the Army of the Darul Islam Heroes, the State Security Body, and the people of Indonesia.

1. *To Cmdr. Bat. IV/I/I*
2. *To Cmdr. Troop I/I/IV*
3. *HQ Terr. Bat. Tasikmalaja*
4. *Bat. IV/I/I via HQ of Darul Islam Heroes Army, Leuwisari.*

IMAM
KARTOSUWIRJO.

Appendix I to Military Decree No. 1

CONCERNING CAPTURED GOODS.

1. All captured goods, including war equipment, are the property of the State (Indonesian Islamic State).
2. These goods will be given to those with a right to them.
3. Those with a right to captured goods are: Men/units of the Army who effect the disarmament, directly or indirectly.
4. The giving of the arms should be made with account taken of the proportionate number of troops, proportionate weight of weapons, and the proportionate strength of the respective groups.
5. Where disarmament is made directly by a certain unit, the State gives the right to the captured goods to that unit.

Appendix II to Military Decree No. 2.

CONCERNING IRREGULAR TROOPS.

1. Since the establishment of the Indonesian Islamic State in the Western part of Java (1948) there are only two belligerent groups, i.e.:
   a. The Dutch authority, the Dutch Army and its instruments.

b. The Indonesian Islamic State, the Indonesian Islamic Army, and all its organs and equipment.

2. It is not permitted that groups, gangs and other units have or create a place for themselves.

3. Irregular troops are all military units which come from the territories of the Republic and enter the occupied western part of Java, especially units covered by the Siliwangi Devision, or other units except those of the Indonesian Islamic Army.

4. Against the irregular troops mentioned above, the Indonesian Islamic State will take the following measures:

    I. a. disarm these irregular troops.

    b. seize all goods belonging to these units/gangs/groups which are needed for the interests of the Indonesian Islamic State.

    II. dissolve these-units once they are disarmed.

5. If when they are being disarmed and/or having goods seized as as mentioned in point 4, I a and b, they made resistance, then the whole of the gang, group, unit is to be considered and treated as enemies of the Indonesian Islamic State and of the religion of Islam.

6. a. Every person from the group, gang, unit mentioned above who is not trusted will be shadowed and thoroughly investigated irrespective of sex, rank and position.

    b. In view of the interests of the State, wherever necessary and as far as is necessary, the Army, the Heroes of Darul Islam, the State Security Body and other organisation of the State, may take any measure in keeping with military law in time of revolution.

*
* *

Similarly also in East Java it happened that measures were taken by certain groups which basically were hostile to our army. A commander of our Battalion, Major Banuredjo, was even murdered. Due to the clever leadership of the Millitary Governor, and particularly to the Commander of Brigade 2, the situation could be brought under control. These groups issued many circulars, attacking and vilifying the Sukarno-Hatta government and the military leaders in Kediri in particular and those in East Java in general.

What they most opposed was the policy of diplomatic struggle.

There were many clandestine pamhlets such as those from *"Gunung Tidar"*, *"Markas Murba Terpendam"*, etc. There were many rumours, such as those concerning the capture and then the death of Commander-in-Chief Sudirman, the destruction of the Siliwangi Division, General Sudirman's agreement to the holding of a "People's Congress" and so forth.

We were set one against the other, as persons *pro* and *anti* the federal structure, *pro* and *anti* negotiations with the Dutch, *pro* and *anti* a cease fire, and so on.

There were many speculations about local difficulties, because there were many groups fishing in troubled waters. Many steps were taken to gain local power, in the military as well as in the civil sense.

It was indeed the case that so many things covered in place from Banten to Besuki, which meant disintegration of the Republican State which was in the midst of a life and death struggle for self-defence against Dutch aggression. In spite of all this, the most dangerous thing of all was the political war and psychological war waged by the Dutch. Those under Dutch orders sought contact with us by all kinds of means, including by making use of our families. There were some who were taken prisoner, as happened to my family, there were some who were tortured, others who were promised the moon, and all of it in order to soften our hearts, to make us prepared to shake hands, to make us lose hope, and the like. Various ministers who stayed in the capital, like Leimena and Djuanda, were visited by the Dutch and promised the moon, in an attempt to disaffect them.

Many rumours circulated amongst the people and in the army.

Therefore, I found it necessary to issue general instruction immediately, directed to the defence of the political and psychological front. On 5 January 1949 the following instruction on Non-cooperation was sent through the chain of Java Command Headquaters communication posts:

JAVA COMMAND HEADQUARTERS
No. 5/M.B.K.D./1949

INSTRUCTION ON NON-CO-OPERATION.

RECALLING: Government Regulation No. 70 and Armed Forces instruction of 9 November 1948.

CONSIDERING: Implementation of the Order of the Day from the Vice President of the Republic of Indonesia dated 19 December 1948, directed to all members of the Armed Forces and Government Departments to continue the struggle by any means whatever:

HEREBY DETERMINES: To issue an
INSTRUCTION ON NON-CO-OPERATION FOR THE WHOLE OF JAVA.

1. All citizens of Indonesia who co operate with the enemy will be considered traitors in time of war, and brought to justice as such in accordance with military law.
2. All civil servants and village officers who have worked with the enemy, especially from the time of the Renville Agreement up to 19 December 1948, in the regions formerly called "occupied territories", are obliged to report themselves again to the Military Government of the Republic of Indonesia, which has been re-established for the whole of Java since 22 December 1948. From here on, point 1 above is in force.
3. All Military Governors, Commanders of Military Regions Commanders of Military Districts, and Commanders of Military Sub-districts will regulate methods of implementation for their respective territories with the assistancee of the commanders of units and civil servants.

NOTE:

a. At bottom, victory depends upon ourselves — that is, upon whether we are still prepared to be made tools of the enemy or not.
b. In order to facilitate the struggle it is necessary to draw dividing lines (demarcation) between patriots and traitors. Every Commander of a Military Regions must list the names of traitors in his region to be dealt with accordingly.

Issued from: The Seat of Command.
Date   :   5 January 1949.

COMMANDER OF THE ARMY AND JAVA TERRITORIUM,
Sgd.   COLONEL A.H. NASUTION.

To:

All military and civil government agencies (With the request that it be passed on to those under them).

*
**

On 7 January another instruction on the extinction of rumours was circulated, as follows:

JAVA COMMAND HEADQUARTERS
No. 6/M.B.K.D./1949

INSTRUCTION
EXTINCTION OF RUMOURS.

RECALLING:

1. With what intensity the enemy is using psychological warfare to break up the unity of the Indonesian people in general, and the Indonesian Army in particular.
2. Government Regulation No. 70.

CONSIDERING: That it is necessary to take strong and firm measures for the safety of the struggle waged by the State of the Republic of Indonesia.

HEREBY DETERMINES:

THE INSTRUCTION ON EXTINCTION OF RUMOURS,

as follows:

1. Spreading rumours is a crime which unsettles security and defence.
2. Infringments of this Instruction are punishable in accordance with military law by military court for isolated region (by Commanders of Military Districts and Sub-districts) and by court matrial (by Battalion Commanders) in keeping with the Instruction from Armed Forces H.Q. previously mentioned.
3. All Military Governors, Commanders of Military Regions Commanders of Military Districts, and Commanders of Military Sub-districts, are ordered to take measures for implementing this Instruction in their respective regions. All civil government agencies are obliged to assist in implementing this Instruction.

EXPLANATION:

1. The enemy is spreading rumours and provocation with the intention of creating a situation of mutual mistrust, mutual accusation, mutual incitement between leader and subordinate, between neighbour and neighbour, between Government and political party, and so on. But by this means he seeks to divide

154

the strength of the State and the people, the Army and the Government itself, with the consequence that we quarrel with each other, fight against each other, so that the Republic of Indonesia can break itself to pieces from within.
2. Then again, rumours are meant to make the people fear the army in order that they will not continue their opposition.

Example:

1. There are now many rumours that the Emergency Government in Sumatra has agreed to a cease fire, that among the government officials there are many working with the enemy, etc.
All of this is in order to make people lose their conviction.
2. Near battle areas there are already many rumours that often shock and confuse the people. Therefore, people should not simple believe everything they hear, expect what is officially issued by the Military Government.

Therefore, government agencies should not accept news which has not been thoroughly checked, and which is not logical. Therefore, everybody should remain at his place of duty and continue his work undisturbed by anything whatever.

> *Issued from* : The Seat in Command.
> *Date*   : 7 January 1949.
> *Hour*   : 08.00.

COMMANDER OF ARMY AND OF JAVA TERRITORIUM,
Sgd. COLONEL A. H. NASUTION.

To:
All military and civil government agencies (with the request that it be passed on to those under them).
Copy: Commander-in-Chief, Armed Forces.

***

On the 12th January then followed an Instruction on non-contact, as follows:

JAVA COMMAND HEADQUARTERS
No. 8/M.B.K.D./49

INSTRUCTION

CONCERNING OUTSIDE CONTACT OF ARMY AND MILITARY GOVERNMENT IN JAVA.

RECALLING: That at the present time doubts and uncertainties occur here and there about the cease fire and negotiations, in connection with the Security Council's resolution, and in connection with the fact that captured Republican leaders have met with enemy authorities.

CONSIDERING: Implementation of the Order of the Day by H.E. the Vice President and the Order on strategy by H.E. the Commander in Chief of the Armed Forces.

HEREBY DETERMINES:

THE INSTRUCTION CONCERNING OUTSIDE CONTACT OF ARMY AND THE MILITARY GOVERNMENT:

1. All military and civil agencies throughout the whole military territory of the Republic of Indonesia are forbidden to contact agencies outside the Republic without the order of their superiors. Such contact will be considered infringement of the Instruction on Non-co-operation.
2. All Military Governors, Commanders of Military Regions Commanders of Military Districts, and Commanders of Military Sub-districts are to take the necessary steps.

EXPLANATION:

In implementing the Vice President's Order of the Day dated 19 December 1948 and the Order on Strategy from the Commander-in-Chief of the Armed Forces, there is only one task possible for the Java Command, namely, to restore the authority of the Government of the Republic of Indonesia throughout the whole of the military territory of Java, similarly also for the military and civil government in Java.

It is to be stressed that the captured authorities automatically do not exercise the function of their posts until they actually and officially resume their responsibilities.

For the Java Command there is an obvious military and administrative hierarchy from bottom to top, and the Java Command accepts orders only from the Commander-in-Chief of the Armed Forces/ Chief fo Staff of the Armed Forces, who is responsible to the Central Government. Therefore, each military and civil agency should remain firm at its place of duty, without heeding news and instructions of any kind whatever which do not proceed along the hierachical line refered to above until our goal has been won.

Issued from: The Seat of Command.
Date   : 12 January 1949.
Hour   : 09.00.

COMMANDER OF ARMY AND JAVA TERRITORIUM,

Sgd.   COLONEL A. H. NASUTION.

To:

1. *All Military Governors/Commanders of Divisions, Military Regions, Military Districts, Brigades.*
2. *All Military Governors/Commanders of Divisions, Military Territories.*
3. *Commando Group of Java Command Headquarters.*

Copies to:

1. *Commander-in-Chief of Armed Forces/Chief in Staff Armed Forces.*
2. *Deputy Chief of Staff Armed Forces.*

On 17 February, after the war had raged for almost two months, in an Order of the Day the Java Territorium Commander depicted the situation of our struggle in connection with political and military strategy, basically stating that the Dutch had failed and that our powers of struggle had remained completely intact. That order reads as follows:

JAVA COMMAND HEADQUARTES
No. 14/M.B.K.D./1949

ORDER OF THE DAY BY COMMANDER OF JAVA COMMAND

Date: 17 February 1949.

To: All members of the Armed Forces and of the civil services of the Republic of Indonesia in Java.

Merdeka!

On this day, when the independence of our State is three and a half years old, and the second colonial attack has been going on for two months, it is proper that we should be fully aware as to what stage our struggle has reached.

157

Three and a half years of struggle which has grown heavier and more intense as time goes on, so that eventually the Republic of Indonesia has control over only one-third of our country, while from within we fight each other, thus diminishing the potential of our struggle. But now, and from now on, we look forward to moments leading to victories that will ensure the fullest independence.

Every citizen should be truly aware, that our enemy has now reached a turning point. He is forced to admit openly that his plans have failed, even that this is because he is being squeezed, both politically and economically, and militarily. So squeezed is he that he is now seeking the most advantageous ways to retreat. He is forced to state clearly his plan of retreat from Indonesia, while he is completely at a loss and without ideas as to how to retreat.

The enemy has failed and is being squeezed politically, because he is unable to destroy the Republic, which now in actual fact even continues to stand firm and is even recognized by the whole world now as a fact. Because the federalists who were created by the enemy himself have turned their backs upon him and are seeking an accord with the Republic, because of the evident strength of the Republic. Because now the puppet federal states of enemy make become more and more unstable through our army attacks the enemy has lost his last bold in Indonesia.

In the international political field he is being squeezed because the United Nations has officially rejected Dutch sovereignty in Indonesia, and the international world is preparing itself to take political and economic sanctions against him, which Asian nations and states have begun to do while they are considering more effective help and recognition of the Republic as the one and only state in Indonesia. Also because the Western states have been shaken by the steps taken in Indonesia and by the birth of the Asian bloc which is basically opposed to the Western states.

Economically the enemy has failed and is being squeezed, because our common people have carried out the scorched earth policy against all his wealth and capital, and now the scorched earth policy and attacks upon estates and roads are being made more intensively all over Indonesia. The economic development which the enemy promised the world has become impossible; the export trade they have been hopefully expecting has become impossible also. If there were no one helping him, the enemy would become bankrupt. Their civil servants and soldiers have received their salaries irregularly these three months, while the value of NICA money continues to fall (the price of rice is already *f*. 1,175 a litre).

Militarily the enemy has failed, because he could not succeed by sudden and brutal attacks in destroying the National Army — the National Army is still even completely intact, and together with the people it is even launching offensives in all regions from Banten to Besuki, thus turning the whole area into a front of total guerilla warfare. It is not possible that the enemy has enough strength to overcome such total war, and throughout the history of war from any country whatever such a total guerilla war has never been surmountable.

From appearances the enemy is winning, but he has achieved only tactical and local victories. Strategically, he has in fact begun to be beaten because he is now tied up and surrounded by total guerilla warfare at whatever point we may endeavour to escape Strategically, he is squeezed and encircled; strategically, we are gradually going over to the attack and to pursuit the enemy.

In the meantime, our Republic outwardly indeed seems to be hard-pressed but in fact our Republic has won complete victory within and without during this second war. Without, we are victorious because now the whole world recognizes the fact of our Republic and bears withness to it. Within, we are victorous because now our Republic has shown that, both politically and militarily, she cannot be destroyed by any force whatever. The foundations of our Republic have never been so obviously strong and complete as they are at present.

In an atmosphere of temporary tactical failures militarily and politically, we must be fully aware of our strategical victories militarily and politically. Therefore, we must from now on continue strengthen our stand yet more and we must be thoroughly aware of our strength. No member of the Armed Forces should waver nor should doubt our ultimate victory any longer. Everybody must remain steadfast at his respective post, working with all his might to the end in order to conclude our struggle with a complete and total victory.

Struggle on, because ultimate victory lies visible before us.

Forever Merdeka!

COMMANDER OF THE ARMY AND OF JAVA TERRITORIUM

Sgd. COLONEL A. H. NASUTION,

*
**

Thus we had to continue to face the agitation from within which attacked the military. This psychological war consisted of insults intended to make the army ashamed, to drive a wedge between the men and the people, and to create a break between army and civilians. Indeed, too often we made ourselves into easy targets through weakness from which enemies disguised as friends could easily reap the benefit. Sometimes, young officers were too arrogant in facing old civil servants. At times, they did not heed the state's structural procedures and acted out of line which confused the civil organisation and hurt people's feelings. And the officers who were insulted, because they did not continuously make forward attacks, frequently lost their head and wildly used up all energy and bullets on battles which were meaningless for guerilla strategy — frequently it was just for the sake of attacking. They neglected old doctrines of people's guerilla warfare. And that was just what the enemy wanted, who felt like a blind man unable to find our troops destroy them with his complete and modern units. Therefore, on 19 February, when the second war had been going on for two months, the Java Command Headquarters issued Decree No. 18. Its contents are as follows:

JAVA COMMAND HEADQUARTERS
No. 18/MBKD/49
D E C R E E.

To all Military Governors, Military Sub-territorium Commanders, Military District Commanders, Military Sub-district Commanders, Commanders of Brigades, Battalions, Companies, Governors, Residents, Bupati, Wedana, Tjamat and Lurah.

1. In several different regions at present there is appearing agitation and provocation against the Armed Forces of the Republic of Indonesia, as follows:

a. *"The army is always retreating, the army does not advance"*, etc.
"If the army does not advance, don't let the people give it food". etc. Such matters an people's tongues are evidently created by certain quarters which are also the source of insults, and we are sure that in the last instance they are originated by enemy spies.

Such agitation and provocation should be eradicated by giving information and by destroying its sources.
It should be consiously understood that within a *Wehrkreise* (the pockets) there is no frout, there is no back line: the front

is in all directions. It should also be consciously understood, that all of the army is not always on the move, but that part of it must stay behind, while another part does administrative work. On the other hand, the army itself should consciously avoid irresponsible measures.

b. At present there are certain groups in the community who continuously and systematically say that the battle are not fought by the army, but by their *laskars* (people's army). Such tactic of psychological war are usually used 'by the enemy to make people lose faith in the army.

c. Misbehaviour by several army men is immediately labelled and sneered at as characteristic of the Army, of the whole Army.

Therefore, it is neccessary that commanders of units, of Military Districts, and of Military Sub-districts issue each week the Army News Bulletin in which the people can read about the war situation, particularly for their respective regions, and in general for the whole country.

2. Here and there conflicts of authority occure between the military government and the civil authorities. In practice there should be unity between the military commander and the regional head, and they should continue to work together. In theory, the regional head is the administrator of civil autonomy and the territorial commander is the administrator of military autonomy, i.e. the *Wehrkreise*, in which the civil autonomy is included as a part. Territorial commanders do not directly interfere with the internal organisation and technical affairs of the civil autonomy which was set up to be total in nature. Removals of civil servants continues to be dealt with by the civil service itself, although there should be mutual co-operation between the two parties.

3. We appeal to and urgently request all officials of the Armed Forces of the Republic of Indonesia and of the Government to take measures to put things in order, or to avoid the atmosphere of agitation and provocation referred to in point 1 for the improvement of matters dealt with under point 2.

Issued from : The Seat of Command.
Date   :   19 February 1949.
Hour   :   10.00.

COMMANDER OF THE ARMY AND JAVA TERRITORIUM,
Sgd. COL. A. H. NASUTION.

Copies to:

1. *The Commander-in-Chief Armed Forces; Cabinet Ministers; Deputy Chief-of-Staff Armed Forces.*

2. *Commander Military Police Corps, all Posts of Java Command Headquarters, to be passed on to Deputy J General Staff Command and Deputy II General Staff Comand of Java Comand Headquarters.*

*
**

There was an increase of local measures by political groups desirous of fishing in troubled waters. In a number of reigons there appeared troops who were unattached within the state structure. Sometimes, those of our own officials who lacked understanding gave their assistance for the formation of defence committiees, such as are ordered in an instruction from a certain party. In fact, it is the right and the duty of every citizen to fight in defence of independence. But it is equally a fact that by neglecting and ignoring, or by appropriating, the legal and official instruments of the Republic implies and result in attacking the state, assisting the disintegration of the state, just as in is keeping with the strategy planned by the enemy. It is a theory of people's guerilla warfare that "guerilla-ism" is to be avoided, even that we must preserve and srengthen law and order and the integrity of the state's instruments. The more bodies there are which seize the competence of state organisations — especially if they compete with them, — the weaker will our struggle grow. From a standpoint of narrow party politics it can be understood that parties endeavour to increase their influence, but it is very mistaken if this is done by taking under control and competing with existing government agencies. Therefore it was felt necessary that I issue and instruction (that of 19 February) in order to maintain and uphold the organisation of the state and army. The contents are as follow:

JAVA COMMAND HEADQUARTERS
No. 19/MBKD/49

INSTRUCTION
RESPECTING

ORGANISATION FOR THE ARMED FORCES OF THE REPUBLIC OF INDONESIA AND THE MILITARY GOVERNMEUT ON JAVA.

RECALLING:

1. The existence of laws, instructions and regulations emanating from the government of the Republic of Indonesia and the Headquarters of the Armed Forces of the Republic of Indonesia,

to face the war situation of the present time; that these laws, instructions and regulations are an adequate basis for carrying ont war efforts and the government activities of the present time;

2. The emergence here and there of situations that are not official, in which the duties and the rights of the Armed Forces of the Republic of Indonesia or of the Government (military-civil) of the Republic Indonesia are appropriated by others;

CONSIDERING:

That the consequences of such matters as mentioned in point 2 above wil result in an overthrow from within of the State of the Republic of Indonesia which was proclaimed by the people of Indonesia on 17th August 1945;

HEREBY DETERMINES:

An Instruction on the Organisation of the Armed Forces of the Republic of Indonesia and the Military Government on Java, as follows:

It is stressed again that it is the task of:

1. All military and civil agencies at all levels to maintain and uphold the organisation and the regulations of the State of the Republic of Indonesia with all the power at their command.

2. Wherever there arise organisations outside the military government and the Armed Forces of the Republic of Indonesia due to the presence of a vacuum or to shortcomings or for other reasons, then all agencies of the military government are obliged to adjust those organisations to, and to include them within, the organization of the Republic of Indonesia's Armed Forces or the military (c.q. civil) government, in keeping with their respective characters. Those who do not comply with this instruction are to be considered to be persons attacking the sovereignty of the State of the Republic of Indonesia in time of war, and are therefore punishable by the military courts in keeping with their crime.

3. This instruction comes into force on the date of issue.

EXPLANATION

1. Military government agencies are: Commander in Chief of the Armed Forces, Comander of the Army and Java Territorium,

Picture of late General Sudirman the Father of the Indonesian National Army (T.N.I.)

Military Governors, Military Sub-territorium Commanders, Military District Commanders, who are in charge of *Wehrkreise* duties, i.e. of military government, territorial command and mobilization.

Republican Armed Forces agencies are: Java Command, divisions, brigades, battalions. Organizations of the Navy of the Republic of Indonesia, Air Force of the Republic of Indonesia, etc. are included in agencies of the military government or of the Republican Armed Forces, except for those on duty with the Armed Forces Staff.

Agencies of the Civil Government are: Governor, Resident, Bupati, Wedana, Tjamat and Lurah, who in accordance with Government Regulation No. 70 are administrators of autonomy in Residencies, Kabupatens, Ketjamatans and Kelurahans. In this connection new organisations wil be set up as far as necessary to implement autonomy within a *Wehrkreise.*

2. Many private organizations are arising that fill a vacuum or some shortcoming of the military (civil) government or the Republic's Armed Forces, or are also as planned by the elements who want to establish an authority outside the State of the Republic of Indonesia which means a violation of the sovereignty of the Republic of Indonesia.

In the order from the Commander-in-Chief of the Armed Forces dated 15 September 1948, the Armed Forces of the Republic are clearly ordered to destroy outright and by appropriate means all actions or intentions to violate the sovereignty of the Republic from without and within.

Whereas the Republic is now engaged in a life and death struggle against foreign enemies, attack from within is extremely dangerous.

3. It is now more urgent than ever before that all members of the Armed Forces of the Republic of Indonesia and of the Government of the Republic of Indonesia, of all levels and in all fields of activity, and all citizens be obliged to understand thoroughly the importance of protecting the organisations and laws (c.q. regulatoins) of the State of the Republic of Indonesia.

The oath of the Armed Forces was pronounced by H.E. the Commander-in-Chief of the Armed Forces on 20 May 1946, namely: to stand or fall together with the State of the Republic of Indonesia. And every member of the Government of the Republic of Indonesia has already taken an aoth as prescribed by law to protect the Republic of Indonesia.

Issued from: The Seat of Command.
Date : 19 February 1949.
Hour : 08.00.

COMMANDER OF THE ARMY AND JAVA TERRITORIUM,
Sgd. COL. A. H. NASUTION.

To:

1. *All Military Governors, Commanders of Military Sub-Territorim, Military Districts, Military Sub-Districts.*
2. *All Commanders of Brigades, Battalions.*
3. *All Governors, Residents, Bupati, Tjamat.*
4. *All posts of H. Q. Java Comand to be passed on.*

Copies to:

1. *Commanders-in-Chief of Armed Forces.*
2. *Ministers of Home Affairs.*
3. *Deputy Chief of Staff of Armed Forces.*
4. *Commander of Regional Military Police Corps.*

It was also necessary to issue a decree to avoid chaos in the government, in connection with the presence of officials in occupied cities. At the apex of the State organisation there was a duality which could be used and taken advantage of by the enemy. The emergency government led by Sjafruddin Prawiranegara, which to us was the official leadership of the State, of course was not recognised by the Dutch. They continued to make contact with Sukarno-Hatta-Sjahrir-Suriadarma in Bangka, who were exiled there as Dutch captives. In the mountains we were very afraid that the leaders in Bangka, as captives who were not independent, as officials who were already non-active, would carry out their own tactics independent of the leadership of the guerilla government. Indeed, it proved later on that there were grounds for such fears. In a number of regions there was a similar situation. Many officials, especially those from the central government who stayed in the occupied towns, continued to maintain contact with their subordinates who had evacuated, or vice versa, those outside the towns still acknowledged the authority of those officials. If this were tolerated, there was no longer any possibility of a single intact leadership, and the disintegration of the state would occur more rapidly.

166

There also a sharp war of ideas against us in that the U.N. Security Council's resolution calling for a cessation of hostilities was being busily discussed. Many people had their own interpretations and standpoints. There were those who thought that the Security Council orders should be obeyed, there were those who thought that the fighting would go on as long as their superiors had given no order. But most dangerous were the individual political interpretation. *"We do not agree with a cease fire, even though ordered by our superiors"*, they said.*"We should obey any orders whatever"*, was the opinion of others. But the sly hand at politics could make the question go deeper. *"The Government wants to continue negotiations, because it has no faith in the strength of the guerillas, this is the bankrupt policy that has brought disastrous consequences upon us till now. It is those Linggardjati, Renville and Bangka groups who have caused those difficulties of ours"*. And so things went on at about the time consultations began between the BFO contact committee and Bangka; the minds of the troops and especially of thoughtful officers were very much disturbed. Here and there, through provocations, there even arose distrust toward superiors, toward the government. Fortunately, in facing this political situation, all problems could be submitted to the person of the Commander in Chief. The Commander-in-Chief sent radiogrammes to all Territorial Commanders in Sumatra and to all army commanders, in order to clear the political atmosphere. He also wrote circular letters to leaders of the people calling upon them to continue to maintain the unity and integrity of the state. Altough he was ill, he took up in full the challenge of political-ideological problems, and thus became a prop and stay for all groups. He gave advice which was followed; that all such matters should be left to him.

My headquarters issued the following Decree:

HEADQUARTERS OF JAVA COMMAND
No. 20/MBKD/1949

D E C R E E
No. 5

I. Because there are persons asking as to what is the position of the authorities of the Republic who are in the occupied towns, we hereby clarify that all officials of the State of the Republic of Indonesia who are in the Dutch occupied towns, are considered to be in a position of being unable to do their work, and are thus not exercising their functions.

II. Because political groups often make their opinions known to offices concerning the Security Council resolution and so on, we hereby affirm once more, that officers should not be provoked into taking steps infringing the sovereignty of the Armed Forces of the Republic of Indonesia, because the duty of the Armed Forces is only the single one, of driving out the enemy from the territory of the State of the Republic of Indonesia.

III. I call upon you to continue the struggle until your duty is done. Do not waver.

> *Issued from*:   The Seat of Command.
> *Date*   :   23 February 1949.

COMMANDER OF THE ARMY AND JAVA TERRITORIUM,
Sgd.   COLONEL A. H. NASUTION.

To: *All military and civil authorities.*

Copies:

1. *The Commander in Chief of the Armed Forces.*
2. *Cabinet Ministers.*

*
**

A most urgent measure for a long guerilla war is the organization of a general people's resistance. Of course, a great deal of individual initiative will be taken. And as was the case in the past, there will be various combat groups *(laskar)*. We had already experienced how difficult it was to unite all these combat groups into a National Army which is united and uniform. We had already experienced how various political groups used the opportunity to create their private armies which were independent of the government. We had also experienced how the enemy himself infiltrated into our organisations of struggle, created conflicts of one against the other, and even formed combat troops which made war upon the Republic. The people also suffered much because all these various organisations of struggle asked sustenance from the people. At a certain poin these bodies were forced, or tempted to take over over control over a certain region, a particular enterprise, a given harbour, only with the aim of meeting their material and financial needs alone.

And eventually the authority of the state was growing dim. Various private armies and private administrations exercised the sovereignty of he states. For the leadership of the army, the situation was yet more difficult. It had to guarantee the safety of its back and flanks against various combat groups acting on their own. It had to arrange

168

a strategy and the execution of orderly defence. As has been expounded at length above, every tendency towards "guerillaism" amongst us was to be avoided and destroyed. The guerilla war would fail, of among the guerillas themselves there was mutual guerilla war. "Guerillaism" will ultimately swallow the guerillas because "guerillaism" takes guerilla action against guerillas themselves.

Therefore, the peoples' burning siprit of resistance had to be properly channeled into an official organisation and one which is orderly. Also the awakening of the people's resistance was not to be left to accident al initiative alone. There are regions which will bring forth many troops, therewill be others also which remain passive. Therefore the strategy of our guerilla war must see to it that the people's resistance extended evenly from one end of the island to the other.

It was in connection with these considerations that I issued an instruction concerning village guerilla roops — the Indonesian name *"pasukan gerilja desa"*, is abbreviated to "Pager Desa" — known up till now as the Indonesian "Home Guard", which was organized village by village. During the First Clash, the "National Guards" in West Java were a failure because various private combat troops still flourished at that time, and the army themselves had not yet come to take an interest in them. During the Second Clash, the "PAGER DESA" developed quickly, and after the war it continued to grow as the village security body. Casualties among "PAGER DESA" members during the war and during security actions have exceeded the casualties in the army itself. The "PAGER DESA" were the embodiment of the true people's resistance. Many of the members have now become regular troops or officers of the village administration. Here also is proof that the "PAGER DESA" contained the selected flower of the village youth. There is now a strong village leadership in the unity between Lurah, village administration,and "PAGER DESA".

The relevent instruction was issued on 25 January, and is as follows:

HEADQUARTERS JAVA COMMAND
No. 11/MBKD/49

INSTRUCTION
VILLAGE GUERILLA TROOPS.

RECALLING:

1. Government Regulation No. 70 and the Armed Forces Headquarters Instruction of 9th November 1948.

2. The existence of general mobilization and the military government.
3. The insufficiency of territorial manpower to man the Military Sub-District Commands.

CONSIDERING:

The need for building up manpower in order to create Military Sub-Distrist Command Troops that mean the extension and intensification of the strength of defence.

HEREBY DETERMINES:

INSTRUCTION CONCERNING VILLAGE GUERILLA TROOPS ("PAGER DESA"):

1. Formation:

The Military Sub-District Commands shall establish in each village one patrol of village guerillas ("Pager Desa") consisting of selected young men.

> NOTE: Experienced ex-service men without significant family burdens should be recruited.

a. Members shall have the rank of soldiers and the commander of the patrol shall have the rank of corporal. The Commander of the Military Sub-District shall be the Commander of all the troops combined for the entire Military Sub-District.

b. All members shall be registered as members of the Military Sub-District and shall later become reserve members of the territorial battalion of the Military District.

c. All members have to be sworn in as members of the army:
   — To be faithful to the Republic of Indonesia.
   — To be faithful to the military law of the Indonesian National Army.
   — To be obedient to their superiors.

The oath is taken by the Commander of the Military Sub-District or by his Deputy, and witnessed by the Lurah.

2. Duties.

a. To conduct guerilla activities under the command of the Military Sub-District Commander.
   — to execute scorched-earth policy.
   — to conduct communications.

- to conduct reconnaisance.
- to carry out a guard over the village.
- to destroy and block roads and rail tracks.
- to destroy the enemy's means of communication.
- and other things considered necessary by the Military Sub-District Commander.

  b. To become reserves for the Armed Forces of the Republic of Indonesia.
  c. To assist the military police within the Military Sub-District Command.

3. a. "Pager Desa" (Village guards) are not accomodated in hostels but shall each live in their homes.
   b. All are voluntary service men.
   c. All are exempted from taxes.
   d. In general, young men without families shall be recruited.
   e. Members shall be on duty by turns.

   NOTE: It must be seen that no repetition occurs of what has happened in the past: that total defence becomes total surety of a livelihood.

4. The Military Sub-District Commander arranges the training of the members with the help of pointers from the Military District Commander.
   Periodically the Military District Commander shall arrange the training of the patrol leaders.

5. For arms, every member shall bring their own swords, spears, knives and the like, and possibly there will be weapons provided by the Military Sub-District Command.

CLARIFICATION.

1. Territorial execution of this instruction has the purpose of training all youth who in time of war can be mobilized in the village and of organizing them in territorial battalions and finally of sending them back to the villages as reserves. This scheme could not be executed until the outbreak of war. With this Instruction, the motter is taken up and adjusted to the situation. By this means manpower is provided for the Military Sub-District Commands while extending and intensifying the potential of the Armed Forces of the Republic of Indonesia by millions of men.

   In every region there already exist various formations differing one from the others.

By this Instruction a uniform organisation is established for the entire military Territorium of Java.

And indeed, it is this time of war which is the best training period for all military and defence bodies, and which must be used to the full. Commanders of mobile battalions should take Village Guerilla Troops with them in their mobile activities as assistance and in order that they may gain experience.

2. In the training of members of the "Pager Desa" special attention should be given to the following aspects.

   a. methods of executing the scorched-earth policy.
   b. reconnoitering the enemy.
   c. conveying news.
   d. security (enemy espionage and provocative news).
   e. the guard and patrol of the village.
   f. how to act, to disappear, etc. when the enemy patrols reach the village; how to save the Lurah, the population, goods, and so on.
   g. methods of destroying and making guerilla attacks upon the enemy's communications; do not allow it to happen that unarmed young men are ordered to attack a well-armed enemy.

3. With such an extension of manpower for the Armed Forces of the Republic of Indonesia, the following can be stipulated, that Mobile Units are first line troops.

   Territorial Units are second line troops.

   Village Guerilla Units are third line troops.

   Dated   :   25th January 1949.
   Hour   :   08.00.
   Issued from: The Seat of Command.

   COMMANDER OF THE ARMY AND JAVA TERRITORIUM,
   Sgd. COLONEL A. H. NASUTION.

To:

   All Military Governors, Military Region Commanders (Sub Territorium Commanders), Military Distric Commanders, Military Sub-District Commanders.

Copies to:

1. *The Commander-in-Chief of the Armed Forces.*
2. *Minister Soekiman for he Central Government.*

3. *To all Governors and Residents.*
4. *To all Commanders of Brigades, Battalions, all posts of Head-quarters of he Java Command, all Bupati and Tjamat.*

*
**

With the issue of these simple instructions, of course there were not enough regulations to organise everything. This was the maximum which we could execute with our simple organisation and administration in so short a time. It was but natural that many errors were made, and many individual measures taken.

Many conflicts occurred between civilians and the military, and between army units Territorial Commands. It often happened also that individuals from the political movement entered the staff of the military administration who were capable of over-awing local civil administrators, so that the position of the latter as representatives of the government was pushed aside. Sometimes the Military Sub-District Commanders became small dictators, who were not to be competed against by anyone at all.

Therefore an Instruction was issued to prescribe the balance between positions held by military and civilian officials within the guerilla government, as follows:

HEADQUARTERS JAVA COMMAND
No. 15/M.B.K.D./49

CLARIFICATION
RELATIVE AUTHORITIES AND COMPETENCES WITHIN THE MILITARY GOVERNMENT.

1. a. After the military government has functioned for one and a half months it is obvious that clarification is necessary concerning the authority within the military government.
   At every level there are three kinds of bodies, a fact which is often not fully understood; for instance, in the level of the Military Sub-District Command there are the Military Sub-District Commander, the Tjamat (Sub-District Head) and the staff of the Military Sub-District Command as staff of the Military Government.
   b. The Military Sub-District Commander, as commander of the *Wehrkreise*, is responsible for the total defence of the *Wehrkreise*. The concept of the *Wehrkreise* in principle includes the following:

1) de facto military defence.

2) de facto administrative defence.

3) ensuring well-being for the people.

c. All three principles must be put into practice in order to succeed in total defence. In order to conduct the military defence, the Military Sub-District Command possesses (may possess) military units from the territorial battalions or Village Guerilla troops in particular to the whole of the people in general. Conditions of general mobilization give the right to the Commander of theMilitary Sub-District to mobilize all forces. For this leadership the Commander of the Military Sub-District is assisted by several members of the army. This is an ordinary territorial duty.

d. De facto administrative defence is conducted by the Tjamat as the Head of the autonomous region under the instruction of the Commander of the Military Sub-District. With autonomy of the *Ketjamatan* (Sub-District) the Tjamat, with the authority of the Military Government, is obliged to regulate administrative matters. Within a *Ketjamatan* all kinds of activities take place in time of war, in the field of mobilizing funds and forces, economy and people, and for these varied tasks the Tjamat needs many assistants; therefore the Tjamat with the authority of the Military Government appoints assistants; for instance, persons to organize public kitchens, public health, etc.

The Tjamat is entitled to use all civil servants in his region.

e. The Staff of the Military Sub-District, which according to the Military Government's Instruction is set up for general purposes, for defence, economic affairs and the needs of the community, is a staff, and not body which can act externally directly on its own.

The Head of every Section always acts on behalf of the Military Sub-District Command, they assist the Military Sub-District Command in solving various problems, in controlling implementation of endeavours, inmobilizing forces, etc. It is adequate if this is merely a small staff.

NOTE: Defence, of course, is conducted by the Army itself. Members of the Staff may be recruited from the military or civilian personnel or from the people.

Through their position on the staff, they are automatically militarized as reserve sergeants, reserve junior lieutenants, etc. (They are regarded as being mobilized). These ranks are not titular. *).

In our military principles, all citizens of the State are as reserve manpower of the armed forces.

2. In practice, it is evident that there are Military Sub-District staffs which have taken over many different kinds of tasks of the Tjamat (such as seeing to taxes, markets, public kitchens and the like). All the civilians tasks are duties of the Tjamat.

Indeed nowadays the Tjamat has a great deal of work, but because of that he can mobilize the necessary forces in the name of the military government. The Military Sub-District Commander determines many kinds of civil endeavours which are needed in connection with the *Wehrkreise*.

Therefore the Tjamat has to take steps for those endeavours and the Commander of the Military Sub-District does not need to be directly involved, for instance in fixing taxes in kind. It is sufficient if he decides that for instance the Tjamat should collect one quintal of rice every month. It is up to the Tjamat how he collects it. The Commander of the Military Sub-District needs only to control implementation and wherever necessary to give his backing in promoting collection.

3. There are also cases in which a Tjamat is appointed as titular officer.

This is not necessary. As a civilian he can continue to implement his civilian duty in keeping with the autonomy of the region, though now he does so for defence purposes, at the order of the Army. Military Tjamats are appointed in regions where there are none or where there can be no Tjamat, for instance in regions which were recently occupied by troops performing "Wingate" movements as in West Java or in the environs of towns where there is too much fighting. In the case of such an emergency, an officer is appointed as military Tjamat, until there is, or can be again, an ordinary Tjamat at work.

This function of military Tjamat in general is automatically taken concurrently by the Commander of the Military Sub-District, in the same way that the Military District Commander takes the function of military Bupati, and the Sub-Territorium Commander that of the military Resident.

---

*) Titular ranks are given in the Indonesian Armed Forces to civilians appointed to perform a specific military function as, for example, with a civilian judge who presides over a military court.

Thus, this is an emergency situation.

4. For a long struggle (depth of the struggle), it is more necessary than in the past for us (the military government) to start activities for the well-being of the people in the field of co-operatives, agriculture, health, education, and so forth.
There are now many capable people leaving the cities and coming to the villages, many dynamic students. Use these people in the staff of the Tjamat. The people must know and be able to feel that independence means happiness for them, which for that reason they must build and defend with their own blood and their sweat. If this does not happen it will not be possible to achieve the fullest mobilization of the people for this long and heavy struggle.

5. Military Distict Commanders and Military Sub-District Commanders are heads ofmilitary government because they have territories. Village cadres are not heads, because they are not commanders of a territory (the villages), they are only workers of Military Sub-District Commands in villages who are seconded to Lurahs. The Military Sub-District is the lowest level of military government. (Village cadres are reserve soldiers or corporals).
In places where there is not or cannot be a Lurah, a low-ranking officer may be appointed as military Lurah. If there is a Lurah later on, or if the situation permits, the civil governt shall immediately reinstate a Lurah.

6. It is evident that there are Military Sub-District Commanders who leave their regions in the company of mobile troops. This is forbidden, because Military Sub-District Commanders must remain in their areas. If for example a greater part of his region is controlled by the enemy, he must continue to attend to his region by illegal or underground methods;
if absolutely necessary he must continue to do his duty from outside his region (but close by).

7. In fact there are Military Sub-District Commanders who have never visited the Lurahs in their territory. All military government heads from the highest to the lowest in rank are required to have good relations with the heads of civil government in their territory, so that they have close personal contact. Work will produce more results if there is personal contact. Because in general military people are younger, discretion is needed and this in fact accords with our character as an Eastern people. Military Region Commanders (Sub-Territorium Commanders)

176

must be united in their duties and daily contacts with the
Residents, Military District Commanders with the Bupati, and
Military Sub-District Commanders with the Tjamat, in order
that our defence can really be total.

On the other hand, civilian authorities for their part have to
realize that there are heads of military government because
of the regulations concerning the state of war. Those who have
to work hard are the Commanders of Military Sub-Districts, the
Tjamat and Lurah. Military Region Commanders and Sub-
Territorium Commanders are the braintrust, the controllers, the
co-ordinators and those who give incentive to practice, because
the Military Sub-District Command can always act executively
as a whole, being a single geographical unit, while Military
Region Commands and those bodies above act only as a combination of geographical areas. Sub-Territorium Commanders and
Military Region Commanders, Residents and Bupati place the
stress of their work upon the Military Sub-Districts/Katjamatan.
Military Sub-Districts/Katjamatan are the very foundation for
the de facto Republic. At higher levels there need not be large
staffs, what is needed are several mobile groups which continue
on and an to visit the Military Sub-District Commands and
Katjamatan. However, it should not go so far that there is no
permanent post, that it is not possible to meet the leadership
every day. The leadership continues to be everywhere (mobile
and with communication posts), but it must be possible for the
leadership to be reached by their subordinates and their superiors at any time.

NOTES:

1. Territorial Commanders of Sub-Territorium, Military Districts,
   Sub-Military-Districts, are there to assist in what is needed
   by operative military units (battalions and brigades in the fields
   of supply, security and local strategy, etc.). Because of this
   teritoriau commanders (Sub-Territorium, Military Districts, Military Sub-Districts) are responsible to commanders of those troops
   conducting operations in their teritories, and the operational
   commanders give orders or instruction to the territorial commanders concerning implementation of what is needed by their
   operation.

   However, the difference of rank must be kept in mind. If, for
   instance the operational commander concerned has a lower rank
   than the territorial commander concerned, then the form of the
   instruction becomes a request and the commanders involved
   must be consious of this fact.

Territorial commanders are concurrently heads of the military government and this calls for work and time which in practice has no limits because of the heavy program of the military government, on the other hand operational commanders, because operations are in general mobile and fast moving, have to concentrate their minds upon the operation and should be free of territorial problems; the one cannot exist without the other, results are possible only through a properdivision of duties, and execution by the respective parties as fully as possible. Wherever operational areas are the same as territorial areas it is well if the operational commander is concurrently the territorial commander of the Military Sub-District, if in the opinion of the Division Commander/Military Governor this is not too heavy.

2. Up till now it has proved that Tjamat and Lurah are the very foundations of the State. They are regarded and felt by the people to be their proper leaders and the persons representing the State. The areas of Ketjamatan and Kelurahan have now proved to be very appropriate for intensive activities in the matter of autonomy. Seen from the practical point of view, it is evident that Ketjamatan are strong enough for a geographical unit; however, because there as of our Kelurahan have been for centuries the lowest autonomous units, we are compelled to take a method of compromise. Kelurahan are to be maintained as autonomous areas in civil matters, and Kelurahan in the sense of military government. In the future, Kelurahan will certainly have a wider area, one which accords approximately with that of the Ketjamatan, such as we see in the region of Jogjakarta, where modernizing and democratising are most advanced.

Issued from: The seat of Command.
Dater   : 1 January 1949.
Hour   : 12.00.

COMMANDER OF THE ARMY AND JAVA TERRITORIUM,
Sgd. COL. A. H. NASUTION.

To:

All Military Governors, Military Region Commanders (Sub-Territorium Commanders), Military District Commanders, Military Sub-District Commanders, Governors, Residents, Bupati, Tjamat.

Copies to:

1. *The Comander-in-Chief of the Armed Forces*
2. *The Minister of Home Affairs.*

C. BASIC INSTRUCTIONS CONCERNING GUERILLA BATTLES

It is a great pity that there was no proper opportunity before the second military action of the Dutch to widen the conduct of guerilla warfare by our people. This has been made clear in the exposition in previous chapters. Therefore after the Dutch attacked, it was necessary as quickly as possible to explain, to clarify or to stress once more the methods to be used. This informations had to be spread quickly, people had to be introduced, it had to be spread widely in a simple way and by popular means which were not beyond the understanding of any our various kinds of officers. Therefore, through following the development of operations, I issued one after the other three kinds of operational instructions to standardize and to unify interpretations. In practice, the Commander of the Java Command is not a commander leading operations, similarly also with the division commanders. They are, rather, the educators of the hundreds of leaders scattered everywhere conducting "small wars". The system of communication, which was given precedence and priority as the first measure, could be the channel for instructions going far and fast and reaching equally all the commanders who who spread out in all directions.

As has been explained, the Dutch, strategically and tactically, attacked suddenly in order to annihilate the Republic and the Indonesian National Army, so that they could set up a National Interim Government.

Their military attack was planned to effect occupation of all important places within two to three months and to obtain control over all traffic roads, to break up and to destroy the National Army and the instruments of the Republic's authority. For that purpose, the enemy tried to demoralise the National Army and the Indonesian people. To make them lose hope. Having in several weeks, occupied all important places, the enemy follower up with extremely intensive and active mopping up operations. Mopping up columns were suddenly roaming every where which were extremely fast-moving. We were pursued here and there without being given much time and room to move aside. In tense terrorization, extensive arrests, arson, machine gunning, cannonades, in brief demoralisation with modern weapons of war and orderly psychological warfare very much to the point. The morale of the

179

Dutch army was strong and enthusiastic and they quickly occupied the capital city. There was no significant defence to block the enemy. Everything went according to plan and in orderly fashion, smoothly and with ease in reaching and seizing their targets.

Therefore, of course, the effect upon our Army and People was also great. There was a great deal of loss of hope, many surrendered, crossed over to the enemy, evacuated to federal regions, remained passively at home, hiding here and there, and searching for protection here and there. Many of our troop units were broken up. This was all the more so with regard to our staffs and our government departments, which became widely scattered.

Many people also felt themselves small and powerless in view of the modern and completely equipped organisation of the enemy. They were downhearted because they were incapable of defending the town and only retreated to move aside. They were ashamed that they were unable to defend every square meter. They felt as though we could only retreat. Insinuations were made against the army. That it was letting the enemy walk all over the towns terrorizing the people. The Headquarters of the Java Command — the MBKD — was said to be Markas Belanda Keliling Djawa" (Dutch quarters roaming around Java).

It is to be understood that many of our people could not bear it. "Why do we just retreat; we must seize the towns again; let us plan a general attack; we must always be in the front line; we'll give the army the back line, we must fight in the front line. " Often sentiments could not be controlled by commons sense. At that stage our tactics were precisely no other than, within two or three weeks, to evacuate the towns and retreat to our pocket centers; to refrain from open battles and only to harrasss the enemy's advance alone; to execute the scorched earth policy. While the Dutch were planning to destroy the Republic and the National Army organisations, at the same time we planned to save our army by returning to the pockets which were its base, along with some small stocks of materials, and with civilian personnel and to evacuate the people to villages and districts. Our objective was purely negative: to prevent annihilation in open battles, to retreat and hide: To mobilise Military District Commands, Military Sub-District Commands and Village defence organisations and the guerilla government.

And so people forgot that there was no front line any longer, there were only the elastic pockets, swelling out when the enemy did not come near, deflating when the enemy came on patrol.

The enemy was compelled to chase us until he became exhausted, the enemy was compelled to patrol everywhere. For that purpose, he was compelled to have many bases, he had to break up his forces until they became detachments and small posts. The enemy had to spread out to break his forces into splinters in order to balance our simple troops. The enemy was forced to become ordinery infantry. His artillery and heavy arms became infantry guards and even mere security police.

Therefore, the real war had not yet begun for us. We were still only preparing ourselves for a people guerilla war. If the Dutch failed to destroy the instruments of the Republic's authority, to destroy the National Army troops in their pockets, their military strategy had also failed their big attacks with everything according to plan would be of no avail, although the enemy could go everywhere, this did not mean that he could occupy all places and take control everywhere despite the fact that he occupied all capitals of Provinces, Kabupatens, Districts and Sub-Districts. If we could compel the enemy to be in that position, if the enemy were compelled to be in such a negative position as long as 6 months, then, as I predicted at that time, the enemy would be compelled to abandon his military strategy, because it was of no avail. Therefore he would have to go back to finding a solution through political endeavours alone.

Therefore, at the very beginning, the location of all our troops were piling all around the Dutch occupied towns, competing between themselves to be furthest forward, to be the most daring. This was the picture all around Jogjakarrta, Solo, Magelang, Madiun, Kediri, Bodjonegoro, etc. Insinuations were made against the "Siliwangi" troops which left Central Java proceeding to West Java that they were reluctant to fight. Similarly also with units of the First Division which were proceeding back to Besuki.

Thus what was needed in the first phase was the making of retreats in order to save the military units, it was not yet time for attacking. Understanding was of course no longer to be had from the people and politicians. Their understanding of war was not adequate. Prior information was naturally impossible. Such information at those critical moment would be interpreted as coveringup defeats in the way which had been customary with war news in the past: "Orderly retreat to strategic positions of greater strength" during the Dutch and Japanese times had covered up their defeats. Also psychological conditions were very difficult among the

181

army itself. They were ashamed at retreating and felt obliged to defend the towns. At those moments the necessary was felt for instruction to clarify the stages of our real tactics which were as they ought to be, to stress the kinds of tasks facing us, to explain the methods of placing troops and the kinds of targets in their order of importance to prevent the troops from piling up without grounds around the towns; to wipe out misunderstanding about the desire to attack towns and seize them again. A long people's guerilla war require the drawing up of orderly strategy, which must be executed with discipline, "guerilla-ism" can not be allowed.

Lt was necessary to economize energy and time to take the fullest benefit from it.

With regard to the dislocation of troops, it had to be recalled that their piling up around the towns made them into the targets the enemy dreamed of. The troops must have their bases far inside the districts and the troops must move around.

Targets must be in keeping with guerilla tactics, that is, to seek out the weaknesses of the enemy and to aboid his strengths. The towns were the bases of his strength. Enemy targets which were weak were their transport convoys and their far-flung patrols. And these were the things which it was possible to destroy by concentrating our strength. It was here that it was possible to execute our tactic ofdestroying the enemy and our efforts to seize equipment. These were the most important military targets for us.

Then came the political targets, namely to create disturbances in the communities of occupied towns; and large scale attacks are not always needed for this, infiltrations, psychological warfare and the like will do. Certainly it was necessary from time to time, at politically appropriate moments, to wage general attacks in order to show that we were still intact and capable of striking in rather large combinations. Our political targets were the enemy's agents, the enemy's employees and traitors who were collaborating with the enemy. People had to be kept scared of working with the enemy. The development of instruments of colonial government had to be made to fail at all times. Occupied towns might not be allowed to feel secure, collaborating employees might not be left in peace and quiet.

Economic targets were of the utmost importance in our guerilla war. The war waged by the Dutch was an economic war for them. Dutch capital was in Indonesia. And for the greater part, their capital was invested in plantation businesses. The development of these plantations had to be prevented by scorched earth. And if it happened that rehabilitation could be started, then we had to make endeavours in order that the work should not go on peacefully.

Every plantation had to be so much guarded by the enemy that it was as though the plantations were themselves fortresses. The crops were to be first destroyed so that they could not be used any more. Our agricultural experts would be asked advice as to what was the most effective way of destroying them. Such a failure of rehabilitation would become failure to export, a failure economically and financially which would be deeply felt by the Dutch. It was these economic interests which were the most important forandation for the enemy's idea of waging war against us in order to save his capital. The expensive Army, an army which is too heavy for that small country of Holland, which was set in motion with great sacrifice, was at stake. The Dutch put up in order to pluck the economic results in the future.

Therefore, the problem of troop locations and targets must be based solely on the strategy of a long guerilla war. Every bullet fired, every drop of sweat, every flow of blood, must be for the achievement of results which had been most carefully calculated.

It was in this connection that, on 31 December 1948 I issued the first instruction on strategy (operation) as follows:

HEADQUARTERS JAVA COMMAND
No. 3/MBKD/1948

WORKING INSTRUCTIONS FOR OPERATION OF MOBILE UNITS

PREFACE.

Every commander must look to the future, must be fully conscious of military developments, etc. and thus be able to organize ways of using troops with the greatest possible benefit (effectively and efficiently).

The first stage of the military situation in Java has lasted two weeks, the phases being:

a The Dutch operations to seize towns and main roads. Meanwhile we made resistance by playing for time (slowing down their actions), in order to make opportunities for mobilizing *Wehrkreise*, through the organisation of the military government and thorough scorched earth.

b. Our oprations re-entered occupied territories and established military governments and waged guerilla war there (Within two weeks the 4th Division had entered West Java).

In the execution of point a, the Dutch were able to obtain quick results, because they had planned an orderly and well-equiped strategy (as had been the case with the Nazi attack on the Netherlands before this), and attacked suddenly on Sunday morning at 3 o'clock in Jogjakarta (in other places at 00.00 hours) without prior declaration. Therefore the Dutch announced to the whole world that they had completed their operations, that the whole of Java was occupied, and so on.

But for us the real war only just about to begin, namely the total guerilla war which was ordered by the Commander in Chief of the Armed Force in his order on strategy. It is this are over stage (the second stage) which is fundamental for us. At this stage, the Dutch have occupied hundreds of places in Java, (towns, factories, estates, bridges, etc.) so that they are broken up to become escort units of the size of a section of a company. They can no longer tell accurately as at the beginning, where are our positions and what our conditions. At this stage, the enemy is no longer the attacker, but on the contrary, is defending himself.

To able to defend himself, he is conducting:

a. local mopping up operations.
b. large scale mopping up operations.

In all their mopping up operations, the Dutch use spies to search who look for where the army are, the youth and leaders, and who show them the roads The information obtained by enemy spies is obtained in the first place from the people. What is known to the people is sure to be known by enemy spies. Reconnaissance flights by piper planes search for groups of people or moving troops and so forth.

Local mopping up operations are executed by the sides of main roads and in the surroundings of their positions (camps) and all around the towns, all of them for an extent of about 5 kilometers.

Large scale mopping up operations are executed by force of one battalion or more, lasting for several days, with the purpose of wiping out the pockets. They usually make encireling actions to surround a wide area and thereafter mop up inside the circle, using several columns.

The conditions of the pockets in West Java have proved that such mopping up operations are not successful, that is the National Army has always been in de facto control of the districts and keeps on attacking towns and main roads. This is the factor which will decide the final victory. The Dutch will fail if they can not possible maintain peace and order. The Dutch can not possible build up a civil administration and can not possibly re-open factories, plantations and traffic. After another half year of such conditions, the whole world, including the Dutch people will obtain proof that the colonial war has failed and that the Republic is the one and only body which can guarantee security, government and prosperity in Indonesia. And after another half year the Netherlands will be bankrupt if she obtains no loans.

TARGETS AND LOCATIONS.

1. After two weeks at war, our troops in general are all round towns as though encircling them, with a great desire to recapture the towns although there are no heavy arms to be able to drive the the enemy away as far as is necessary.

It seems that the aim of all troops is merely to enter the towns. In reality every brigade and battalion commander ought to organize targets properly and not waste manpower and materials.

Where are the targets?

Several attacks on towns would prove that towns can not easily be recaptured.

Meanwhile the enemy would make large scale mobile attacks from behind against the troops encircling the towns, and this could destroy our units. Against the towns we need only mobile army cells which protect our Military Sub-Districts and exert pressure upon the towns — thus small military units able to play hide and seek with the enemey on patrol.

The basic targets for the scoud stage are the enemy's communications.

The encircling of towns in reality can only be successful through wiping out the traffic between towns. Roads and bridges must be destroyed barricaded and mined and so forth continually. Convoys should be our targets. Trains should be stopped. Trafic between towns should be severed. In order to prevent this, the enemy would have to guard every bridge and every 2 kilometres, but this is impossible. The enemy will continue to execute mopping up operations all along the roads, but even this will be impossible, if the locations of troops are far from roads. The severing of traffic will have big consequences in the fields of the economy, of military and political affairs (including the cutting of telegraph wires).

2. It is obvious that the enemy can not possibly maintain peace and order with his army alone. Therefore, he will try to do so by political means, that is to obtain civil administrators, village administrators and the people. The enemy has begun to distribute medicines, foodstuffs, etc. in the towns and along the roads. He will begin to make propaganda, for instance, a hamlet or market will

be suddenly surrounded and the people will be compelled to listen to propaganda. We must see to it that the enemy does not obtain Lurah and Tjamat. If we can ensure this, the enemy will appoint his accessories to become Lurah or Tjamat, but these people have no followers. It is also our duty to have such Lurah and Tjamat set aside. The enemy will establish a police force. This too must become our target, that is they must run away to us with their arms, or else we must disarm them. Such Lurah, Tjamat and policemen should be our second target.

3. Though there is no peace and order yet, nevertheless the enemy will try to open estates and factories, because these are the sources of capital for the enemy. For capitalist states, the problem of Indonesia is a problem of plantations and factories. We must make the opening of plantations and factories a failure. We have burned them all down earlier, or if it has not yet been done perfectly, we have to continue the scorched earth activities. If the enemy opens them, we have to see to it that he gets no labour, apart from what we purposely place there for strategical purposes. If a factory or a plantation is already running we then have to continue our attacks, so that it will not be able to work. At last the enemy will arm their employees and establish plantation or factory police. They must then be our targets, plantations and factories must be our constant targets.

4. Towns must be kept in an agitated condition through the infiltration of small units especially allocated to this task. Also through attacks upon electricity, water supply and telephones. And as far as possible also through psychological warfare. At times when there are conferences of important installation of officials, we should intensify our infiltration attacks.

5. Especially to get supplies from time to time we launch attacks, for instance against convoys or against parts of towns.

With the above exposition it is evident that the location of mobile troops must be adjusted to the targets. They should not be concentrated around towns, but must be so located that they can keep on attacking transport, attacking communications between towns. Also the concentration of troops around towns, as existed earlier around Semarang, Surabaya, etc. will be dangerous, because they can be attacked easily by the enemy from behind and also from the front. On the other hand, activities of mobile troops within the towns are needed at times, in order to strengthen the military government and to keep on exerting pressure against the towns. Neither should mobile troops be allowed to stay on in *kyoten* *)

---

*) Kyoten: Japanese term for fortification.

because it is certain that the enemy will conduct mopping up operations there. Mobile troops must be on the move a great deal so they are always making an effect and cannot be easily encircled. When mobile troops are resting they should not concentrate in one place but have to scatter; if they are attacked suddenly, they should save themselves by scattering in small units (one section) so that they can move easily and can be destroyed only with difficulty. Basically, mobile units have to be mobile and take action in small units (guerillas). In this way, they can not be destroyed and also they can move easily, even though they have to cross areas under guard by the enemy. As well as this it will be easy for them to get supplies.

But we must also remember that under such conditions, communications become more difficult. Therefore, every commander of a patrol, a section, a company, etc. must keep on arranging communications with their superiors, their subordinates and their equals. Every unit must also be fully concious of the fact that we are no longer acquinted with back and front, but that at all times we can face the enemy from the front, the backs or from our flanks and so our moves are not cognisant of advance and retreat as in former times, but only "hide and seek".

With these methods, we spend a minimum time guarding against our own destruction and continue to the maximum to make difficulties for the enemy so that he will later fail completely. Indeed our warfare is different from ordinary warfare. Our warfare is war specifically suited to Indonesia at the present time.

Reminders: Because this is a long war:

1. this instruction should be passed on to subordinate commanders.
2. we must keep on being mobile in character, operating with small units (guerillas).
3. targets and the location of troops should be in harmony.
4. we must always remember that there is no front and back any longer.

Issued from :	The Seat of Command.
Dated :	31 December 1948.
Hours :	10.00

COMMANDER OF THE ARMY AND JAVA TERRITORIUM,
Sgd. COL. A. H. NASUTION.

To:

All Division Commanders.

All commanders of Brigaders (to be passed on to Battalion commanders), Commanders of Military Regions (Sub-Territorium commands).

*
**

Within about one and a half months, almost all troops occupied the pockets which were their bases. Invasions of the Pasundan region and the pupet "state" of East Java were almost all completed. And so gradually guerilla pockets spread evenly throughout the entire island of Java.

This was what we aimed at in the first stage. In this way, the whole of the island was filled with hundreds of pockets. After our troops had reached their destination, passing through the gaps guarded by the enemy, so solidation of the pockets was begun. We began to build cadres and territorial officers, many persons being recruited from the region concerned itself. We then influenced the village officials who were gradually made staunch followers of the Republic or who were attacked if they were faithful to the enemy, or else a new administration was directly appointed.

Our civil authority gradually spread out from the cells of our troops, like water spreading all around the source of a spring.

Automatically we no longer recognized the borders of the Renville agreement; we had gradually to regain the entire island. It was thus natural that the first phase was the most difficult. The enemy had already established his administration in many places and it was functioning. We came along as armed gangs which merely created disturbances. Many of the people felt harassed. Many of the people were passive, even here and there they showed a hostile attitude. Trusted persons still had to be sought and to be closely watched. Our propaganda had still to be begun. A long time was needed with intensive activities of agitation and propaganda, intimidation and terrorization, in order to be able to influence the people and to make them into sympathetic friends. Later on, we had gradually to make them into friends who activily assisted us.

Here and there, patriots emerged who voluntarily joined us. The struggle for independence had deteriorated when the pockets had been evacuated, but it was not dead, it still burnt beneath the surface. On the other hand, there were also many former pockets of the Republic which had been filled by other fighting organisations

188

which no longer fought for the Republic but for another state, and a different ideology. In West Java a new guerilla state had been set up the Darul Islam, complete with an army, a territorial organisation, local government and village officers and a police force. In other places, similar organisation had been set up which were of a left revolutionary character. There was not much room in the country side left open for the National Army of the Republic. Darul Islam was already well-rooted among the people of the mountains of Priangan and Cheribon. The loyalty formerly given by the people to the Republic was now given to Darul Islam. Their fanaticism was even greater through the presence of their religious convictions, which was in keeping with the character of people who were faithful to their religion.

Organisational methods and the tactics of the National Army of former times were taken over and the benefit reaped — they were even improved upon. The period of pause between the "Renville" and the moment when the second clash broke out was a pause for the National Army, but for those who were left behind in the pockets, this was a period filled with sufferings and trials, filled with bitter experiences, filled with lessons valuable for the development of a system of fighting the Dutch. These experiences also gave them advances which we could not immediately overtake.

In fact, the situation in the pockets was also different from what it had been in the past. In the past, many of the people and the civil servants had evacuated along with the National Army to the mountains. Now in general they had returned to the district, kabupaten and residency cities.

Also many of the original inhabitants had removed, or had evacuated in reverse direction to the towns, because they could not bear the consequences of the tactics of terror used against each other between the guerillas and the anti-guerillas. Many villages which had been formerly deserted in their entirety were now obliterated, with thick jungle in their place.

Former friends such as the *kiai* (religious leader) and prominent villages were no longer to be met with. The atmosphere was cold, an atmosphere in a community which could not yet be trusted, The situation was not secure. These were the difficulties faced in the federal regions at the very beginning.

In Republican regions, such as the greater part of Central and East Java the atmosphere was different. Here we felt an atmosphere such as that during the ealier Firth Clash when the enemy invaded West Java and the most easterly region of East Java. And the experiences of the first clash had been analysed and was used to organise the pocket system more perfectly. Because of this, in the initial period, the hottest places were the Renville territories of the Republic.

At the stage reached after one to two months of fighting it became evident that the distribution of troops was not yet in keeping with the needs of our strategy, namely to spread the pockets evenly from Banten to Besuki so that the entire island would become a single field of widespread and intence guerilla war; to exert pressure primarily upon central towns, the most important traffic routes and the plantation areas; to agitate the federal "states" made by the Dutch and make them totter. It was evident that the troops were distributed too much in the mountainous areas of the south regions and not enough in the northern regions which actually should have been the primary targets. The movement for guerillas in the pockets was not yet evenly spread in the northern regions. In this connection it was necessary to review the placing of troops. They needed to be pushed up towards the north. It was also necessary to decrease the number of officers in the south and the centres in the surroundings of Jogjakarta in order to spread them in the "minus" areas. Therefore a second operations instruction was issued as follows:

HEADQUARTERS JAVA COMMAND
No. 13/MBKD/49.

INSTRUCTION
WORK FOR THE STRATEGY (OPERATIONS).

Nature: Secret, solely for Commanders of Divisions, Military Regions, Brigades, Sub-Territories, Military Dictricts and posts of Java Command H. Q.

The fundamental of the Order on Strategy no. 1/stop/48 issued by the Commander in Chief of the Armed Forces,, is to make the entire territory of Java and Sumatra into a battlefield. Because by this means, the enemy will have insufficient forces to defend himself and also in this way it will not be possible to destroy the National Army through largescale operations by the enemy's modern divisions. For this reason "wingate" actions were launched invading the accupied territories, which now have been completed throughout so that the whole of Java can beome one large battlefield from Banten to Besuki. However, after one and a half months of war, it is evident that there are still shortcomings in the sense of location, actions, commands and coordination.

Keadaan Sekarang: Kantong² kita terutama dibagian² Selatan dan kota² jang ditekan umumnja kota². Keresidenan dan Kabupaten diwilajah ini. Perhubungan² jang tergonggu adalah diwilajah ini. jang kurang pentingnja bagi musuh dibanding dengan jang dibagian² Utara.

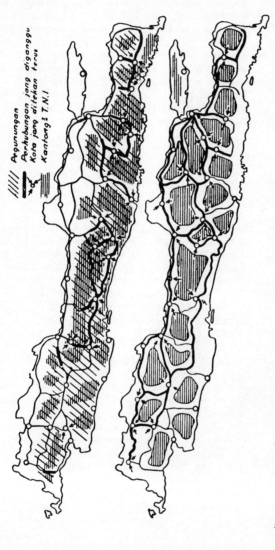

////// Pegunungan
Perhubungan jang diganggu
Kota jang ditekan terus
Kantong² T.N.I

Keadaan jang seharusnja: Kantong² merata dan tenaga lebih terpusat ke Utara, dimana kepentingan² jang lebih besar bagi musuh. kota²pusat (Djakarta, Bogor, Bandung, Tjirebon, Tegal, Semarang, Pati, Tjepu, Surabaja, Malang, dsb. Jalan lalu-lintas jang penting² puta jakni djalan Djakarta - Semarang - Surabaja - Malang disamping Bandung - Purwokerto - Djokja - Solo - Madiun - Surabaja.

Keadaan sekarang: Kantong-kantong kita terutama dibagian-bagian Selatan dan kota-kota jang ditekan umumnja kota-kota Keresidenan dan Kabupaten diwilajah ini. Perhubungan-perhubungan jang terganggu adalah diwilajah ini, jang kurang pentingnja bagi musuh dibanding dengan jang dibagian-bagian Utara.

Situation at present: Our pockets mainly are situated in the South and towns in general which are being pressed are those in Keresidenan and Kabupaten in this region. Communications which are disturbed are in this region, are less important for the enemy, in comparison with those in the North.

pegunungan	=	mountenous areas.
perhubungan jang diganggu	=	disturbed means of communication.
kota jang ditekan	=	towns under pressure.
kantong-kantong T.N.I.	=	pockets of the T.N.I.

Keadaan jang seharusnja: Kantong-kantong merata dan tenaga lebih terpusat ke Utara, dimana kepentingan-kepentingan jang lebih besar bagi musuh, kota-kota pusat (Djakarta, Bogor, Bandung, Tjirebon, Tegal, Semarang, Pati, Tjepu, Surabaja, Malang dsb.) dan lalu-lintas jang penting-penting pula jakni djalan Djakarta — Semarang — Surabaja — Malang — disamping Bandung — Purwokerto — Djokdja — Solo — Madiun — Surabaja.

Situation ought to be: Pockets should be in harmonious positions and energy should more centred to the North, where the enemy concentrate its important purposes, big towns (Djakarta, Bogor, Bandung, Tjirebon, Tegal, Semarang, Pati, Tjepu, Surabaja, Malang, etc.) and important means of communication, like roads between Djakarta, Semarang, Surabaja, Malang, besides Bandung, Purwokerto, Djokdja, Solo, Madiun, Surabaja.

192

1. Location and Actions.

a. At this moment, the strategical distribution of troops is by no means in accord with what is mentioned above. A number of areas in the centre of the island have numerous troops, and several coastal areas (Semarang, Pati, Madura) have not enough troops, whereas, for instance the Semarang area (with neighbouring Pati) is the centre for Central Java.

The distribution of troops must be improved by the Divisions. (See following map).

b. In the tactical sence, it should not happen that troops are placed on the borders of towns (static) and all along the roads. That would only make the enemy's mopping up operations easy, and we would not have enough manpower to fill all places. Such things must be achieved by movements (mobile).

Example of a *Wehrkreise* of one brigade:

At a secure place far from towns and main roads, the brigade commander sets the primary base where also the central office of the administration and other departments are located. On the borders of the towns and alongside main roads, small military cells are placed to keep on promoting activity by the Military Sub-Districts and the people to constantly harass the enemy or their accomplices, to disturb communications etc. to play „hide and seek" if the enemy approaches so that it is possible for them to be overpowered by the enemy. In fact this ought to be the duty of territorial battalions (every Military District Command has one such battalion armed in the ratio of 1 : 3), but because during implementation of reconstruction, too many arms were given to mobile units, in general territorial battalions are not effective. They must now be given units in the form of sections, if there are no other forces. Meanwhile mobile battalions conduct actions (are constantly mobile) in their *Wehrkreise*, attacking in turn communications, towns, plantations. For unexpected (unforeseen) eventualities every battalion should always keep in reserve one fourth of its forces, which should not join a particular action.

In this way:

— Many targets will be hit (a wide area will be controlled).
— It will be difficult to be found and destroyed by the enemy.
— It will be light on the people's supplies.
— All Military Sub-Districts will feel protected.
— Troops will have an effect everywhere.

Once a month, the brigades will organise a general operation against some special target, for instance, a capital city or a convoy, or a group of plantation buildings which can be effectively seized and destroyed. In the case of battalion targets greater importance should be given to destroying or seizing targets, rather than harassing activities. It is better to mobilize one company to destroy 5 trucks or one plantation, or to seize 10 bolts of cloth than merely to diturb towns. Infiltration by small units is adequate for disturbing towns, to burn things down, to kidnap collaborators, to upset one section of the town, etc.

2. SECURITY (PROTECTION).

It is evident that insufficient importance has been given to guarding, to reconnaissance, to keeping places secret, etc., these detivities are even much laughed at as "being afraid" or "lacking in bravery". Many move in ordinary columns without taking security measures, or rest without guards being stationed, etc. In the months of guerilla war ahead, everyone will feel for themselves, that there were many casualties, which would not have been necessary had adequate security measures been taken: It is not a matter of "afraid" or "brave", but a matter of the safety of our troops, of the forces for our struggle, and every commander has the obligation of saving his troops. It should be fully realised that in a *Wehrkreise* there is no longer any front line and back line; but we face the enemy from all directions, from the north, south, west and east. Every unit must face possible eventualities from all directions and therefore there must be security measures for all directions. It must also be fully realised that pockets are not fixed (static) regions. The enemy can and possibly will cross over and pass through the entire pocket region. But the enemy can not possibly control it, because we keep playing 'hide and seek' with him.

This is the system to be used by the units, the Military Sub-District Commands, the local government officers and the whole of our people.

3. THE COMMANDS.

There are units which no longer feel that they belong to a command, because there is not enough or no communication, because there are not enough or no instructions and news, because their superior commanders are "too mobile", so it is not possible to meet them to settle things. Instructions have already been issued in regard to communications, by what means the eyes and hands of commanders are felt everywhere, through command posts and the constant sending of reports, instructions, etc. visits by individual commanders or by commanding groups (staff officers) who go the rounds and the like. But in his mobility, the commander must

194

always be within reach of the commanders under him via a certain post. Day to day business must also be conducted through the respective posts.

4. COORDINATION.

Brigade commanders must constantly give priority to coordination between battalions. At sector borders, liaison officers from both sectors are to be appointed and also from the staffs there should be officers who can move quickly to defence points. For brigades, divisions and the Java Command, there are the same needs in these matters.

5. TECHNICAL ASPECTS.

Finally, I ask for the fullest attention to the technical aspects of operations, of furlough, of supply, of communications, etc. as taught in connection with the needs of the *Wehrkreise* and guerillas. These always require that measures be taken by small units spread out. Battalions on the move should not be combinations of companies on the move, but combinations of sections. This is for example. By such means it is difficult for the enemy to find and destroy us and easy for us to pass through regions controlled or patrolled by the enemy. Similarly also, supplies will be more easily obtained with the people's assistance. When encircled, troops ought to break through the encirclement by spreading widely in very small units or person by person, and then when through the encirclement, gather together again at a time and place fixed beforehand.

It is also necessary at all times to be careful in making reconnaisance, in the sending of reports, in research, in the execution of orders, etc. Finally, it is desirable that every member of the Armed Forces of the Republic of Indonesia regard this time of war as a period of training for the integration of the Republics Armed Forces, so that in the future they will become a military force strong and great in keeping with the greatness of our Country and in keeping with the significance and position of our Country in the world, a significance now proved by the whole world's agitation over the question of Indonesia In the future Indonesia will continue to possess a similarly important position in the world.

Issued from :	The Seat of Command
Dated :	1 February 1948
Hours :	08.00

COMMANDER OF THE ARMY AND
JAVA TERRITORIUM.
Sgd. COLONEL A.H. NASUTION.

To:

1. The Commander in Chief of the Armed Forces.
2. Deputy Chief of Staff of the Armed Forces.
3. Chief of the Military Police Corps, Java.
4. Central Administrative Office.
5. Cop Sec.
6. 9th Brigade.
7. 10th Brigade.
8. 12th Brigade.
9. 3rd Division.

We gathered together all troops which had not originated from Jogjakarta-Solo-Kedu to be sent gradually to regions in West and North Java. Officers were released from "plus" regions to be sent to strengthen the leadership of "minus" regions. Battalions were also encouraged to move with greater mobility in order to intensify the guerilla war yet further, in order that larger areas should be harassed.

Carelessness also began to be noticeable because the people's help was so good. The people were hiding our soldiers so that it was the people who guarded them. This custom resulted in the fact that security and the mounting of guards was not emphasised. We were increasingly being surrounded and kidnapped. Too many thought that waging guerilla warfare was just mere sniping at the enemy, while other factors were not thought important and were neglected.

In investigating our experiences and the results achieved during two and a half months, it is evident that there were advances. In general the pockets had been consolidated. Our troops had been given the first testing. A screening was being conducted smoothly in the midst of the practice of war. The conviction that we could not be defeated and destroyed had become strong. Morale continued to heighten. Living together with the people in the villages had created solidarity. Certainly, there was still a great deal for us to improve, but what was of the greatest primacy was that we stood firmly on our own two legs, filled with confidence in ourselves and in our own people, the sources of our strength.

Thus besides our endeavours which gradually improved organisation, leadership and operations, it was also necessary constantly to instil the basic idea that, as a people's guerilla army and in order to achieve the final victory, we might not be static, a there must always be progress. There had to be conscious awareness

196

of the steps which had to be taken to follow the extremely long road filled with difficulties and trials, which led in the direction bearing us eventually to victory: to develop from small guerilla units into the troops of a regular army, from troops harassing the enemy to troops pursuing the enemy.

Therefore, on 4 March, I drew up the third Operations Instruction, as follows:

HEADQUARTERS JAVA COMMAND

No.: 24/MBKD/49
Nature: Secret
OPERATIONS INSTRUCTION

To:

All Commanders of Divisions, Sub-Territorium Military Command and Deputy General Staff Commands, Posts of the Java Command H.Q. mobile Staff Officers, Commanders of Brigades, Battalions, Military Sub-Territorium and Military Districts.

Copies to:
Commander in Chief of the Armed Forces,
The Inspector-General.

I. PREFACE.

1. With the success of our plan during the last two and a half months, namely that all units remain intact while fighting, there is enough evidence for our conviction since the beginning that the National Army cannot be destroyed and will finally achieve victory. It is, however, necessary to improve and to care for all military requirements, that is organisation, determination, equipment, leadership and the most important, morale.

With regard to morale it has now been clearly proved that the morale of the National Army is high, in keeping with them of all military bodies fighting for independence.

Concerning equipment, what must be a constant effort is to care for it economically and to work out tactics in order that we can obtain equipment and weapons from the enemy, as is the case with supplies for every guerilla.

Concerning the leadership, the conditions which must be recalled at present are: perfecting communications, contacts between superiors and subordinates which operate automatically, through mobile staff-officers, through farsighted planing which takes experiences into account. Leadership should be felt all the time.

With regard to organisation it must be kept in mind at all times that it is organisation which can guarantee our potential to become a power in the struggle. Without an orderly organisation it is not possible for us to struggle for long.

Regarding determination, it is necessary that we always remember that spirit and determination must be maintained side by side.

A burning spirit must be used effectively, that is, we should not just fight alone courageously, but leaders should always make calculations for the sake of efficiency and effectiveness. For every casualty there should be a clear gain, every attack should be made in accord with calculations, and the whole must remain within the bounds of a single programme of continuing action. In this way, the courage of the soldiers will not go for nothing.

Therefore our leaders must continue to perfect and to bring into accord one with the others technical matters, the tactics and strategy of our struggle.

2. The strategy of our struggle is evident in the Instruction on Strategy No. 1/stop/48, namely to launch "Wingate" invasions in all directions, conducting actions to save time, the mobilization and activisation of *Wehrkreise* so that eventually in a short period of time, from Banten to Besuki there will be a single and intense guerilla battlefield, co-ordinated in keeping with a certain plan of strategy.

With such methods it will not be possible for the enemy to have sufficient forces, finance and time to counter our activities, so that eventually he will have to give up his hopes.

At the moment the enemy abandons his hopes, in principle we have already won. At this moment we may be convinced that this moment has already been reached. The aim of the Dutch to destroy the National Army and thereafter to destroy the Republic, has now failed in the witness of ourselves, of the enemy and of the whole world.

On the other hand, the plan for our tactic still operates, the objectives of our strategy have not diminished in the least. In places where the mobile troops have become our first line, our territorial army our second line, we are now building our third line, namely the Village Guerilla Troops which will produce hundreds of thousands of cadres, unlimited numbers of cadres.

Meanwhile it is necessary only that we continue to improve the execution of our strategy, that is, to regulate the stress of our pressure upon targets as effectively as possible, namely upon the enemy's centres and the communications between those centres and the economic targets. By doing this we positively secure the de facto Republic up to the borders of the towns, so that we continue to control the greater part of the Territorium.

The Instruction on Strategy No. 3/MBKD/48 determines the kinds of targets which are effective militarily, economically and politically. The Instruction on Strategy No. 13/MBKD/48 determines the strategic and tactical execution of those movements in keeping with the region concerned. We go further into the execution of technical and tactical aspects of our activities below.

We recall the division of duties in our Army between mobile troops (rapid movement) which must attack on the move, and territorial troops which must tie the enemy down and constantly harass him.

Because organisational execution of this division of duties could not be completed when the war broke out, in practice therefore, the greater part of our mobile troops were used for stationary duties in the regions, so that there are still insufficient effective attacks which are executed on a large scale (brigades, divisions). However, it can be seen that in practice some brigades on their own initiative have organised mobile attacking units which have determinedly conducted actions day after day, attacking by day and night, on and on, as a continuous operation. Indeed it is true that with guerilla actions, that is by taking measures in small units (patrols or *kumi*) which act on their own, or even in battalion formation, or even in brigades, there will be no obstacles to our actcivities. Occupied towns can be entered and by concentrated attacks heavier losses will be inflicted on the enemy, attacks can be made to shake the enemy's bases, and the trust of the people in the enemy can be shaken or broken.

After co-ordination and consolidation have been effectced in accordance with the needs of the various localities, the time has then come for the divisions to launch real offensive actions with the force of one battalion or more, and by reaching this level of operations, it will be possible to destroy the enemy more effectively and to seize weapons. We must remember that at a certain time we must progress from purely guerilla activities to guerilla activities plus ordinary warfare, that is when the enemy's power diminishes and our power increases.

II. At all times in this war, we have two kinds of activities, namely withstanding the enemy (defensive) and attacking him (offensive) in strategy and tactics. In the defensive activities we are confronted by enemy activities:

a. **Local mopping up operations.**
b. **Large scale mopping up operations.**
c. **The kidnapping of our leaders.**
d. **Psychological warfare.**

CONCERNING a.

For the enemy there always be security in the towns and along important trafic ways. To obtain this, the enemy keeps making mopping up operations, by patrols of platoons or larger units up to companies, along highways, on the edges of towns and in pockets within the cities.

The results of their operations depend primarily upon the enemy spies and upon the ways on which we save ourselves. Those ways must be of such a kind that we can not be swept up by the enemy. It is therefore clear, that it is only security and the close guarding of secrets which must be our prime concern. And when the enemy takes action we must disperse and save ourselves individually or in small groups and gather together again later on when the enemy has passed.

In executing such astions, whenever possible the enemy should be put into disorder by sniping by one person, who changes his position frequently to fire from many different directions. The individual characters of soldiers and cadres should obviously be developed, in order that they can act on their own initiative. In this way, it will not be possible for us to be swept out of our pockets on the borders and within towns and along roadways, but at most will be chased away for a while, only to return later on.

If operating with approximately one company, the enemy will send troops to close in on the places to be cleared, while other troops will conduct the mopping up within the enclosed area. What is then important is that we get out of the enclosed places individually and unite again in another place, namely the reserve which has been fixed beforehand by the commander.

CONCERNING b.

The enemy directs these operations against our fortifications in extensive regions where a battalion or brigade has its base. The enemy operates with at least 1 battalion, supported by cannon, aircraft and at times by cavalry and tanks. Such an operation frequently takes several days. The enemy first send out their investigators and spies to act as their guides later on. Usually the region will have first been investigated or photographed from the air.

The enemy commanders will even first investigate their respective sectors from the air. The enemy conducts the operation in such a way, that troops are usually at our site very early in the morning, at 4 to 5 o'clock, and right away encircle us and mop up as explained in point a.

The way of facing this measure is only as explained in point a, that is, by security and a dispersing action.

Security is guarded by a system of command posts, which are camouflaged and move from place to place, by periodically moving their troops, by daytime disguise among the people, by using false names, etc. In continuing this total war, passive and active security measures become increasingly important. The basis of safety is security (see Instruction on Communications regarding security of command posts).

If the enemy appears, we must endeavour to defend ourselves by means of mobile "hide and seek" actions with small units; causing confusion amongst the enemy by sniping from various angles, and shooting from different directions; afterwards, attacks should be made at night -time in order to harass the enemy.

When encircled by the enemy, first attempts must be to save the troops of a unit by means of dispersing and getting out of the encirclement. One at a time individuals can save themselves by hiding under the growing rice, corn, etc. and getting out of encirclement at night. It should be remembered that in the case of such attacks the enemy usually has prepared detailed plan beforehand, so that our duty confined only to saving our soldiers and amunition and in harassing the enemy alone.

Because we are involved in a long war, eventually every fortified place will suffer such attacks several times; therefore, commanders should have plans to face any eventuality so that there will be no confusion. We should not be bound to front line defence, but have plans suited for pockets and hide and seek tactics.

Meanwhile the damaging of main roads and village roads, and the making of changes to them will increase our security.

The ways in which the people save themselves are also important; it should not occur that there are many casualties shot and taken prisoner; this matter is the duty of the Military Sub-District Commander.

CONCERNING c.

It is important in any war to destroy the leaders and their command posts. For this purpose, the enemy uses selected spies and in general uses commando troops trained for action in our rear and amongst us, operating in small fast-moving units. To face this situation there are only security measures and the setting up of places of command far from roads. It often happens that security is not sufficiently stressed on the part of the army itself.

CONCERNING d.

It has often been discovered how sharp is the psychological war, how weak is our defence against it, and how many have succumbed from our side during these three years. By means of spreading provocative and untrue news, by giving provocative information about every event, the psychological war has purpose of creating an atmosphere of suspicion, of bringing about splits and, if possible, mutual attacks and the like, so that our potential will break from within, so that the tactical plans of our struggle cannot be implemented because our leadership has no opportunity to lead and our troops have no opportunity to fight, because they are bound by constant internal conflicts.

Corps solidarity and discipline for the entire Army and an unhesitating point of view at every post are badly needed, and more than ever under present conditions. It is also important to give information to members of units and to those in their environment (see Instruction to Overcome False News). It must always be remembered that our enemy is foremost in psychological warfare.

ADDITIONAL

The methods of organising everything mentioned above, must be determined by the condition that we may not be wiped out, if necessary, we go away temporarily but eventually we continue to take action in our respective pockets.

Mopping up operations which cannot possible clear us out even though executed times, will guarantee that final victory is on our side. There are already sufficient proofs while technical matters and tactics are good enough to ensure that we can not be swept out of the pockets even though they are in the middle of the towns themselves.

In the matter of attacks (offensive) there still are many things needing improvement. It still often happens that we attack only for the sake of attacking, without any calculation or a plan in readiness which it is possible to execute. It still often happens that our attacks are only a single measure alone and not a chain of measures and activities in keeping with time and place. There are still insufficient daytime attacks. A consequence of all of this is to increase the

202

enemy's mobility, therefore we must perfect the tactics and technical aspect of attacks. It is even more necessary that commanders of brigades and lower units must concentrate their powers and thoughts upon operations alone. A concentration of arms is also needed upon the troops which have the duty of taking the offensive. Arms are not individual possessions, but the property of our struggle. Arms for attack such as mortars and *tekidantos* (Japanese mortar-like weapons), should be economised for the purpose of offence.

Our measures of attack are of two kinds, namely those which constitute:

a. **constant (permanent) harassing of the enemy, so that peace and order will not be possible for the Dutch in the towns, on the roads, on the plantations, etc. (territorial).**

b. **destruction of the enemy or his equipment or the seizing of his equipment (cars).**

CONCERNING a.

For a defence ensuring that even the most remote place becomes a centre of guerilla warfare so that there is nowhere secure for the enemy and his accomplices it is necessary that every occupied town, every route for road traffic, every plantation, every member of the enemy's local administrative staff and police, and finally every inhabitant of occupied regions should be harassed uninterruptedly.

This ought to be duty of the territorial troops, of which there should be one battalion in every Military District Command supported by Village Guerilla Troops. However, for various reasons for the greater part this duty is still the task of the mobile troops, a fact which compels every brigade and battalion commander to organise small units especially for these constant harasing activities. Gradually this task should be transferred to the territorial troops as far as possible. The objective is that through these continuous small actions the enemy's soldiers, civil officers, inhabitants of the occupied areas aad those regions themselves, will gradually grow more and more disturbed, so that finally they will lose hope and lose their confidence in their government and troops.

This is actually the task of the territorial troops, which in every pocket should consist of several people who are well enough disguised but who can periodically snipe, set fire to targets and kidnap collaborators, start whispering campaigns and conduct other similar subversive endeavours.

203

A high degree of initiative and individuality is needed for the pockets in towns. It has often been proved that students are good for this heavy task.

Communications

On highways connecting cities, there should always be disturbances in the shape of sniping, of mines and nails on the roadways, of barricades and damages to bridges. By this means, no convoy will be free and civilian traffic can not exist. For every 20 Km a few carabine rifles are enough, apart from these, there are mines, nails, etc. At least barricades should be placed in the middle of roads every night so the enemy is compelled to dismantel them first in order to move. It is very effective if holes are constantly made in the roads which will be enlarged by rain, so that the enemy's repair work increases so much that he cannot pay for it. Every possible thing available from stones to wood must be placed in the roads every night. In this way, the war becomes a contest of wills. All electric and telephone cable should be kept on being cut.

Actions against plantations and factories

Continuous efforts should be made as psychological warfare. Sniping, burning, and kidnapping of employees can be organised without end so there is no security for plantation and factory workers by the Military Sub-District Commander. The objective is simply that they should not feel secure.

Actions against the enemy's local government officers, police and other NICA accomplices

These persons should also be constantly disturbed by means of threatening letters, etc. in their homes, and on their journeys, so that they will be unable to work peacefully and are at all times subjected to a war of nerves. Several clear examples, such as steps taken against some Tjamat, some Lurah or others who have become NICA accomplices, will keep these people scared.

ADDITIONAL.

It should be remembered that we can create disturbances with extremely few arms, provided we do it constantly and keep on in a systematic way, so that the enemy cannot possibly hare any sense of security. It is this feeling of being constantly thretened which will provide the basis for the enemy's defeat, because slowly but gradually the enemy will lose all faith in his troops and government and at last will lose all conviction that the enemy army and government can bring peace and order, so that both in our country as well as overseas the conviction will eventually grow that it is only the Army and the Government of the Republic of Indonesia which are the single organisation able to secure peace and order in Indonesia.

Finally it must be constantly borne in mind that basically this war is a political struggle. Defeat of Dutch policy is our basic aim. And without the presence of collaborating inhabitants for the Dutch to rule, the Dutch are at bottom defeated. For this reason also the Instruction regarding Non-co-operation is very important.

CONCERNING b.

Attacks ought to be the duty of fast-moving battalions using the tactics and technique of small units of troops. They must move each time for specific results, that is to destroy or seize and not merely to harass the enemy. We clarify again here the technical implementation of what is called our "Wingate" action. (Mobile guerilla actions attacking from behind and in enemy occupied regions are popularly called "Wingate" actions by our troops). One division in a "Wingate" action is in fact hundreds of platoons conducting "Wingate" actions, hundreds of small groups on the move, but still under leadership within an organisation and in co-ordinated action, moving through loopholes in the enemy's defences, and even through loopholes in enemy occupied towns. In short, there are no places they hannot pass through, and if thay are attaiked it is difficult to fight them because they disperse and become hundreds of small platoons.

It is necessary that every sergeant, corporal and soldier take the initiative on their own, every patrol and platoom must feel like a complete army, capable of fighting alone, should they be cut off from others. In every squad there must be a division of its own tasks, so that the squad is able to arrange its own supply, security, communications and other things on its own. The capability of units will be higher if they have sharpshooters, reconnaisance men, weapons experts, etc., and still higher yet if every member is able to do everything. To this end we keep on training our men in order to perfect our tactics at this present time. By this means we should be able, for instance, to bring one brigade back and forth from Djakarta to Surabaya, making attacks on the way.

It is necessary to have a program of attacks which is tactically complete, based upon co-ordination of one after another by the Brigade and Division commanders so that it becomes a complete programme for one month, and so on. Every attack should always be devided into a number of tasks, namely the task of investigation and preparation, the task of misleading the enemy by action drawing him off to the places we desire, the task of cutting up or isolating or tieing down the enemy, so that the fundamental task of attacking the real target becomes lighter, the task of seizing equifment in use and other necessary things.

For instance if we are going to attack a town, then, to throw the enemy off guard, we begin to make continuous attacks for several days upon the roads used by convoys to that town, also mobilising the people's forces as far as possible. Because of our determined and stubborn action in cutting traffic, the enemy will draw off more forces to that place. Then we leave a small number of our troops there, merely in order to tie the enemy down, and as suddenly as possible we attack the town from all directions. This attack must be made by the means we call a "Wingate" action, described above. With small units consisting of one patrol, or a third of a patrol, we should hide ourselves beforehand in pockets within the town at night time, and then all together begin to attack. In this case the attack can be launched in daytime because with the small units and the presence of actions all over the whole town, we will have rather large chances for safety, so that we will be difficult to be destroyed. Also in this case, there must be a division of tasks and a division of sectors in the attack upon the town. During the attack of course the enemy will take cover in their shelters and only after reconnoitering will he send out troops with tanks, bren carriers, etc. Because of the situation wherein small groups of our troops are mixed everywhere amongst the population, the enemy will have no opportunity to use cannon or to machine-gun from the air. We must plans where and how to destroy the enemy. For example, by means of setting buildings on fire, etc. in one or two quarters of the town so that the enemy will moae those places. We should prepare barricades on the roads going to those places. It is necessary to keep trying to take the enemy by surprise.

There is thus the basic task of destroying the enemy by trapping him, there are those who trap him, and there are those who merely harass him by means of sniping, of barricading roads, conducting scorched earth policy, etc. The division into kinds of tasks and sectors for tasks must be worked out beforehand.

In such actions, attacks should be gradually lengthened to two, three or four days and so on, by means of hiding in pockets within the towns or on the edges of towns. In this it is possible to carry out an extensive program to cause the enemy losses, to seize equipment, to scorch the earth, to take their collaborators prisoner, etc. We must also organise way of leaving the city and the place where every unit of troops should go to rest, and then later move to attack the second, thord, etc, target.

Because of he probability of unforeseen circumstances, it is necessary for there to be close connections between commanders and their subordinates. They should always have officers to communicate with their subordinates who can make contact at all times. Simirlarly, this also applies to communications with neighbouring troops.

With the switching of the enemy's attention and forces to a town, we rapidly change to another target, for instance the capital of a district where there is a NICA *Wedana*, where we suddenly attack the enemy local government employees, police building and other things belonging to the enemy. These actions, moving consecutively to other things according to calculated plan, will keep on increasing our military standards and in this way heavy losses will keep on being inflicted on the enemy. This procedure can be organised in the first phase in the brigades, later on in the divisions, while bringing the people to participate through mobilisation and agitation so that their will to attack will continue to burn. By these means, eventually the present tactical situation will certainly change. At present in general from a tactical point of view the enemy attacks us; however, with our programme arranged by careful calculation and through continuing and determined actions, we will be able to change the tactical situation so that it will be ourselves who hold the initiative.

Strategically our position is now stable and the enemy has already come to a dead end. When we have already reached the phase in which tactically we are constantly able to destroy the enemy, there will be no more mopping up operations by the enemy and we will rise to the phase of pursuing the enemy. And this must be possbile because the enemy does not have sufficient forces.

We take as our principal targets first one thing and then another upon which our attacking forces will launch attacks in concentration. We must hold the initiative and the enemy must be able only to react. In order to achieve this, we must keep on perfecting our strategy, our tactics and our techniques.

Our technique and tactic in attacking towns, attacking convoys, attacking plantations, attacking Kabupaten and District capitals must continue to be perfected by solving the problems collectively, using past experiences and holding to our basic strategical objective. In regard to the technique and tactic of attacking convoys themselves,

207

it is necessary to arrange a division of tasks and sectors. The tasks must be organised of shooting at convoys, of rushing the convoy and seizing arms, of setting them on fire, etc., of placing roadblocks fore and aft of what must be attacked, of isolating by obstacles and of breaking up road surfaces. The people can be of great use, especially at night time. Through such a concentrated attack there is a real possibility that the whole convoy can be destroyed, arms can be seized, etc.

Through such a systematic programme, it can be expected that at a certain moment the enemy, from lack of forces, will leave his guard posts in district towns and plantations, so that our de facto territory will become more and more compact. Moreover, through our continuing successes he will have to leave the remote towns in Kabupaten and so on.

All this will be increased by perfecting our technique, our tactics and strategy, and by proceeding upwards from battalion attacks to brigade attacks in which the tasks have been organised in accordance with time and plan, and in which the tasks of misleading the enemy, enclosing him, attacking, etc., have also been organised.

Concerning the seizing of arms, natural targets are police, plantation guards, enemy patrols and convoys which can be destroyed by our concentrations.

Tekidanto weapons and mortars should be our prime objective, because as long as we do not possess these weapons we can not fight larger units. These weapons are needed for our ability to attack. In short, we need to seize arms for offensives. It is advisable that every commander should always watch the advances of his troops in the field of techniques, tactics and strategy from month to month, because in this way the world will see also the degeneration of the enemy from month to month, and the enemy will be pushed back onto the big cities alone, and so on. Finally, from our guerilla battalions there will be born complete battalions, from guerilla brigades complete brigades, which at last will be able to launch open warfare to chase the enemy completely out of our country.

On the one hand, the enemy will become increasingly weaker, increasingly less; on the other hand we will become increasingly stronger, increasingly more. On the one hand, the enemy will have increasingly less posts, on the other hand our pockets will become increasingly larger, so that it will be easier to maintain the larger units in compact form, rising from companies to battalions, and so on. In this way, on the one hand, the enemy's regions become less and, on the other hand, the territory of our bases increases. The tactical actions of the enemy will increasingly shift from the offensive to the defensive, while for us, it is precisely the opposite.

Gradually by these means we shall destroy and chase the enemy away, so that ultimately the enemy will lose all hope of being able to dominate us again.

Issued from: The Seat of Command.
Dated : 4 March 1949.

COMMANDER IN CHIEF OF THE ARMY AND JAVA TERRITORIUM,

Sgd.

COLONEL A.H. NASUTION.

A Guerilla-member using a radio-apparatus confiscated from the enemy.

COPY

THE ROYAL NETHERLANDS INDIES ARMY
ROYAL ARMY
T — BRIGADE

From :   Commander T Brigade

To   :   Cdr. 5RS   C 5-5 RI   C 2.2 RVA   C 7 Vew   C 4 MP IV
          Cdr. B pat. ARVA (Maguwo)   Cdr. LVT Maguwo   Cdr.
          Vbd A-T   Cdr. Ml Smg.   Head IVG-T   Cdr. Tpn Det-T
          Cdr. 5 Givd Indo: Cdr. B Div   Hd. A & K [1]

No: 817/op 4/SECRET/MOST URGENT

Enclosure : 1 oleograph   Jogja, 1 February 1949
                                                 Time : 13.00 hours

Order for the mopping up by 20 hours of the territory bordering:
Opak river proceeding towards Jogja, Imogiri (9208), on 3 February 1949.

I. PLAN.
    On 3rd February 1949 the following is to be executed:
    A. Mopping up territory south and east of KOTAGEDE
       (9318).

II. THE ENEMY.
    A. See inteligent reports.
    B. The enemy will presumably try to evade us by sharing off
       in a south-easterly direction.
    C. The enemy in this territory possesses a fairly good morale
       and is well armed.

III. OWN TROOPS.
     Known.

IV. PARTICIPATING TROOPS.
    A. Combat Troops West:
       Cdr. CC RS;
       4 platoons 5 RS + IVG unit + men
       4 MP IV. [1]

---

[1]   Various Dutch fighting units etc.

B. Combat Troops East:
   Cdr CC. LVT
   Coy Airforce troops + 4 men

C. Closing-in Group South:
   Cdr CC 5-5 RI
   3 platoons 5-5- RI [1])

D. Closing-in Group North:
   Cdr. Platoon C 7 Vew.
   1 platoon 7 New + 15 men of Staff-guard + 4 men of
   Mine-squad 5 LS

E. C-C Cr Platoon 15 RS
   Cr platoon 5 RS + Pi Platoon + Mine-squad 5 + bulldozer 5 Givd.
   4 MP IV. [1])

F. 1 Battery 5 RS RVA

G. Auster

V. EXECUTION (For route of march see oleograph)

A. Combat Troops West is to march on the night of 2 — 3
   February at such a pace that at dawn they reach Djidjiran
   (9214).
   (9214). After mopping-up operations, two groups of two
   platoons each are to make an advance break in a general
   northerly direction at fast pace, after which Kotagede
   (9318) is to be thoroughly searched. The North Closing-in
   Troops come in at the fastest pace possible.

B. Combat Troops East are to march on the night of 2 — 3
   February at such a pace that they reach Koeden (9817) at
   dawn. They are to start mopping up operations immediately in the settlements along the general axis of the action.

C. The Closing- in Group South is to be responsible for
   ensuring that the closing-in line of the south bank of the
   Opak River is ready at 03.00 hours. (See oleograph)
   The closing-in is to be lifted as soon as the Eeast and
   West Combat troops have passed in a northerly direction
   at 18.00 hours.

D. The Closing-in Group North is to be responsible for
   ensuring that a closing-in line is prepared at 030700 hours
   to the north and north-east of Kotagede (9318)

---

[1]) Various Dutch fighting units etc.

E. Cdr. Platoon 5 RS + Pi Platoon mine-squad 5 RS +
bulldozer 5 GiVd:

Cdr Platoon 5 RS is to march in at 030630 hours along the
line of Jogja-Kotagede (9318) and restore this line.

VI. ARTILLERY.

A. 1 Battery in position at Maguwo airfield.

B. Battery to be ready to fire at 6000 hours on ... February.

C. Main direction: South.

D. Artillery WNMR at the combat borders east and west.

E. 1) Auster to be used for reconnaisance and observation.

   2) Auster to be in the air at dawn above the terrain of
      action.

   3) At its own initiative, the Auster may fire at enemy
      concentrations it observes. Safety to be taken into
      account, eg tpn (vnml closing-in line south).

VII. LSK.

A. If necessary apply for air support at Staff T.-Brigade.

B. Upon application make use of air support — tgm-forms.

C. Targets to be indicated by cloths on the ground; the
   distance to the target is to be shown by strips across the
   tail of the arrows (1 cross strip = 100 metres).

VIII. COMMUNICATIONS.

A. Cdr. Communications A arranges reception by a radio
   network of Combat Troops West, Closing-in Group South
   and Combat Troops East.

B. V. Communications A is responsible for the radio communications of Corgr 5 RS with the Staff of T Brigade.

IX. EMERGENCY MEASURES.

A. The border lines indicated in the oleograph between odln
   are not to be violated. Cn. are responsible that there shall
   be no firing over the borders.

B. Indications: yellow cloths on ground.

C. In case the Auster requires dmv cloths on the ground to
   indicate the tpn position, a red Verey bulet shall be fired.
   It shall only be in case of emergency that the Auster
   applies in this way for the position of eg tpn.

D. The roads indicated on the oleograph for the route for marching are in general the axis of the action. Cn can deviate from these routes is reports, for instance on observation of the enemy, require this.

Confirmation of receipt with code word ZILVER.

COMMANDER T- BRIGADE
0/1 HEAD KT OPR.

Copied in accordance with the original:
SUTARSO, Sgt Major
Sie II Staff Ri 14/STXIV, Bureau C.

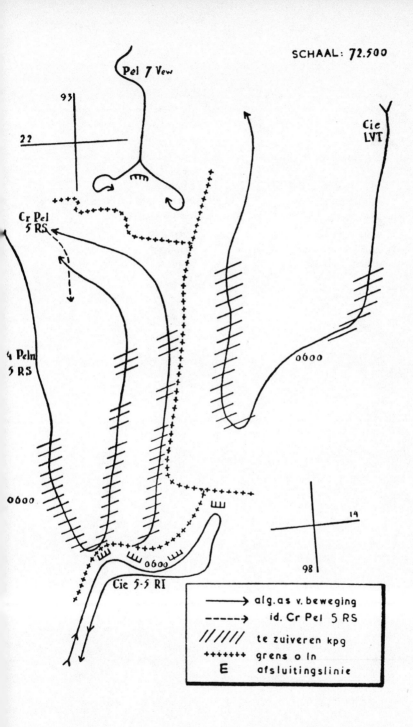

SCHAAL: 72.500

Pel 7 Vew

93

22

Cie
LVT

Cr Pel
5 RS

4 Peln
5 RS

0600

0600

0600

Cie 5·5 RI

14

98

→————→	alg. as v. beweging
- - - -→	id. Cr Pel 5 RS
//////	te zuiveren kpg
++++++	grens o ln
E	afsluitingslinie

CLARIFICATION

Schaal	=	Scale.
Pel.	=	Platoon.
Cie.	=	Company.
Cr. Pel.	=	Platoon Commander.
alg. as v. beweging	=	general axis of action.
id. Cr. Pel. 5 Rs.	=	idem. Commander of 5 Regiments Platoon.
te zuiveren kpg.	=	settlements to be mopped up.
grens odln	=	borders odln.
afsluitingslinie	=	closing-in-lines.
Lampiran dari operatie order T-Brigade	=	(Enclosure to Operations Order from T-Brigade).

COPY
MIDDLE JAVA TERRITORIAL COMMAND
No.: AK/35 G/60 04/SECRET

Enclosures: Three convoy schemes (Jogja, Solo, Blora)
List of sectors and sub sectors Cdt with position
Three communication schemes.

CONVOY ORDERS MIDDLE JAVA TERRITORIAL COMMAND.

I. GENERAL.

    a. This order is not allowed to be carried by personnel of convous, escorts and indirect security guards.

    b. In telegramms regarding convoys, the convoy lettermark only is to be mentioned (Jogja convoy Letter A, Solo convoy letter B, Blora convoy letter C.)

II. a. According to a scheme issued bi-weekly (cq weekly) convoys on the following routes Jogja — Semarang (Salatiga) and return Semarang (Salatiga) — Solo and return Blora — Solo and return shall be driven by AA Tcien and transport platoons of the Army Transport Service.

    b. Should there be vehicles unable to participate in convoys due to size, speed and weight, special arrangements shall be made (slow convoys).

Applications to join convoys are to be submitted 4 $\times$ 24 hours before the departure date to Cdrs of T. Brigade, V. Brigade and 3 — 7 RI. For departures from Semarang (Salatiga), applications to Cdr B. Dist. (Head A & K), departures from Jogja, Solo and Blora respectively to Cdrs T- Brig., V. Brig and 3 — 7 RI.

III. COMPOSITION.

    a. Convoys are to be composed of groups each consisting of a maximum of 60 cars.

    b. The front car of each group should carry a blue flag and the last car a green one. The second last car is to carry a red flag, the last crane car for sweeping roadblocks to carry a white flag. These flags to be provided and later returned to the convoy commander.

217

c. All vehicles are to be provided with a number by the convoy commander indicating the groups (not necessary when there is only one group) and the number of the vehicle in the group.

d. Casual convoys may travel, provided they keep to the safety measures and provided that the sectors and subsectors have beer notified.

Other vehicles are allowed to follow the tail of the convoy.

IV. COMMAND.

a. The convoy commander is an officer of AAT. Should the units have the strength of 1 company or more, the Convoy commander commands and the officer is attached to him as technical advisor.

b. The convoy commander is to ride as a matter of principle in the front group but never in the front car.

c. Every group of a maximum number of 60 vehicles is to be commanded by an officer.

d. The convoy commander is to contact Sector commander (C T Brig, Tpn Cmd, Smg) and subsector cdrs (Bat cdtn, Esk and Adtn branch) (see enclosure IV) and should lead his convoy in accordance with the local instructions which are based on these orders.

V. GUARD FOR SAFETY.

a. Indirect.
The (sub) Sector cdr shall at a given moment start off a patrol and the placing of roadblocks along the road indicated and shall indirectly safeguard the convoy with special attention to the terrain and location of roads in connection with actions of the enemy.

b. Direct.
1. Tno shall be separated from the indirect guards on safety on all the aforementioned convoy routes between Coffeepot-Jogja, Tengaran — Jogja, Tengaran — Solo and Demak — Blora, and cars shall be given escort through the subsector Cdrs concerned according to the directions from the Sector cdrs (Brig. Cdr, Troop Cdr, Semarang).
2. A part of the guard put on roads for marching should be able to be switched immediately so that the convoy can be given aid in emergencies.

3. The (Sub) Sector cdr is responsible for protecting the convoy at indicated parts of roads.

4. At the borderline of subsectors the escort receiving the transfer is to take the responsibility for protection.

5. The strength of the escort is to be a minimum of 30 soldiers with a minimum of two brenguns per group of vehicles.

6. If possible an armoured vehicle (not an armoured car) should ride in front at a short distance ahead of the convoy and indicate any mines; the road surface must be continuously searched and examined. Behind this armoured vehicle, an armoured car can be placed.

7. The bottom of all vehicles should be covered with sand bags.

8. Should the convoy be hindered by some obstacle, the front vehicles should pull in to the left side of the road, the drivers and other personnel should immediately leave the vehicles. Drivers should remain in the neighbourhood of their vehicles. The escort should by speedy action break the obstacle zn in co-operation with the Cdr responsible for the protection of the part of the road concerned.

The Terr tvs Tpn Cdt Central Java
w.g. JK Meyer
Gen Major

ARMY
TERR IV/DIV. DIPONEGORO
RES. INF 14/SUB TERR XIV
SECTION II

Copied in accordance to the original,
Sie II Staff R. I. 14.
MASHUD SIDIK
Corporal Infantry.

The late Lt.-Col. Slamet Ryadi

D. INSTRUCTIONS FROM OTHER LEADERS
GUIDE FOR GUERILLAS
ISSUED BY THE LATE LIEUTENANT-COLONEL SLAMET RIJADI, COMMANDER OF THE 5TH BRIGADE, „PENEMBAHAN SENOPATI", DIV. II IN JAVA, DATED 23 MARCH 1949.

I. MILITARY
INTERNALLY

1. Build up strength (co-ordinate/consolidate units) so that in every territorial region there really is a single body of armed forces under one command.

2. Build up the strength of the masses so that there really is a true people's defence (see H.Q. Java Command's Instruction).

3. Form cadres, so that reserve troops are created in every centre, *rayon* and sector which can be used at any moment.

4. Perfect all defence organisations (communications, reconnaisance, etc.) in every territorial region so that they use similar methods (see H.Q. Java Command's Instruction).

EXTERNALLY

1. The basis of the tactics we use are: Guerilla warfare.

2. Forces have to be divided into platoons (small groups).

3. Actions should be fast, and methods of disappearing and of gathering must really be throughly seen to.

4. Surprise attacks must be launched.

5. The placing of platoons should be of such a kind that in every territorial region there is a "spider web" defense.

6. The cutting of communication lines must be seen to at all times.

7. Stoppages of traffic must be made on roads at all times (by trigger bombs, barricades).

8. If the enemy intends to strike at us (mopping up operations, etc.) we must not be destroyed, but must disappear; when the enemy is in a weak or bad position through carelessness we must attack.

9. It is adequate to make attacks with small but effective forces.

10. Do not attack enclosed places (defended objects).

11. Do not make night attacks upon the nemy's camps if they cannot be entered at all (to fight man to man).

12. Utilise all weapons in the best possible way. (Remember: one shot by one sniper which hits the target is more valuable than an unsuccessful general attack against a city!)

13. Care for weapons as well as possible (Remember: arms are the soul of an army.)

14. Strike and don't be struck (Cover against sight and fire should always be remembered, or attack suddenly and immediately disappear.)

15. The best defence is to attack. Do not let the enemy attack us: the enemy may come any direction whatever, but it is we who must attack the enemy first; therefore every guerilla units must be flexible, mobile and dynamic; reconnaisance must be very good.

221

16. Every guerilla unit must always be on the move amidst the people, like fish in water (they may not and cannot be separated); therefore strong measures must be taken against every act which hurts the feelings of the people (cuts the people off from the guerillas).

17. Keep guerilla secrets as well as possible. (Plans which are known to the enemy means half-way to defeat already.)

18. Do not be over-daring to die, but dare to live by killing the enemy. (Before a guerilla dies, he should have killed 100 enemies.)

19. We must be able/dare to use all opportunities to kill the enemy without regard for any obstacles (rain, night time, etc.).

20. We must at all times nurture the will to resist and to attack which we have. (The will to attack means already half-way to victory.)

21. Perseverance and the preparedness to suffer until our objective is won.

22. We must at all times be filled with initiative to destroy the enemy; this does not mean the abolition of the command. Resistance without leadership means chaos.

CLARIFICATION

Instruction concerning the above have in fact been issued already, but because it is evident that mistakes are still found in several territorial regions, every commander must always try to put the methods of fighting into practice which are outlined above. Many of our soldiers have died unnecessarily, being encircled etc., because of mistakes made by commanders who were insufficiently active in executing the tactics of guerilla warfare.

It must be remembered that we cannot win, in "organised fighting" but on the other hand by the "assassins tactics" we use, step by step the enemy will surely be destroyed and will not be able to dominate us.

To have the worst of the equipment situation does not mean to have the worst of it in battle. We can surmount this situation by using equipment as efficiently as possible and to the greatest advantage.

At present, the enemy is certainly provoking us to show ourselves and to make attacks upon their defences which will result in our concentration and our easy destruction by the enemy.

Attacks at night, or general attacks against enemy fortifications will have no meaning, if not accompanied by an attack of complete destruction against the enemy (man to man fighting).

Acts of "letting people see that we are fighting" and the like must be stopped. We do not look at whether a fight is heavy or not, but at the results of the battle. To kill as many of the enemy as possible with the least possible number of bullets, this is the aim of every guerilla. Do not be flattered or become angered quickly, for this will result in unnecessary death or casualties made in vain. Praise to any guerilla or his own feeling of satisfaction depends upon the results which are the outcome of each time he takes action. The resistance we are now making must be conducted according to plan, perfectly executed in one set way, and also under one command.

At present, our system of fighting is about to enter the "ambushing phase" which goes on to the "annihilation phase" and further to the "occupation phase" and to the "pursuit phase". This means that our activity is just now limited to stopping the enemy, to holding him up and to attacking undefended objects. We cannot yet begin to seize towns, but this does not mean that guerillas within the towns or in the enemy's midst should cease their activities; no, it is precisely guerilla activities — by the means already decided — which we must increase. However, it is not yet time for large scale attacks to seize a particular town. It should be remembered that attacks by big forces can easily be destroyed (at present, the enemy is still strong and well-equipped), and that this will create a sense of unity among the enemy. On the other hand, continuous guerilla activity coming from unknown directions, causing few casualties, but going on without stopping, will bring results: we will not be able to be destroyed and the enemy will become demoralised. Thus to proceed to the "annihilation stage", guerilla commanders should await for instruction which of course will, be issued at the most appropriate time. Also in proceeding on to the "occupation phase", every guerilla fighter has to wait for the command and continue to guard discipline, in short: to remain in the places they occupy, and so on; likewise with regard to the "pursuit phase".

In order to increase the results of our operations, every guerilla commander should pay real attention to every instruction and to the matters above; they should also execute them in such a way that every guerilla will know his duty and in what direction he will be taken.

II. POLITICAL

1. Nurture unity so that we return to the Proclamation of August 1945.
2. Defend/stabilise the Government of the Republic of Indonesia, which at the present time is in the form of the military government.

EXTERNALLY

1. An attitude of non-co-operation with the Dutch (see: H.Q. Java Command's Instruction).
2. The guerilla policy. We must smash/sabotage every effort by the enemy concerning this which will strengthen their purpose.
3. Take strong/firm action as the apparatus of destruction by the State of the Republic of Indonesia against the instruments of the enemy government/collaborators (by kidnapping, killings, etc.).

CLARIFICATION

In a number of places lately friction has begun to appear between left and right which is truly disadvantageous to our struggle. Therefore, every guerilla must try to overcome the friction and to turn those persons' every desire and purpose back to what it was when we proclaimed our Independence on 17 August 1945.

The only question is to be free or to die. Do not let us split from within only because of a quarrel as to what characteristics we will give our State, while the state which we are quarrelling about is itself still physically threatened in the real sense of the words. Therefore every guerilla must take strong measures against these dangers in an organised manner. Remember the activities of the Netherlands Indies Forces Intelligence Service.

Every guerilla must also know for what we are fighting, in conection with the fact that here and there people hold the opinion that "the government has been wiped out" and the like, which opinions are in fact truly dangerous for our struggle. In order to continue our struggle, we must continue as state against state. Do not let our resistance degenerate into a people's rebellion, which would mean a retreat for us because what we have built during these two and a half years would be lost, with the consequence that, both internally and (which is most important) externally, we would become weak and would be defeated. Therefore every guerilla must take strong measures against the elements with those anarchic ideas, but, it must be remembered, this must be done in orderly fashion. The attitude of non-co-operation which has truly become the attitude of every patriot must be carried out with all consequences. Indeed, at this moment there should be a clear dividing line as to whether one is a patriot or a traitor. There is no middle of the road attitude for us. Either a person is a feudalist or a person assisting us with money and other goods. If it is evident that a person is working together with the enemy, we will strike. Do not let us be shaken by money, a girl's smile, or mere sweet words. The feeling of nationalism is the highest feeling in the heart of every patriot and cannot be bought with money, goods, etc. This feeling should be displayed by the voluntary sacrifice of all we possess.

Further, real attention must be given lest the guerillas can be shaken, influenced by party ideologies or by political party members.

What we want is only to be Free, or to die. Only later, once the State is Independent, may those persons begin to give characteristics to our State from then on. Free from all political currents, we must will this: **As long as the Dutch are here, guerilla warfare will never end.**

Be on your guard against the N.E.I. Intelligence Service activities which want to split us; be on your guard against irresponsible political party members. We will smash every endeavour which will place obstacles in the path of our struggle, which will split us from within, just as we will smash the enemy.

III. ECONOMIC

INTERNALLY

1. Strengthen our economy so that the livings of our guerilla troops will not be affected.
2. Organise the people's economy so that with the cutting of communications between one region and others, the people's living will not be affected.

EXTERNALLY

1. Economic guerilla war against the enemy.
2. Economic blockade against the enemy.

CLARIFICATION

It is evident that living conditions for guerilla troops in one region are not the same as those in others, because these are greatly dependent upon physical conditions — whether a region is a minus or surplus area. Although this is so, if a regulated economy can be organised in every regions it goes without saying that conditions for our guerilla troops will surely be good.

Remember that the economy is a fundamental for military affairs. An army cannot be strong or win a war if the economy is upset and disorganised. Therefore every centre, *rayon* and sector must pay real attention to these matters and must be able to support themselves or make their own arrangements in keeping with conditions in their respective environments. Because of the fact that the centre can not possibly provide upkeep, is even at present in exhausted condition, every *rayon* (we say *rayon*, because these are middle-sized regions with natural boundaries) must become autonomous regions with regard to economic affairs, which they must see to themselves, with the supply section of the military government executing what is required.

But under such conditions, military units must not allow feelings to arise that they are free of all ties because they are able to live on their own, or feel superior because they are able to make provision for their own troops, but must realise that in guerilla warfare conditions must be so. It is for this reason also that guerilla units may not be cut off from the people, because economically they are dependent on the regions they inhabit. Remember that the food supply of guerilla troops depends upon their good and close relations with the people. Indeed, the centre can not possibly make provision as it should; it is able merely to assist from time to time. Therefore it is wrong if a certain unit feels superior because during some long time past it has been able to live on its own without any provision (assistance) from the centre; that is how a guerilla unit ought to live. But this does not mean that the centre is released from its responsibility. No; every member of the staff, every commander must at all times make efforts corresponding to the size of their region (sector, *rayon*, centre, Military Governor's region, etc) to make living conditions easier for the guerilla troops.

It should also be remembered that a region should also have direct economic relations with others, which means that surplus regions should also bear the burdens of neighbouring minus areas.

The execution of the above becomes the responsibility of the commander of the front in every military government which has direct relations with sectors, *rayons*, and centres; he must act wisely in order that the people's economy can continue to function and be undisturbed — even, through the addition of experts from army personnel in the respective area, it should become increasingly organised and strong.

Remember: Every guerilla acting in orderly ways must take firm/strong measures also against persons upsetting the economy. It must be possible to put practical methods into operation. For instance: Public kitchens which prove to be unwieldy and consume too much expenditure, should be replaced by family kitchens for the use of every platoon lodged with families indicated by the military government.

We must intensify our economic guerilla warfare against the enemy. Every region where the enemy holds authority must become a region in which the enemy is not able to organize the economy/ exploit the products. The enemy must feel demoralized and confronted by chaotic conditions everywhere. Stock piles of foodstuffs must be a target, places for economic exchange in enemy areas must continue to be made disorderly. We must fix the exchange rate or else we must act. Every guerilla must take the stand that it is better to be destroyed rather than that a single thing be consumed by the enemy.

In executing the above we must sometimes sacrifice our feelings, because we frequently observe that the people in enemy occupied areas are also suffering. But we should remember that every endeavour strengthening the enemy occupation means suicide. Therefore with or without sacrifice, economic guerilla warfare must be undertaken. We have already sacrificed much, our people have already suffered much; there are no exceptions; the whole of the Indonesian people who are fighting for freedom are suffering.

IV. ORDER

Every commander of guerilla troops is required to execute the above guide and pass it on to every guerilla in order that each knows his duties and position and that all know their purpose.

God willing, with our united forces, we will certainly win.

Indenpendence or death! We remain in the midst of our troops.

Dated: 23 March 1949.
COMMANDO GROUP PPS.
Commander Brigade 5/II,

SLAMET RIJADI.

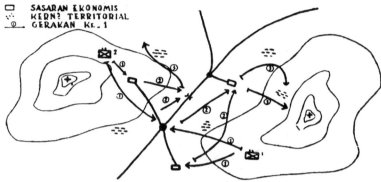

SASARAN ᴱKONOMIS
KERN² TERRITORIAL
GERAKAN Kᴇ-1

Schema	— Scheme	Kern² Territorial— Territorial Centres
Sasaran Ekonomi — Economic Targets	Gerakan ke-1 — First Movement

2. DOCUMENT FROM THE HEADQUARTERS OF THE SUMATRA COMMAND. (PART XII).

As in Java, so in Sumatra also consolidation of our defence was achieved around the "Rum-Royen Agreement". On May 1, the Operations Section of the Sumatra Command Staff issued a document showing our advances and containing various guides for the improvement of the further struggle. From this document it was evident that the enemy's activities had already reached their climax, although immediately after May 7 his patrolling in all sectors became somewhat more active and he newly took occupation of a number of small places. However, on the other hand, the National Army rose to a new level in binding together and connecting with one another various local defence activities into a wider framework which became the point of beginning for intensification of the guerilla war. This clear from the document mentioned above which was issued in the same week with the "Rum-Royen" statement that, through means of a compromise, was to bring an end to the people's resistance **Part XII of this document runs as follows:**

"Although we had known from the beginning that guerilla tactics were the basis of the warfare we were practising, nevertheless preparations for guerilla war had not yet been made, or not much had yet been done, so that in the first phase of the Second Dutch Attack we took a heavy military blow which caused the breaking up and dispersal of our troops in all directions not according to any specific plan.

"In the period between the First and Second Attacks, when in fact we had sufficient time and room to make preparations for a people's and a guerilla war, they were not used as they should have been, so that in fact we obtained a strategic defeat against the Dutch before the Second Attack began by not using that time and room, and at the time before the Second Attack it was as though we held the opinion that we could face the Dutch army by the means used by troops with modern arms and equipment.

"It was because of this opinion that it seemed as though preparations for guerilla war were forgotten, and in general our troops were placed in a stiff defence of lines facing the direction from which the enemy would make his attack. At merely the first blow alone it was already evident that we could not face the enemy's attack with that linear defence, our lines of defence were broken through, the enemy made encircling moves of other kinds so that our troops were forced to split and disperse, retreating in this direction and that in order to avoid danger (destruction).

"Our troops continued the armed resistance by making small-scale attack, each group acting as it wished, without orderly planning and leadership, and in this way we automatically turned from earlier tactics to those of the guerilla. Gradually, our guerilla activities, which had no specific objective at the beginning, each unit acting as though in accordance with its own will, began to be consolidated and organised so that it could be said that the attempt had been made to link those guerilla activities into a guerilla action covering the whole of Sumatra.

"Through the issue of Instruction No. I/107/SU II/49/R and through this present text, the attempt is made to regard and to relate guerilla activities in every Sub-Territorium one with the others, in order to be able to taken action in a large-scale and over-all relationship.

"At the first pressure from the enemy it was obvious that our troops did not have fire-power the equal of the enemy's nor striking power sufficient to withstand and to delay the enemy's moves, and automatically the system of lines was abandoned. As a consequence of that lack of firing power, we were not able to conduct battles on open battlefields, we were not capable of a shooting duel with the enemy; this was felt intuitively by our troops, so that of themselves they entered upon the guerille phase. Indeed this is the one and only tactic by which we can face the enemy who in the matter of arms and equipment is far stronger than us. And it also this tactic which is feared by the enemy, as is evident from his demands at the time of the "Renville" agreement for the withdrawal of our guerilla troops from the pockets, and later on (when the negotiotions began) from his request to put an end to the guerilla war (erpecially guerilla warfare under the military governors).

"With the enemy's recent break-through of our lines, made with a blitz tactic, they hoped through this one blow alone to be able to destroy the National Army, so that they could free themselves from the danger of guerilla war and eliminate it. They have been disappointed in this hope, for it has proved that at the first blow our troops were only taken by surprise alone, no kileld — they even did not fall unconscious; we were able quickly to orrgɪnise our armed forces again and to continue the resistance as guerillas supported by the people in the system of a "people's defence". Guerilla warfare is a tactic in defence which is executed by an army that feels itself far weaker in arms than the attacker; through this means of fighting which is continued for long periods of time, the enemy will have no opportunity to organise himself in all fields, they will even become increasingly weaker both physically and psychologically. It can therefore also be said that "the guerilla tactic is a tactic of squeezing out the enemy's life blood".

The basic tactic of the guerilla as the principle of every clash is to advance in order to smash the enemy and to retreat in order not to be smashed by the enemy; or, in other words, the basic tactic of the guerilla is to retreat and advance in order to avoid blows and to strike. But in a guerilla war, both of these moves are performed simultaneously, by fast, ingenious, skilful moves. For this reason the first requirement for guerilla troops is that they have the ability to move from place to place, to move over very large areas. This is the absolute condition in a guerilla war, that there is nothing at all which is static, but that everything is dynamic. And so that these actions are light in their movenments, they are not performed by large bodies of troops but by quite small units, even groups of 10 to 15 persons are adequate.

The troops may not be tied down to one place, defending that place at all cost, but always move around here and there within a certain area. Therefore Instruction No. I/017/SU II/49/R of this document is based upon guerilla tactics; this means that in those plans no static characteristics are to be found, but that everything is based upon the characteristics of mibility, manoeuvre ability and dynamic action. But this characteristic of wide-spread movement does not mean that the movements of guerilla troops have no purpose and objective; because they really do have purpose and objectives, these movements have to be able to be steered and commanded by one hand oble to contact all troops lying with its reach.

For this purpose therefore, there must be guerilla regions within which the guerilla troops live and conduct their movements which are under the leadership of one commander who connects one movement with the others and relates them to the purpose and objective already decided. For the guerilla region there can be taken, for instance, one *Kabupaten*, in which there will be guerilla bases *(Ketjamatan)*, which see to all the needs of the guerilla troops in conducting their activities (supplies, equipment, rest places, and so forth).

In order to facilitate his leadership and lighten, it, the commander of a guerilla region will divide it into sectors, each led by a sector commander. Thus the movements or activities of each sector are organised by the commander of the guerilla region in such a way that those activities have a purpose and a relationship within a certain plan. Above these guerilla commanders there are other, higher commanders, namely the commanders of Sub-Territoriums, who regulate the activities of the guerilla regions in their territories.

The Commander of the Army of the Sumatra Territorium has determined that authority in the matter of defence is given over to the hands of the commanders of the Sub-Territoriums (the military governors), but that the Commander of the Sumatra Territorium maintains the right to make suggestions/provide guides so that each Sub-Territorium has a specific plan in order that the over-all plan for the Island of Sumatra may be executed. With such a structure as this, our guerilla war is not a "wild" war, but on the contrary has a fixed structure with plans and lines of authority which are also fixed, that later on, at the right time will be able to launch a simultaneous retaliatory attck, and so be able to guarantee the success of our guerilla war in reaching its objective.

A circle of guerillas is made by our troops around one or more places occupier by the enemy and these are gradually decreased in size, so that eventually we are able to gain a stronghold over the enemy in those places.

If the enemy attacks us in strength, cutting through the lines of our encirclement, and we feel unable to face him directly because he is too strong, then the enemy is allowed to enter in the first place; then, when the enemy returns to his base, we follow him, making small-scale attacks by sniping and so forth, and our positions gradually extend further forward yet. By such means, bit at a time, we draw in the lines of encirclement and exert pressure upon the enemy; but we must always be ready to disappear if we are attacked by the enemy. We might call this the tactics of the snake's constriction, for it is like snake's action in twining around the body of its prey: when the prey draws breath, swelling out its stomach (in our case, when the enemy makes a sally), then the constriction is somewhat eased (our guerillas retreat or disappear), but at the moment that the prey expells breath, so that its stomach is contracted (in our case, when the enemy returns to his base), then the snake's contriction is gradually increased (our guerillas reappear, follow the enemy and gradually push themselves further forward yet) so that bit at a time the prey is stifled and crushed to death.

In order to give greater assurance of success for the operations of the guerilla troops forming the guerilla circle, so that the danger of surprise attacks from behind will be diminished and to prevent the enemy's attempts to eliminate the gaps to be found in his lines of operation, we must take certain measures, that is to put "stoppers" in places where the terrain is advantageous to us in front enemy positions. Neither are these stoppers stationary, but are also characterised by mobility, so that our defencee is not stiffly facing the direction from which the enemy is likely to come.

In conducting this defence, troops must not be characterised by waiting for the arrival of the enemy arms in hand, only to fight if the enemy attacks, but must keep on, every day, going to and attacking the enemy with lightning actions, making counter-patrols, harassing the enemy's positions, using the regions of the "stoppers" as bases for their sorties, so that by this means the enemy will have no opportunity to make preparations for the launching of attacks.

To be able to keep on conducting these activities, the troops making the "stoppers' should be divided and take turns, so that when one part is attacking, the other is at the ready in the stopper waiting the possible arrival of the enemy from any direction. In our movements out from the guerilla circles and stoppers when conducting the tactics of snake-like constriction, there must be close-co-ordination of the actions of one unit with the others, for if they take steps on their own which have no connection to those of others, or have no clear objective, the desired results will not be obtained.

From this it is again obvious how important it is to have a single leadership which organises, combines and leads the movements of our guerillas, and a leadership able to have an over-all view of conditions upon the basis of which it will take action to achieve a purpose and to execute a plan.

Further, what we must use as our guides are:

* Do not fight in a frontal attack on an open field if it is not necessary and fighting power is not equal.

232

* Retreat when attacked by a stronger enemy.
* Attack and smash small units of enemy troops.
* Inveigle the enemy to enter traps.
* Harass and attack lines of communication and convoys.
* Use the elements of time and room for action to the greatest advantage.
* Do not form concentrations to become targets for the enemy, but be many small targets so that the enemy is forced to divide his troops into small forces which will be easy for us to wipe out.

Guerilla war is a tactic of defence made by the side defending itself which does not feel capable of facing the attacker directly. This is not a passive defence; on the contrary, it is a very active defence conditional upon the initiative and great activity of guerilla troops. It is required that wherever the enemy may be he shall always be harassed, attacked, and sabotaged, with the regions ot enemy authority disrupted, and the enemy himself disrupted materially and morally. By this means, the enemy will obtain no opportunity to make military, economic and political consolidation, but will eventually be at his wits' end and be unable to live further on Indonesian soil.

A guerilla war, executed actively and in orderly fashion, will become a power strongly fostering and advancing our political forces which are conducting a political struggle against the enemy, so that at last the enemy can be struck politically and military. Thus when the moment comes that the enemy has already suffered deterioration in his powers and his morale, we will change over from the tactic of defence as guerillas to the tactic of attack by launching simultaneous attacks throughout all the regions under the enemy's authority. For fundamentally, victory cannot be won by mere defensive tactics all the time; the defensive tactic is a stepping stone to the tactic of attack in order to exercise the decisive and/or death-dealing blow. Whether the duration of time is long or short between defence and attack depends upon our perserverance in the widest possible sense, also upon the perseverance of the whole of our nation in conducting the present over-all struggle.

In brief, in the last analysis, the activities of our guerillas must constantly have the objective, night and day of disrupting the enemy positions wherever they may be, of surrounding the enemy's positions and his lines of communication by complicated measures, like ants gathering round sugar, and by attacking and harassing the enemy every day, every night, in rain and in heat, although it may be many small actions, so that feelings of doubt and perplexity arise in the enemy's ranks which will vitiate all the enemy's efforts to effect consolidation in the military, economic and political fields, and so that our people in enemy areas will be fully convinced that the state of the Republic of Indonesia still stands in its greatness and cannot be wiped out by anyone at all.

*
**

DOCUMENT FROM THE STAFF OF DIVISION I ON JAVA

Later on, the then leadership of Division I made announcements about the definition of, guides for, and the organisation of the people's defence which was increasingly stiffening and deepening the understanding of and the capability for a long guerilla war.

CONCERNING THE PEOPLE'S DEFENCE

The meaning of people's defence:

There are many people who do not understand the meaning of people's defence, even persons who sit amongst the leadership of the people's defence lack understanding of its meaning or have only a vague idea about it.

What in reality it "People's defence"?

An advanced state with complete and modern apparatus is able to gather up the strength of its state with which to strike at the enemy. What is he meaning of gathering up all the strength of a state? All citizens between the ages of 19 to 50 years are called up and mobilised. The men become members of the army and police. This is called military defence. The women replace the men in the fields, in the factories and businesses. This is called economic defence. There are also those who enter the field of social defence. Apart from that, all persons over 50 years of age are also mobilised, to take the place of young persons in the offices, colleges, in information and so forth. For ease, all of this is referred to as society defence.

How about the children between 6 and 19 years of age? They continue to go to school, for what would happen if later on there should be no young people ready to take the places of those who fell in the state's struggle. Those approaching adulthood are given military training or else help in all fields (police, information work and the like). The remainder are only babies and children between

234

the years of 1 and 5, plus old persons who have no strength any longer. The total of these is approximately 5 per cent of the total population.

Apart from this last group constituting about 5 per cent, *the whole of the people participate in defence. In all fields the respective duties and tasks are tackled more energetically than before, which people working together very closely.* In a foreign language this is called *"Total People's Defence".* From the outline above, it is clear that what is meant by people's defence is not merely fighting as many people mistakenly understand it.

Now,how about our state? The state is newly born, it is not yet modern and does not yet possess instruments complete in every way. To call up all men between the ages of 19 to 50 is not possible, because communications are broken or are very difficult. To arm them all is likewise not possible, for arms are insufficient. Factories in fact are not numerous, and of the few most have been destroyed. Conditions are similar for businesses. Thus it is evident that in our country women can not yet be mobilised to replace men workers; it is even the case that many men no longer have a set field of employment. In what kind of employment can they work? In agriculture, on the wet or dry rice fields? Land for agriculture and rice fields is no longer sufficient for the whole population, although we do still see that there are empty lands. Thus our economic defence can not yet be 100 per cent.

How about social defence? Every day we see evacuees who have not yet been seen to, and many of them are unemployed; the Red Cross wants to expand, medicines are non-existent or insufficient. Similarly also with society defence. There are already many schools now, but parents feel it is not necessary to send their children to school, and wait for the future when there is peace, and the like. All of this is not only because our state is young, but also comes about in consequence of past colonialism.

Examining these matters, it becomes obvious that our people's defence is still far from perfect, or in other words, not all of the people yet participate in a total people's defence. And it not all the people yet participate in total people's defence, this means that we do not yet possess real defence.

This is not caused by our people not wanting to know what it is that is called people's defence, but through lack understanding and also through the additional fact that our equipment for seeing to all this is inadequate in every way and out of date in every way (the consequence of colonial ill-treatment).

235

Is it possible that we can build a people's defence in such conditions as surround us? It is possible, so long as we know how to conduct is, what are its methods, and, what is most needed, as long as we understand what is the meaning of people's defence. It is not possible for us to copy the methods of advanced countries in order to create a total people's defence in our state which is still young and where everything is old-fashioned (the consequence of Dutch colonial education which kept us to orthodox ways).

Is it possible that we can attract the greatest possible number of the people into participation in defence, so that it constitutes a total people's defence? It is possible — and indeed that is precisely the objective of the people's defence. Through means that are simple and inadequate in every way, it is possible for us to gather up the greatest possible powers of the people, so that it can be said that the whole of the people are participating in defence. But it is precisely what those ways are which we need to understand and to study thoroughly, so that in the future we will not fail in the middle of the road.

Those ways are as follows:

1. The people must gather up their energies ready to assist the government in all fields (economic, social, financial and in the community).
2. The people must report to the government every lack to be found in society, and put their practical opinions forward as to how to solve those lacks, or the results consequent upon those lacks.

These are some examples:

1. Schools are closed because of a shortage of teachers. The people's defence can bring forward the opinion to the government that, for the time being, the shortage of teachers can be overcome by the government making it obligatory upon evactuated civil servants to teach in the places where they have taken refuge.
2. Road blocks have been removed by the Dutch, telephone wires have been strung again. The people's defence can mobilise the people to put the road blocks back again and to roll up or cut the telephone wires also.
3. The people's defence can convince the inhabitants of a locality of the importance of rice barns, of government promissory notes, etc.
4. The people's defence can train the young men to become reserve troops, to take the place of men of the mobile units when they are at rest in the rear.

236

5. The people's defence can mobilise the people to guard security, to assist the Military Police, the State Police, the Village Police, etc.
6. The people's defence can bring forward persons to assist the village commander in their villages.
7. The people's defence can open up fallow lands owned by individuals through the collective method of *gotong-rojong*.
8. The people's defence can gather together persons clever at repairing damaged agricultural implements.

Many other things could be taken as examples showing that under our conditions, in which there is not enough of anything and in which the means and equipment are so simple, we can yet build up a people's defence with wide-spread tasks so that the whole of the people participate in defence. We do not need to be ashamed before states which, as is explained above, are advanced and have modern equipment complete in everything.

As can be seen from the above examples, the tasks (field of endeavour) of the people's defence are extensive and must be capable of mobilising the people in the best possible way. For this reason, the leadership/management must consist of prominent persons from the ranks of the people themselves who have already obtained the people's confidence and who are honest and have a sense of responsibility for the state and nation.

But it is very necessary to remember that, although its tasks are extensive, the people's defence is not a separate body of the government which as though it stood besides or above the existing bodies, may issue announcements, make regulations and give instructions etc. on its own. That is not at all what is meant. Organisationally, the people's defence is a framework provided for the mobilisation of the masses in order that they can assist the administration. From another angle, in conformity with the factual situation, the people's defence can present its opinions, recommendations and requests to the government.

The people's defence has this objective: with the inadequate and simple equipment and means at its disposal to gather up and to mobilise the greatest possible powers of the people, so that as far as possible the people participate in defence.

FOR THE PEOPLE'S DEFENCE

A guide for the people's defence:

In the very first place what needs to be remembered and taken thoroughly into account is that the nature of the work of the people's defence is to assist, to convince and to mobilise the people in order to help the government.

1. WHERE THE REGION HAS BEEN OCCUPIED BY THE ENEMY

The basis of the work is to defend and maintain the de facto political and military authority of our government.

a. Political de facto authority:

    i. To obstruct the setting up of an administration made by the Dutch:

* Kill the henchmen of the Dutch.
* Disrupt Dutch trust in their henchmen.
* Blacken the characters (morals) of henchmen of the Dutch, especially if they are influential people.

    ii. Cultivate awareness of our administration in every inhabitant:

* Every instruction, regulation, statute and announcement made by the government and the administration is required to be conveyed to the population.
* Ask the population to make reports about the strength, activities and movements of the enemy.
* Convey to the population news of the military situation and radio news from abroad.
* Assist the population by trying to obtain the goods for their daily necessities (through a co-operative, for instance).
* Keep on collecting for the Rice Barns of the Struggle (it is also good to do so by giving out reduced quantities).
* Encourage the population to continue to pay taxes etc.

b. Military de facto authority:

    i. Guarding at watch-houses by our people should be used to disturb security (this means that we have no intention whatever of guarding security in enemy-occupied regions, whatever may happen).

    ii. Show the way to our troops when they pass, provide cover (sanctuary) to members of our army who are hard-pressed by the enemy.

    iii. Show the wrong paths to the Dutch and then tell our nearest troops.

2. WHERE THE REGION IS PATROLLED BY THE ENEMY

a. The government and people's organisations return immediately once the danger has passed.

238

b. Keep up the people's spirit:

  * Bring in information officers (Propagandists).
  * Visit persons who have been visited by the enemy, or who have been forced to follow the enemy, or persons who have suffered seizure of their possessions by the enemy or had a member of their family taken away by the enemy, or persons who have returned after being forced to do something for the enemy's needs.
  * Together with the Military Police arrest the traitors to the nation and those who would sell the state.

c. Foodstuffs for the people and the Rice Barns of the Struggle must be hidden away carefully so that it is not easy for the enemy to find them, for example, in the jungle, in market gardens and the like.

d. Encourage every inhabitant not to co-operate with the enemy and explain the consequences of conducting a tactic of co-operation.

e. Mobilise the people to take in the harvest at night time, for in the day it is possible that the Dutch will come on patrol.

f. Road blocks must be put up again (rather far from the village) and bridges should also be damaged.

g. When the authorities (for example, Lurah, the village secretary, etc) are negligent, they are to be admonished; persuade them to perform their duties, assist them with manpower/ideas, keep close beside them but do not compete in giving good offices; do everything for state and nation (everyone has an obligation to give their services).

3. WHERE THE REGION HAS NOT BEEN DISTURBED

Pioneer the way so that the region can stand on its own (be autonomous) and meet its own needs (be self-supporting).

a. Economic:
   i. Launch slogans for multiplication of products of the soil.
      * Pay attention to seedlings, stocks, irrigation and manpower;
      * Watch the conditions of agricultural animals;
   ii. Watch methods for collections for Rice Barns for the Struggle.
   iii. With the advice of the Forestry Service investigate the possibility of cultivating forest lands.
   iv. Fisheries.

v. Village co-operatives, Village Rice Barns, storage of food-stuffs against hard times.

vi. Pioneer the centralisation of financial resources.

(In all these matters keep in mind the economic plans of the *Ketjamatan* or Village military government).

b. Social:

i. Eradication of infectious diseases.

ii. Popularise the Javanese herbal remedies.

iii. Encourage the population to receive evacuees and to make collective purchases of daily necessities which are not easily obtainable.

iv. Have lodgings in readiness for our troops.

v. Prepare evacuees to do work in conformity with their capabilities (as assistants in the Military Sub-District Command administration, in information work, in education, in opening-up land and so forth).

4. SLOGANS WHICH MUST BE HEEDED/IMPLEMENTED:

i. Every patriot must be non-cooperative with the Dutch.

ii. Every person who does not love the country is a traitor.

iii. There is no bridge between non-co-operation and co-operation.

iv. Education must be continued.

v. The whole of the people participate in defence.

THE ORGANISATION OF THE PEOPLES'S DEFENCE

Concerning the organisation of the people's defence:

The mobile troops, the territorial troops and the people have each their respective tasks in facing the Dutch, but each needs the other to be able to fulfil those tasks.

The mobile troops have the task of attacking and smashing the enemy in places where he is weak. But to perform this duty, the mobile troops need bases, supplies, transport power, guides, etc. It is the territorial troops which see to these things with the help of the people (contributions in the form of manpower, products of the soil, etc.).

The territorial troops together with the people have the task of defence. The de facto political and military authority of the Republic must continue to be maintained in each region (territorium). To be able to perform this duty, protection is needed from the mobile troops against large-scale attacks by the enemy, and help is also needed from the people, both in the form of goods (wealth) and in the form of manpower.

The people have the task of producing as much foodstuffs as possible and of assisting the administration in all fields. And the people need the protection of the mobile and territorial troops.

The whole of this is regulated by the government so that it constitutes orderly team-work with the services, both military and civil, and with an organisation of the people's defence ("PERA") which mobilises the people and arranges that the people's assistance is effective and efficient.

In this way the whole of the people participate in defence (Political, Economic and Military). And what materialises is a total people's defence.

With regard to the character and nature of the People's Defence:

From the outline above, we can draw the conclusion that the organisation of the people's defence assists, supplements and mobilises the people.

In no sense at all is it intended that the organisation of the people's defence constitute a body in its own right, standing above or beside the government, issuing its own announcements etc. No, this organisation is a part of the government, that is its character.

With regard to the Structure of the People's Defence Organisation:

Our experience during the whole time we have been at war against the Dutch shows that the de facto authority of the Republic, politically and militarily, can be easily defended and maintained in the *Ketjamatan*. In the *Ketjamatan*, the organs of the government (the Commanders of the Military Sub-Districts, the village cadres, the *Tjamat* and the *Lurah*, still have mutual connections, the government department services in the *Ketjamatan* can be easily co-ordinated and activated. Security can be easily ensured and seen to. Apart from this, the area of the *Ketjamatan* are composed of a group of villages, and these are the foundations of our agrarian society which are very easily organised.

In connection with this, and also in connection with the facts that the people's defence organisation is a part of the administration and that the government strategy bases its struggle upon defence in the *Ketjamatan*, it follows that the people's defence must base its organisation upon defence in the *Ketjamatan*.

In the centres of military administration which are Residencies, the people's defence organisation is a command which is purely legislative in character, whilst in the *Ketjamatan* and Villages, apart from legislative matters, it is also for executive affairs.

241

As a minimum, the people's defence must be able to build an attitude among the people of consistent non-co-operation, and be able gradually to heighten the quality of people's defence until the people become trained in guerilla warfare.

Although the people's defence organisation is a part of the administration, however, and primarily because of its character in mobilising the people, the leadership of the organisation must be given into the hands of persons who are influential in the community. It is only formally that it is led by the commanders of the territorial troops (who are the heads of the military government) to deal with matters connected with technical military affairs. By such means all dualism and impotencies will disappear from the people's defence.

Things to be done:

The military government of the Residencies divides its activities in these fields into various levels:

1. To explain and to make it plain and clear what is the meaning of people's defence, as well as what is the nature and character of the people's defence organisation.

2. To indicate what are the targets for the attention of the people's defence (general tactics) in military, political and economic fields, in the light of our experience so far. Also to give guidance to the leaders of the people's defence in the *Ketjamatan* and villages.

3. To set up (again) people's defence organisations in all *Ketjamatan* and throughout the villages in conformity with the concept above.

E. THE ADMINISTRATION OF JUSTICE BY THE MILITARY GOVERNMENT

Besides the directives given in the fields of war movements, supply, communications, etc., the need of the guerilla war was felt immediately for courts of justice in the pockets. Before the First Attack — at the time when Kasman Singodimedjo was head of the Army department of Justice — the government had already drawn up the requirements for military justice. These regulations were not aimed at the needs of wartime, but were merely requirements for ordinary peace time. It also appeared to have been a matter of consideration that National Army officers could not then be entrusted to perform duties in courts of law because they lacked sufficient education. Thus these duties were coupled to the work of existing civil courts and prosecutors, and so technical aspects were placed above matters of principle.

The problems of military justice are difficult to pass over to persons unacquainted with a military climate. Wartime conditions demand a different treatment of justice from that of peace. The battle fields can not be served by civil prosecutors and courts, even though they are given the official right and duty to do so. The regions of jurisdiction under civil courts are not based upon the organisation of military regions but conform with civil requirements.

And so the First Dutch Attack proved that the existing regulations were useless, because they could not be implemented. We looked for prosecutors and judges but they could not possibly be obtained. Thus reality demanded that there should be military justice, that there should be charges and there should be courts. In consequence of the vacuum, people took justice into their own hands. Whoever felt himself strong immediately acted as judge in accordance with individual interests. Many were the irregularities, miscarriages of justice and wrongs that we were forced to let be. Many also were the lower commanders who acted as judges on their own without any control. It became difficult to differentiate murder from a sentence of death, difficult to differentiate between kidnapping and arrest, difficult to differentiate between robbery and confiscation.

In spite of all the endeavours made throughout the "Renville" period to effect alterations to existing statutes, and to provide politic directives for a time of war, all had been completely without result. Certainly, little attention was given to the forthcoming war. There

were too many political incidents which all prevented the concentration of our powers and thoughts upon war and fighting.
Questions politics and diplomacy towered above all other affairs.

The Madiun Affair provided new evidence. Thousands of people
were taken into custody and their cases could not be settled. The
military authority, which had been newly organised after Colonel
Gatot Subroto became military governor, had no points of guidance
to be able to fulfil its duty in the field of justice. For the second
time, we were compelled to take action outside the existing laws,
which could only be justified by "emergency laws" or "revolutionary
laws" because of the non-existence of the legal guides which should
have been there.

At the time of the Second Dutch Attack, the Republic of Indonesia, a state under the rule of law, had still been neglectful of
regulating the needs of justice in wartime. Minister Susanto Tirto-
prodjo had made a very brief directive which was circulated only
amongst a few persons close at hand, and which, in general, was not
concerned with the special interests of war, let alone being adjusted
to the organisation of a guerilla administration. Because he immediately went off on tour in East Java, it was very difficult for us
to contact him in order to discuss a final arrangement, and measures
taken in the field of justice which had no basis in law were on the
increase. Meanwhile, in West Java, individual regulations had also
been made by Major Gani in the name of the Military Governor.
It was better that there should be a legal basis, even though most
simple, than that there should be none at all. Our struggle as a state
needed the existence of regulations as foundation for the act of
pronouncing sentence.

I entrusted the Military Police with the making of a draft for this
purpose. Eventually, Major Widia and Ali Budiardjo, political
adviser to Deputy Chief of Staff of the Armed Forces Simatupang,
drew up a concept. With this draft as working material, the Staff
made contact with Prosecutor-General Tirtawinata, through the
help of Commissioner of Police Sosrodanukusumo who had already
joined forces with the military government. As the outcome of his
active help, a practical draft was formulated which, in my opinion,
met the needs.

Tirtawinata's draft took the fact of war as its base. He provided
for a summary procedure, which was the only one we could use. He
regulated the prosecution and the judicature severally for military
and civil purposes, which in practice could be implemented by
local commanders and local government heads, and the whole was
adjusted to the organisation of a guerilla administration. Everything

244

was brought under the responsibility of the military administration, the terms used being military courts and civil courts of the military administration.

Military courts were set up in every Military Sub-District Command, every Military District Command and in every region under a Military Governor. The tasks of Judge Advocate were performed by officials of the military police corps. The execution of sentences was adjusted to the needs of guerilla war under conditions of total people's defence. However, everything was always based upon law.

The civil courts of the military government were likewise established in every *Ketjamatan* and *Kabupaten*, this being a practicable structure. And for the "front line", that is, where there was no military government as yet, or where it could not possibly function, such as in the midst of regions where battles were frequent, it was made possible to set up special courts, which of course were temporary in character, existing until such time as "second line" conditions prevailed in the place in question.

I was extremely grateful for the drafting of this regulation. Immediately I sent special couriers to the Central Government Commission in Java — this body consisted of Kasimo and Suroso, for Susanto and K.H. Mansur were on tour in East Java, Sukiman had returned home to Jogjakarta so that he was captured, and Supeno had been shot by the Dutch — to obtain immediate validation. Minister Kasimo, as leader of Government Commission executive in Java, signed it straight away in approval.

It will be well to set down here that important regulation on guerilla justice.

HEADQUARTERS OF JAVA COMMAND
EMERGENCY REGULATION
1949, No. 46/MBKD/49

THE COMMANDER IN CHIEF OF THE ARMED FORCES OF THE REPUBLIC OF INDONESIA,

RECALLING:

The need for an emergency regulation governing military courts of the military government and civil courts of the military government, governing special military courts and concerning the methods of executing sentences of imprisonment;

CONSIDERING:

The President's Order of 19 December 1948;

HEREBY DETERMINES:

1. To revoke the "Emergency Regulation governing special judges and prosecutors and the methods of executing sentences of imprisonment" issued by the Central Government of the Republic of Indonesia, dated 30-1-'49, No. 3/1949.

2. To determine the following regulation:

EMERGENCY REGULATION GOVERNING MILITARY COURTS OF THE MILITARY GOVERNMENT, GOVERNING CIVIL COURTS OF THE MILITARY GOVERNMENT, GOVERNING SPECIAL MILITARY TRIBUNALS, AND CONCERNING THE METHODS OF EXECUTING SENTENCES OF IMPRISONMENT.

PART I

CONCERNING MILITARY COURTS OF THE MILITARY GOVERNMENT

Article 1

The military courts throughout Java and Madura shall be abolished and replaced by the Military Courts of the Military Government.

Section 1. Concerning the structure and powers of the military courts of the military government

Article 2

"Military Courts of Military Under-Districts" throughout Java and Madura shall be conducted by:

i. Military tribunals of the Military Government for areas which are Military Sub-Districts.

ii. Military Tribunals of the Military District for areas which are Military Districts.

iii. Military Tribunals of the Military Governors for areas which are under curfew.

Article 3

i. The seat of a Military Tribunal of the Military Government shall be the same as the seat of the Commander of the Military Sub-District.

ii. The area under the jurisdiction of a Military Tribunal of the Military Government shall encompass the Military Sub-District.

Article 4

i. The Military Tribunal of a Military Sub-District shall be composed of the Commander of the Military Sub-District as chairman with two first officers as members who are appointed by the Commander of the Military District, and a member of the armed forces to act as Clerk of the Court who is appointed by the Commander of the Military Sub-District.

ii. The Military Tribunal of a Military Sub-District shall try all cases of crime and infringement of the law committed within the area under its jurisdiction by members of the Armed forces who hold the rank of non-commissioned officer or private.

iii. Should a certain crime or infringement of the law be committed by someone from the rank-group of non-commissioned officer or private together with someone from the rank of officer, the Military Tribunal of a Military Sub-District shall not be entitled to try the case.

iv. Should a non-commissioned officer or a private commit a crime or infringe the law together with a civilian, then the case shall be tried by the Military Tribunal of the Military Sub-District.

Article 5

i. The seat of the Military Tribunal of a Military District shall be the seat of the Commander of the Military District.

ii. The area under the jurisdiction of a Military Tribunal of a Military District shall encompass the Military District.

Article 6

i. The Military Tribunal of a Military District shall be composed of the Commander of the Military District as chairman with two first officers as members who are appointed by the Commander of the Military Sub-Territory, and a member of the armed forces to act as Clerk of the Court who is appointed by the Commander of the Military District.

ii. The Military Tribunal of a Military District shall try all cases of crimes and infringement of law committed within the area under its jurisdiction by members of the armed forces with the rank of first officer below that of captain.

iii. Should a certain crime or infringement of the law be committed by a first officer with a rank below that of captain together with an officer of higher rank, the Military Tribunal of the Military District shall not be entitled to try the case.

iv. Should a certain crime or infringement of the law be committed by a first officer with a rank below that of captain together

247

with a non-commissioned officer or private, or together with a civilian, then the Military Tribunal of the Military District shall try the case.

Article 7

i. The seat of Military Governors' Military Tribunals shall be the same as the seats of the Military Governors.

ii. The area under the jurisdiction of a Military Governor's Military Tribunal shall encompass the area under the jurisdiction of the Military Governor.

Article 8

i. A Military Governor's Military Tribunal shall be composed by the Military Governor or his Deputy as chairman and two middle-ranking officers as members who are appointed by the Army Commander of Java Territorium, and an officer to act as Clerk of the Court appointed by the Military Governor.

ii. A Military Governor's Military Tribunal shall try all cases of crime and infringement of the law committed within the area under its jurisdiction by members of the armed forces from the group of officers with rank from captain to lieutenant-colonel.

iii. Should a certain crime or infringement of the law be committed by an officer of the rank mentioned in clause ii. above together with on officer of a rank above that of lieutenant-colonel, the Military Governor's Military Tribunals shall not be entitled to try the case. Such cases are to be brought to justice by the military tribunals referred to in Article 15 below.

Article 9

What is meant by "members of the armed forces" in Articles 4 to 6 inclusive above is members of the lawful army, navy and air force, similarly also members of units which have been militarised and permanent employees who work in the armed forces.

Section 2. Concerning the laws and procedure which are to be used

Article 10

i. The criminal laws which shall be applied by military courts of the military government referred to above are those contained in:

a. The Statute Book of military criminal law, as amended;
b. The Book of criminal Statutes as amended by Statute No. 1/1946;
c. Statutes governing criminal law (Statute No. 1/1946);
d. Statutes and other regulations containing criminal law.

ii. The procedure which shall be used by the military courts of the military government is a summary procedure guided by the provisions of Article 337 of the Revised Law Code.

Section 3. Concerning the Prosecutors in the military of the military government

Article 11

i. The Prosecution in the military courts of the military government shall be conducted as follows:

a. In the Military Tribunals of Military Sub-Districts:
by a first officer who shall be appointed by the Head of the Sub-Detachment of the Military Government Police.

b. In the Military Tribunals of Military Districts:
by a first officer who shall be appointed by the Head of the Detachment of the Military Government Police.

c. In the Military Governors' Military Tribunals:
by the Head of the Security Section of the Military Governor's staff, or by his Deputy.

ii. In the performance of their duties, the prosecutors in the military courts of military government referred to in clause i. above shall take as guide: all regulations in force for the "Counsel for the prosecution in the District Courts" as contained in the Revised Law Code (Article 46 foll.)

Section 4. Concerning decisions of the Military Courts of the Military Government

Article 12

All decisions of the military courts of the military government, whether from the Military Tribunals of the Military Sub-Districts, the Military Tribunals of the Military Districts, or the Military Governors' Military Tribunals, can not be reviewed.

Article 13

Every decision of the military tribunals of the military government operable within at most 7 (seven) days after the judgement has been pronounced.

Article 14

The Prosecutor concerned is the person who must execute the sentence of the military tribunals of the military government.

Section 5. Concerning Special Military Tribunals

Article 15

Should an officer with the rank of colonel or higher commit a particular crime or infringe the law, the case shall be brought to justice by a special military tribunal which shall be set up by the topmost leadership of the armed forces. This special military tribunal shall also try all cases of crimes and infringements of the law comitted by officers with the rank of colonel or higher together with members of the armed forces of a rank lower than that of colonel.

PART II
CONCERNING CIVIL COURTS OF THE MILITARY GOVERNMENT

Article 16

Civil courts throughout Java and Madura shall be abolished and replaced by civil courts of the military government.

Article 17

The civil courts of the military government shall be divided into:

A. Kabupaten Courts.

B. Police courts.

KABUPATEN COURTS.

Article 18

i. There shall be *Kabupaten* courts in every *Kabupaten*.

ii. The seat of the *Kabupaten* courts shall be the same as that of the *Bupati* (Head of the *Kabupaten*, second-level autonomous region).

iii. The area under the jurisdiction of the *Kabupaten* courts shall encompass the area of the *Kabupaten*.

Section 1. Concerning the structure and powers
of the Kabupaten courts

Article 19

i. The *Kabupaten* courts shall be composed of the *Bupati* as chairman with at least two prominent persons as members who shall be appointed by the Military Governor, and a civil servant to act as Clerk of the Court who shall be appointed by the *Bupati.*

ii. Should it be considered necessary in view of the size of the area under jurisdiction of a *Kabupaten* Court, or the amount of work of its chairman, the Military Governor may put one or more special chairmen to work at each *Kabupaten* Court.

iii. If one or more special chairmen work at a particular *Kabupaten* Court, the work connected with the administration of justice must be so organised by the chairman of the *Kabupaten* Court that the special chairman/chairmen can hold sittings in the various places considered necessary within the area of jurisdiction.

Article 20

Each sitting of a *Kabupaten* Court is lawful only if that sitting is attended by: chairman, two members and the clerk of the court.

Article 21

The *Kabupaten* Courts shall bring to justice the criminal and civil cases which formerly fell within the competence of the District of Justice.

Section 2. Concerning the laws and procedures which are to be used

Article 22

All regulations which were in force for and were applied by the former district courts of justice shall be in force for and shall be applied by the *Kabupaten* Courts; however, in trying criminal cases the summary procedure must be used as is referred to in Article 337 of the Revised Law Code.

Section 3. Concerning the Prosecutors in the Kabupaten Courts

Article 23

i. The Prosecution in the *Kabupaten* Courts shall be conducted by an officer of the Police of the military government who shall be appointed by the Head of the Detachment of the Military Government Police.

ii. In performing their duties, the prosecutors at the *Kabupaten* Courts shall apply the regulations in force for the "Counsel for the prosecution in the District Courts" as laid down in the Revised Law Code, but in their application of these regulations they must adjust them to present circumstances.

251

Section 4.   Concerning decisions of the Kabupaten Courts

Article 24

No decision of the *Kabupaten* Courts can be reviewed.

Article 25

i. The Prosecutor concerned is the person who must carry out the sentences of the *Kabupaten* Courts.
ii. The methods of carrying out decisions shall be as stipulated in Articles 325 clause 1, 325a, 329, 330, and 331 of the Revised Law Code and Article 11 of the Statute Book on Criminal Law.
iii. If, because of conditions, a sentence of death can not be carried out in accordance with the method described in Article 11 of the Statute Book on Criminal Law, that sentence can be carried out by firing squad.

B.   POLICE COURTS

Article 26

i. There shall be police courts in every *Ketjamatan (Keonderan, Kapanewon)*.
ii. The seat of the police courts shall be the same as the seat of the *Tjamat (Panewon)*.
iii. The area of jurisdiction of the Police Courts shall encompass the area of the *Ketjamatan (Keonderan, Kapanewon)*.

Section 1.   Concerning the structure and powers of the Police Courts

Article 27

The Police Courts shall be composed of the *Tjamat (Panewon)* as Judge and a civil servant to act as Clerk who shall be appointed by the *Bupati*.

Article 28

The Police Courts shall bring to justice all criminal cases which were formerly tried by the Sub-district Courts.

Section2.   Concerning the laws and procedure which are to be used

All regulations which were in force for and were applied by the former Sub-district Courts, shall be in force for and shall be applied by the Police Courts, with the proviso that the application of these regulations shall be adjusted to present circumstances, and that, in

252

trying a case, the summary procedure is to be used which is stipulated in Articles 4a to 4c inclusive of the Sub-district Court Regulations.

Section 3. Concerning the execution of Sentences by the Police Courts

Article 29

The person who shall carry out the sentences imposed by the Police Courts is to be a member of the Military Government Police appointed by the Head of the Sub-Detachment of the Military Government Police.

PART III
CONCERNING THE SPECIAL COURTS

Article 30

i. If in a certain area of Java or Madura no regional military government has yet been set up, the commander of troops no less than one company in size which are present in that area may establish a special court to try all criminal cases in which the accused are both members of the armed forces and civilians; however, should the accused be a member of the armed forces with a rank higher than that of the commander of troops concerned, the said court shall not be entitled to try the case.

ii. Should this latter happen, the officer making the detention concerned shall give the accused over to the commander of the battalion of which the said officer's unit is part.

iii. The powers set forth in clause i. above may also be exercised by the commander of a body of troops no smaller than a company, which is present in a region which, because of enemy activities, has been left by the military government.

iv. The matter referred to in clause ii. above shall also apply in cases where conditions are as stipulated in clause iii.

v. In the exercise of their duties, the special courts referred to in clause i. above shall take as guide the rules laid down in this Regulation.

PART IV
CONCERNING THE METHODS OF CARRYING OUT SENTENCES OF IMPRISONMENT

Article 31

i. If, because of existing conditions, a sentence of imprisonment can not be carried out in the usual way, the method of carrying

253

out that sentence can be replaced by the payment of a fine of Rp. 1.000,— (one thousand rupiahs) for each month or part of a month of the period of imprisonment.

ii. If the payment of a fine in accordance with Article 31 clause i. is not possible, the method of carrying out a sentence of imprisonment can be replaced by a term of forced labour for a period one-half as long as that of the period of imprisonment.

iii. A person undergoing a sentence of forced labour may stay in his own village or in the village where he committed the crime or infringed the law, but he must appear every day to give his labour to the village where he lives, whilst the kind of work that he is to do shall be set by the *Tjamat* whose area covers the said village.

TRANSITIONAL ARTICLE

Article 32

If, before this Regulation comes into force, but subsequent to 19 December 1948, a decision has been reached in a criminal case and a method of carying out a sentence of imprisonment fixed which is at variance from the provisions of this Regulation, then those measures shall be held to be lawful and in accord with this Regulation.

CONCLUDING ARTICLE

Article 33

This Regulations shall come into force at the time of its issue.

Determined at the seat of Command on 7 May 1949.

IN THE NAME OF THE COMMANDER-IN-CHIEF OF THE ARMED FORCES OF THE REPUBLIC OF INDONESIA

(Sgd.) Col. A. H. NASUTION,

Commander of the Army and Java Territorium.

Approved and Ratified on 20 May 1949
ON BEHALF OF THE CENTRAL GOVERNMENT COMMISSION OF JAVA,
in the name of the Minister for Justice,
(Sgd.) I. Kasimo,
Minister for Prosperity/Military Government.

*
* *

F. GUERILLA GOVERNMENT IN THE VILLAGES AND KETJAMATAN

In ordinary warfare there are base regions, connecting regions, and regions of operations; this is the order from the back to the front line. And so there is the base line, lines of communication and front lines; every thing needed moves from the back to the front; the operational fronts develop through the sustenace received from the base lines. For a guerilla war with its pockets there are no front and rear lines. Fighting goes on in all directions; the base is the people, at the very least a part of the people, and the base regions are the hamlets and villages where those people live. Thus there are people who give their full support, there are those who are half and half, and those with a hostile attitude. It is an absolute condition for guerilla warfare to gain control over these people, to attract the assistance of these people.

Even in an atmosphere of revolutionary spirit when revolt is aflame it is still necessary to have an orderly organisation to regulate the people's assistance, to organise and to canalize the people's struggle. This is possible only through the leadership which the people recognise as such, through using the channels which are there already amidst the people. To make new leaders and to create new channels is too difficult and is certain to take a very long time. The people's customary laws, the administrative system, religious matters and other factors will determine the methods of organisation and of canalizing effort.

It was for this reason that, in the midst of our guerilla war against colonialism — which also required that there be efficiency — from the very beginning I always urged that *Pa' Lurah* and his village officers be the leadership of the people in the people's defence. For centuries it is they who have been the heads of the village communities, the heads of their administration, the heads of their institutions of customary law. It is they who are the direct choice of the people. It is they who are the chairmen in the decision-making procedures of the village people. In practice, they are still firmly entrenched in the midst of village society throughout the Country. Centainly, the revolution has shaken their position. The characteristics of many of them are still reminiscent of the feudal era, and in various areas they even form small princedoms. However, the social distinctions continue to be at bottom what they were in

255

former times; the *Lurah* and his village council are still the centre of village life. The authority of the state, the administration of the state which has changed from that of the Dutch to that of the Japanese, then to that of the Republic, with changing cabinets, even with altering structures of provinces, residencies, etc at the higher levels of administration, are all based in the last resort upon *Pa' Lurah* and his village officers, upon the village administration and upon village society. Through religion and the nationalist movement thare have arisen new centres of influence which compete with the village council; the executives of political parties, of co-operatives and of workers' organisations, the Moslem religious leaders and others are also to the fore in village society. In general, however, when conditions are critical, *Pa' Lurah* is still the one and only person to rely upon or to be dependent upon for leadership, although he may be a person lacking in education and general knowledge, lacking understanding of the nationalist movement and of economic matters. In spite of all, his position has existed for many generatins both in the administration and as the leader of customary law; he is felt to be these things and is accepted as such by the village people; he is often considered to be the wealthiest man or the person able to control the ringleaders in the village. The village community cannot change very quickly, the village community is well-known for its conservatism in maintaining traditional knowledge and its non-acceptance of new things. As a community whose thinking is agrarian which lives close to its wet rice fields and its vegetable gardens, such conditions are indeed only usual.

This village community consists of the government's most obedient citizens. Whatever comes from the government is accepted with the utmost loyalty. Agitation and propaganda had been commenced in the colonial period in order to activate and anti-colonial spirit, which was often interpreted as anti — *Lurah*, opposed to paying the *Lurah* through free work on his lands, anti-village work orders, anti-tax, etc. But in my experience in several regions during the First and Second Dutch Attacks, in general this had not yet affected the old relationships greatly, apart from a number of localities. But also how difficult it was to restore stability to the village communities once they had been disrupted by confusion in the administration, by the depredations of armed gangs, or brought to chaotic conditions throught to chaotic conditions through agitation.

In investigating what organisation of the people's defence and what organisation of guerilla government would be most efficient for our needs, I came to the conclusion that it was the structure of the village and the position of the *Lurah* and village officers that must be their foundations. It must not be allowed to happen that these were altered and weakened; on the contrary, they must be maintained and strengthened in order that the fullest possible benefit could be won from them for the people's struggle. The village administration could be given the characteristics of a guerilla administration and be entrusted with its tasks under the authority of military law. The struggle for the de facto authority of the Republic must become a struggle for de facto village administration. Supplies for and costs of the state could be guaranteed only by the village administration its farming community.

Experience frequently showed also that the intellectual levels of the *Lurah* and village officers ought to be raised in order that they might follow the developments confronting them, but in war time it was difficult to make improvements. It was also felt that the area of many villages was no longer in conformity with present conditions; in general their areas were too small to be able to become autonomous guerilla administrations strong enough to be small "de facto Republics". There had indeed been much growth since the bounds of the villages had been set in by-gone times; roads had shortened communication routes and time, the increase of population and expansion had amalgamated several villages into one, and the like. However, for the planner in time of war, it was not possible to seek changes; the most important thing was to care for the existing situation and to draw the greatest possible benefit from it.

Therefore, in composing the guerilla administration, we made the village administration into the lowest authority of the military government. The *Lurah* was provided with assistants — cadres and young men who were chosen by the *Lurah* and trained by the army, who were called village territorial cadres. They became the *Lurah's* most important instruments in dealing with matters of security and defence. Later on the *Pager Desa* were also set up who became "Home Guard" troops for *Pa' Lurah* to carry out guard and other duties required by the army, as a relay pool for couriers, as guides, as orderlies, as soldiers' assistants and to participate actively in guerilla activities.

The village community and administration was intended in the sense of a basic unit of defence, economic and social affairs, able to stand on its own. It was therefore extremely important to convince members of the army they should respect the *Lurah* and his village officers and not order them about or exact demands from them; troops should treat them as though they were their own fathers. At times soldiers wanted to be waited upon as though they were lords in feudal times; they asked for fowls to be cooked; they asked for the head of the family's bedroom as their own. At times village cadres felt more important than the *Lurah*, and considered themselves to be military *Lurah*. Such excesses were of course numerous, for they were caused by the lack of prior preparations and through insufficient understand and lack of intellectual development. It was often considered that the military had the right to give anyone orders. If these things were to occur frequently the name of the army would degenerate in the eyes of the people.

The members and functionaries of the army were required precisely to respect *Pa' Lurah* and his village officers. The army, in fact, ought to assist him in his work. A guerilla army must be felt to be protector and helper of the people. For this reason therefore, there must be specific functionaries for all measures taken in the village, just any soldier might not be allowed to interfere and give orders arbitrarily.

The village guerilla administrations were grouped together in *Ketjamatan*, to which we gave the character of military governments during the war and which came under the commander of the Military Sub-district who was usually a lieutenant. He was the representative of the army who conveyed all requirements to *Pa' Tjamat* for implementation or for forwarding to *Pa' Lurah*. In our methods of guerilla warfare, where the pockets were only of several hours' walking distance in extent, it was these *Ketjamatan* which had the administrative structure with an area sufficiently compact for direct administration. A most it was only the *Ketjamatan* bordering main roads which were cut in two by the enemy patrols along those roads: there were, however, enough gaps for crossing over from side to side and at night time the separation was insignificant. The head of the *Ketjamatan* military government, the Commander of the Military Sub-district, and *Pa' Tjamat* were the leaders for the execution of village defence the guerilla administration. It was they who promoted activity, fostered, co- ordinated and supervised execution in the villages. Of course, excesses often occurred. At times, a too-energetic young officer clashed with an elderly *Pa' Tjamat* who worked slowly and carefully. At times, the village officers felt the Military Sub-district Commander to be a nuisance and somebody dominating over them. Of course, there were many conflicts of authority, for it was only the basic principles which had been set out for the complete whole. And aften the Military Sub-district Commander thought of himself as a little dictator, the person with the greatest authority and power in the whole *Ketjamatan*.

It was therefore of very great importance to create understanding, to provide regulations and give guidance to make the military

258

governments of the *Ketjamatan* and *Kelurahan* sound and to facilitate their work. At the time of the earlier conference on 11 November 1948 in Army Headquarters, Jogja, I had asked the Residents to forward my brochure on village defence to all the *Tjamat* in their territories; it seems that the greater part had not reached their destinations when the Dutch attacked. Delivery in the guerilla period became much more difficult; it was difficult to produce books and difficult to deliver them.

As Commander of the Army, Java Territorium, I gave to Colonel Bambang Supeno, Chief of Staff of Java Territorium. the task of collecting Instructions, Regulations and Directives for the needs of the Military Sub-district Commanders which had been compiled with the help of other ministries, especially that for Internal Affairs. Basic information was needed, understanding of the tasks for the fulfilment of duties, the relative proportions of different authorities; guides for work were needed in defence, economic matters, social affairs, health, police, justice, information, finance, etc.; methods of execution were also necessary which would not weaken existing structures and the village officers and *Lurah*, but, on the contrary, would strengthen them. From the beginning I had been opposed to the structure of people's defence that had been organised earlier by the Ministry of Defence which did not rely upon and was not dependent upon *Pa' Tjamat, Pa' Lurah* and his village officers. Irrespective of the insults of being feudal and colonial which are usually thrown at them because of their history in past times, it was a fact that they are the lawful leaders of the people and that they are recognised by village society.

Thus it was possible for the Headquarters of Java Command to issue the "Working Guide for Military Government in the Ketjamatan", which runs as follows:

WORKING GUIDE FOR MILITARY GOVERNMENT IN THE KETJAMATAN.

A. GENERAL

I CHARACTER AND DUTIES.

The military government is an organ of the state under the protection of the army, which has the obligations:

a. To canalize all forces for defence in our community (the national potential) to the struggle of our state.

b. To unify (co-ordinate) and activate civil manpower.

259

c. To take responsibility for and to execute de facto military defence, de facto administrative defence and the execution of measures for the people's welfare.

EXPLANATION

Re a. What is called society's powers of resistance are all the powers of its people less the minimum of manpower needed for the daily necessities of life.

Re b. The system of working adapted to the *Wehrkreise* calls for the simultaneous co- ordination and activation of all civil manpower. For this purpose, the military government has the obligation of protecting and ensuring the safety of the instruments of the state, for which it must remain above all political parties and groups. This is all the more true when we call to mind the extremely important position of our local government officials in their task of helping to canalize the people's powers of resistance (they have direct contact with the people.)

Re c. These three (de facto military defence, de facto administrative defence and execution of measures for the people's welfare) must be made to work to that total defence can result. For the conduct of that military defence, the military government possesses mobile troops and territorial troops or village guerillas in particular and the whole of the people in general. The presence of general mobilisation gives the right to the head of the military government to mobilise all manpower. The de focto administrative defenceis conducted by the regional head (the Resident, *Bupati* and *Tjamat* of autonomous regions) in the name of and at the tactical instruction of the head of the military government.

II. STRUCTURE

a. Organisation.

The structure from top to bottom is as follows:
1. Commander in Chief of the Armed Forces
2. Commander of the Army and the Java or Sumatra Territorium
3. Military Governor
4. Military District Government *(Keresidenan)*
5. *Kabupaten* Military Government
6. *Ketjamatan* Military Government

For the sake of uniformity and ease in understanding it is better if we use only the following abbreviations:

1. PBAP 2. PTTD/PTTS 3. GM 4. PMD 5. PMKB 6. PMKT [1]).

---

[1]) Translator's Note: These are abbreviations of the Indonesia terms.

b. Officials of the Military Government in Java.

1. The head of the military government in Java is held by the Commander of the Army and the Java Territorium.
2. The post of Military Governor is held by the Divisional Commanders.
   3. The head of the Military District Government is held by the Commanders of the resistance regions/*Wehrkreise*.
4. The head of the *Kabupaten* Military Government is held by the Military District Commanders.
5. The head of the *Ketjamatan* Military Government is held by the Military Sub-district Commanders.

NOTES:

At the level of the Military District Government there are some differences in rank of the heads of the Military District Government; for instance:

1. In Division I, the Brigade Commander is concurrenly both Commander of the Military Sub-Territorium and Head of Military Diatrict Government.
2. In Division III, there are heads of Military District Government who are Brigade Commanders (8 and 10), and there are also those who are Military Sub-Terrirotirum Commanders. This has now been adjusted with the most senior rank.

c. The Staffs of Military Governors, Military District Governments and Kabupaten Military Governments.

The Staff of the Military Governor consists of: a territorial branch from the Divisional Staff under a Middle-ranking Officer, and a civil branch under the civil governor.

The Staff of the Military District Government consists of: a territorial branch from the Sub-Territorial Military Command, and a civil branch under the Resident.

The Staff of the *Kabupaten* Military Government consists of: a territorial branch from the Military District Command, and a civil branch under the *Bupati*.

EXPLANATION.

The Commander of the Army and Java Territorirum by virtue of his post is concurrently the head of the military government (administration), in which task he is assisted by the Ministry of Internal Affairs, bodies from other ministries and the Java Territorial Staff. Political leaderahip is held by the Central Government Commission on Java, of which the Commander of the Army and Java Territorium is a member.

The Military Governors holds the highest authority over defence and the military government and has as executive organs the Division (for defence) and the military government which is composed of a combination of the Territorial Military Government and the civil governor. The Divisional Chief of Staff is concurrently Chief of Staff of the territorial branch of the military government, and the Governor is the chief of staff of the civil branch of the military government.

The Military District Government holds the highest authority over defence and the military government, and also has executive organs in units of troops (brigade and territorial troops) and the military government which is composed of the Military Sub-Territorium Commander (territorial) and the Resident (civil), respectively as chief of staff of the territorial branch of the military government and chief of staff of the civil branch of the military government.

The *Kabupaten* Military Government is in the hands of the Commander of the Military District as its head, while the executive organs under it are the Military District Commander as chief of staff of the territoriral branch of the military government and the *Bupati* as the chief of staff of the civil branch of the military government.

NOTES:

In general, from this level down, the commanders of the sub-*Wehrkreise*, the (battle) sector and sub-sector do not concurrently hold office in the *Kabupaten* and *Ketjamatan* military governments, because these become increasingly executive organs in which it is felt to be increasingly difficult to unite the responsibilities for fighting and for administration.

EXPLANATION OF THE DIAGRAM SHOWING THE STRUCTURE OF
THE MILITARY GOVERNMENT.

1. The diagram clarifies the limits of authority of the commander of a unit of troops who is concurrently a head of the military government.

2. Military Governors and heads of military governments of localities which are Residencies possess two staffs:

   a. A military staff and,
   b. An administrative staff.

262

3. The military staff is the one to attend especially to military matters, whilst the administrative staff attends to everything concerning the administration of the military government.

4. The heads of lower level military governments (from the military governments in localities which are *Kabupaten* downwards) only possess an administrative staff alone because this post is not held concurrently by the commander of a unit of troops.

5. This administrative staff is one which is given its duties by the territorial staff together with the staff of the civil administration.

6. a. The head of military government in localities which are *Kabupaten* is not a post held concurrently by a battalion commander in view of:

   * His duty in his unit is as the executive of the military unit, and therefore the commander can not possibly be concurrently the head of the military government, for this is also a task as executive in matters of military goverment and could thus interfere with/over-burden his duty as commander of the military unit.
   * To be concurrently head of the military government would tie him down because of its geographical character, and this could interfere with his mobility.

   b. Wherever conditions require it, a battalion commander may temporarily hold concurrently the post of head of the military government at the directive of the commander of a resistance area, until such time as conditions allow of the post of head of the military government being taken over by the Military District Commander.

7. In execution of the military government it must not be allowed to happen that the community feels that there are two authorities in existence, namely the military authority and the civil government authority. The community must feel that there is only one authority of the Government in existence and that is none other than the authority of the military government alone. The diagram affirms the existence of a single authority by a double line showing the hierarchy from the top down and, vice — versa, from the bottom up.

8. In the ranks of the civil government there is still a direct connection from the top to lower levels, shown in the diagram by: ...... This connection is not one of authority but merely has the character of control, stimulation, and investigation.

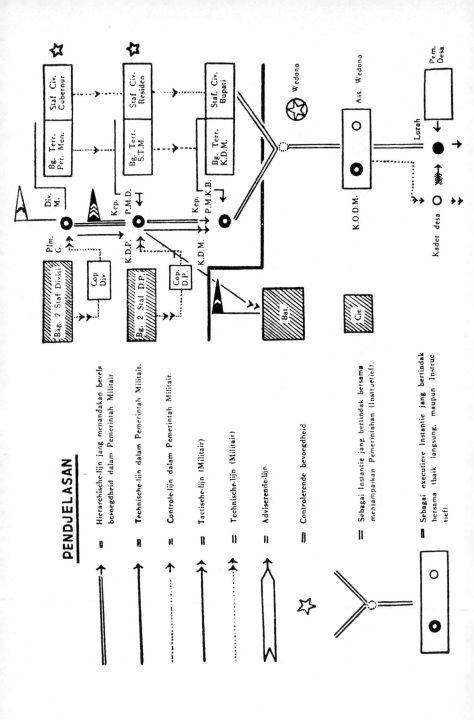

PENDJELASAN

Hierarchische-lijn jang menandakan bevels bevoegdheid dalam Pemerintah Militair.

Technische-lijn dalam Pemerintah Militair.

Controle-lijn dalam Pemerintah Militair.

Tactische-lijn (Militair)

Technische-lijn (Militair)

Adviserende-lijn.

Controlerende bevoegdheid.

Sebagai Instantie jang bertindak bersama menjampaikan Pemerintahan (Instructief).

Sebagai executieve Instantie jang bertindak bersama (baik langsung, maupun Instructief)

PENDJELASAN		CLARIFICATION
Hierarchische-lijn jang menandakan bevels bevoegdheid dalam Pemerintahan Militer	=	Hierarchy-lines which indicate competence-orders in the Military Government.
Technische-lijn dalam Pemerintahan Militer	=	Technical line in the Military Government.
Controle-lijn dalam Pemerintah Militer	=	Control-line in the Military Government.
Tactische-lijn (Militair)	=	Military tactical line.
Technische-lijn (Militair)	=	Military Technical line.
Adviserend-lijn	=	Advising line.
Controlerende bevoegdheid	=	Controlled competence.
Sebagai instantie jang bertindak bersama menjampaikan Pemerintahan (Instructief)	=	As an Instance which jointly carries out instructive (Government) Policy.
Sebagai executive Instantie jang bertindak bersama (baik langsung, maupun Instructief)	=	As an executive Instance which jointly carries out (direct and instructive).
Schema Susunan Pemerintahan Militer	=	Scheme of the Military Government.
Plm. Div. G.M.	=	Division Commander of the Military Government.
Bag. 2 Staf Divisi	=	Section 2 of Division Staff.
Bg. Terr. Per. Men.	=	Territorial Section Senior Officers.
Staf Civ. Gubernur	=	Governor Civil Staff.
Cop. Div.	=	Division Operational Commander.
Kep. P.M.D.	=	Head Territorial Military Government.
K.D.P.	=	Regional Operation Command.
Bg. 2 Staf D.P.	=	Section 2 Regional Operation.
Bg. Terr. S.T.M.	=	Territorial Section of Military Terr. Staff.
Cop. D.P.	=	Regional Operation Commander.

K.D.M.	=	Military Regional Command.
Kep. P.M.K.B.	=	Head of Military Government of Towns.
Bat.	=	Battalion.
Cie	=	Company.
Bg. Terr. K.D.M.	=	Territorial Section for Military Regional Command.
Staf Civ. Bupati	=	Civil Staff of Bupati.
Wedono	=	District head.
K.O.D.M.	=	Sub Military District Command.
Ass. Wedono	=	Under District Head.
Lurah	=	Village Head.
Kader Desa	=	Village Cadre.
Pem. Desa	=	Village Administration.
Org. Pertahanan Desa Rakjat	=	Organisation of Village People Defence.

---

9. In consequence of history and of the people's deeply-rooted ideas, the *Bupati, Tjamat* and *Lurah* are the figures who provide a specific hold in the people's eyes for their understanding of government and its existence. Therefore, beginning from the military governments of *Kabupaten* and Sub-districts it is necessary to have an attitude made manifest in joint action — joint action by the Military District Commander together with the *Bupati*, and joint action by the Military Sub-district Commander with the *Tjamat*, in the sense of the powers of the military government (the existence of a single authority alone) concerned with dealing with the execution of the tasks of civil administration (such as collection of taxes, the gathering of foodstuffs, etc). These matters continue to be conducted by the *Tjamat* and *Lurah* as members of the civil administration (see clarification issued by the Headquarters of Java Command, dated 1 January 1949, No. 15 MBKD/49).

10. In the military government, the *Wedana* are officials included in the staff of the *Kabupaten* military government as supervising officers (on tour).

11. The *Lurah* are the ultimate cells of the military government. Village and Hamlet Cadres are the *Lurah's* assistants in questions related to village defence.

12. The thick line (———) in the diagram shows the legislative and executive authority.

Further elucidation appears unnecessary.

B. KETJAMATAN MILITARY GOVERNMENT.

I. STRUCTURE.

The post of head of the *Ketjamatan* Military Government is held by the Commander of the Military Sub-district, who is assisted by the staff of the military government.

This staff consists of military members of the Military Sub-district Command and civil officials under command of the Military Sub-district Commander as head of the *Ketjamatan* Military Government. The two together constitute a single staff in which there are four divisions:

a. General affairs
b. Economic affairs
c. Social affairs
d. Defence.

NOTES

This does not mean that the Military Sub-district Command takes on the form of the *Ketjamatan* Military Government, or that the civil departments under the *Tjamat* are abolished. Both the Military Sub-district Command and the civil organisation continue to exist, and must even be strengthened. A part of the employees of the civil departments, in keeping with their respective capabilities, are united into the staff of the *Ketjamatan* Military Government, with the obligation of assisting the head of the *Ketjamatan* Military Government in solving many different kinds of problems, in investigation, in carrying out undertakings, in activating and uniting military and civil departments with parallel work, and the like.

Additional.

In forming this staff it is permissible to take outside personnel. For example: evacuees personnel from other services or students.

In this case, the most thorough investigation must be made into the origins, etc, of this personnel; it must be guarded against that enemy agents or disruptors are not included.

Relative Degrees of Authority.

The position of the *Tjamat* in this staff is directly under the *Ketjamatan* Military Government, which is responsible for total defence in the bounds of the *Ketjamatan.* Questions which arise must be solved jointly and external measures must also be taken jointly.

Should the Head of the *Ketjamatan* Military Government be prevented from performing his duties, it is the Deputy Commander of the Military Sub-district who deputises for him, and not the *Tjamat.*

The Method of Settling Differences of Opinion.

Should there be a difference of opinion regarding execution of the tasks of the military government which are concerned with civil affairs and/or the general public, the *Tjamat (Panewu)* has the right to submit his objections to the Head of the *Ketjamatan* Military Government who shall make a decision in agreement with the *Bupati.* Should such agreement not be reached, it shall be the Head of the Military District Government who has the right to make a decision after hearing the points submitted for his consideration by the Resident.

II. TASKS.

As the highest agency within the bounds of the *Ketjamatan*, the *Ketjamatan* Military Government is charged with the conduct of total defence within that area, that is:

1. De focto military defence
2. De facto administrative defence
3. The well-being of the people.

1. DE FACTO MILITARY DEFENCE.

The territorial task is: to supply the armed forces, to see to security, recreation, information, communications, social care, family care and order.

The task of the people's defence is:

> Passive: Signalling the enemy's position, ensuring that the people are ready to participate, preparing for evacuation and for the contribution of such manpower, wealth, domestic animals etc as may be needed.

> Active: Upsetting traffic and communications, harassing estates, collaborators, etc.

The direct duty in assisting operations lies primarily in the making of investigations, as guides and as persons completing scroched earth tactics.

The position of the Village and Hamlet Cadres is as assistants to the *Lurah* in the execution of his day-to-day duties.

The position of the *Pager Desa* (the village guerilla units) is as the cells of the people's defence in the village.

2. DE FACTO ADMINISTRATIVE DEFENCE.

The civil departments as services under the *Tjamat (Panewu)* perform the task of de facto administrativ defence in the name of the *Ketjamatan* Military Government.

For the tasks of de facto administrative defence see the brochure by Colonel Nasution entitled *Guides for Village Defence by Local Government and Village Officials'*.

On the one hand, the purpose is that the Dutch will be unable to establish an administration, and, on the other, that the administration of the Republic of Indonesia will continue to operate by means of playing "hide and seek" with the enemy.

* Eliminate collaborators.
* Ensure security and proper working methods for local government and village officials.

SCHEMA
PEMERINTAH MILITER KETJAMATAN

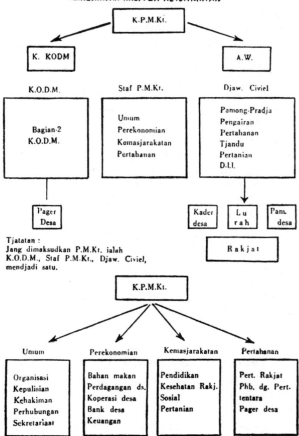

K.P.M.Kt.

K. KODM

A.W.

K.O.D.M.

Staf P.M.Kt.

Djaw. Civiel

Bagian-2
K.O.D.M.

Umum
Perekonomian
Kemasjarakatan
Pertahanan

Pamong-Pradja
Pengairan
Pertahanan
Tjandu
Pertanian
D.l.l.

Pager
Desa

Kader
desa

L u
r a h

Pam.
desa

Tjatatan :
Jang dimaksudkan P.M.Kt. ialah
K.O.D.M., Staf P.M.Kt., Djaw. Civiel,
mendjadi satu.

R a k j a t

K.P.M.Kt.

Umum

Perekonomian

Kemasjarakatan

Pertahanan

Organisasi
Kepulisian
Kehakiman
Perhubungan
Sekretariaat

Bahan makan
Perdagangan ds.
Koperasi desa
Bank desa
Keuangan

Pendidikan
Kesehatan Rakj.
Sosial
Pertanian

Pert. Rakjat
Phb. dg. Pert.
tentara
Pager desa

CLARIFICATION
SCHEMA
SCHEME

Pemerintah Militer Ketjamatan	=	Ketjamatan Military Government.
K.P.M. Kt.	=	Head of Military Government Ketjamatan.
K. K.O.D.M.	=	Head Sub Military District Command.
A.W.	=	Assisten Wedono (Under District Head).
K.O.D.M.	=	Sub Military District Command.
Bagian-bagian K.O.D.M.	=	Sections of Sub Military District Command.
Pager Desa	=	Village Guard.
Staf P.M. Kt.	=	Ketjamatan Military Government Staff.
Umum	=	In General.
Perekonomian	=	Economy.
Kemasjarakatan	=	Society.
Pertahanan	=	Defence.
Djaw. Civiel	=	Civil Instance.
Pamong Pradja	=	Government Officials (Civil servants).
Pengairan	=	Irrigation.
D.l.l.	=	etc. (and so forth).
Kader Desa	=	Village Cadre.
Lurah	=	Lurah.
Pem. Desa	=	Village Officials.
Rakjat	=	People.
Tjatatan:		Note:
Jang dimaksudkan P.M.Kt. ialah K.O.D.M., Staf P.M.-Kt. Djaw. Civiel, mendjadi satu	=	What is meant by Ketjamatan Military Government is that Sub Military District Command, Ketjamatan Military Government Staff, Civil, Instance, become one.

271

K.P.M.Kt.	=	Head of Ketjamatan Military Government.
Organisasi	=	Organisation.
Kepolisian	=	Police.
Kehakiman	=	Justice.
Perhubungan	=	Communication.
Sekretariat	=	Secretariat.
Bahan Makanan	=	Food stuffs.
Perdagangan d.l.l.	=	Trade etc.
Koperasi Desa	=	Village Co-operation.
Bank Desa	=	Village Bank.
Keuangan	=	Finance.
Pendidikan	=	Education.
Kesehatan Rakjat	=	People's Health.
Sosial	=	Social.
Pertanian	=	Agriculture.
Pert. Rakjat	=	People Defence.
Phb. dg. Pert. Tentara	=	Communiaction with Military Defence.
Pager Desa	=	Village guard.

* See to information.
* Ensure the continued existence of order, operation of the law, collection of taxes, etc.

THE WELL-BEING OF THE PEOPLE.

Apart from the duties described above under Section 2, the civil departments as agencies under the *Tjamat (Panewu)* also conduct efforts in the name of the *Ketjamatan* Military Government to ensure the well-being of the people.

Duties for Ensuring the People's Well-being.

As the basis for a long struggle, the people must feel and be fully aware that they struggle with their blood and sweat for their own happiness.

The people have already experienced the cruelties of the enemy, and are in a position to compare Dutch times with Japanese times and with the period of Independence. The people have already felt the benefit of land reform (conversion, etc). At bottom, the peple struggle for the own interests. For that reason we must make efforts at all times to improve their conditions in questions of economic matters, education, health and the like.

CLARIFICATION.

It is clear from the above that questions related to de facto military defence are left to the Military Sub-district Command, whilst questions related to de facto administration and securing welfare for the people are left to the *Tjamat (Panewu)* for forwarding to and execution by the civil departments and by the people. It is to be noted that both these agencies perform their tasks in the name of the *Ketjamatan* Military Government.

By this means the military and civil tasks can be differentiated so that all tasks can be performed under the supervision and protection of the *Ketjamatan* Military Government and so that confusion of tasks is not necessary.

CLARIFICATION CONCERNING RIGHTS AND POSITION.

Rights.

The rights of the reads of the Military Government above the level of the Ketjamatan Military Government is a legislative (planning) right, and for that reason they have the right to issue regulations with punitive sanctions, while the Head of the

Ketjamatan Military Government merely possesses an executive right, meaning that he merely executes the regulations from his superiors. Should the interests of the area bring him to issue his own regulations, the Head of the *Ketjamatan* Military Government may issue special regulations so long as they do not conflict with the regulations from his superiors and have no power of sanctions. If sanctions appear necessary, proposals should be made to this end to the *Kabupaten* Military Government. It must be noted that the military government as we intend it may not take the form of a military dictatorship in which members of the armed forces take direct action with regard to the people. All measures and all connections with the people must be made through the *Tjamat (Panewu)*.

Position.

From the outline above the conclusion can be drawn that the position of the military government constitutes the second line of defence of the State, behind the mobile defence.

From the structure of the military government it is clear that the *Ketjamatan* Military Government, as the lowest military agency which executes regulations via the *Tjamat (Panewu)* isho sends them to the Village Heads for forwarding to the people, occupies the most important position and the heaviest obligations. Therefore, the *Ketjamatan* Military Government needs to exercise tact and wisdom in performing its tasks in order to ensure the smooth operation of the military government. It can be said that the *Ketjamatan* Military Governments are the foundations and the backbone of the military government in general, because it is plainly evident that our total defence is based upon all the strength which there is in the people.

POLICY IN THE EXECUTION OF TASKS.

One command.

Although there must be a single command, in the execution of day-today tasks joint measures are badly needed by the *Tjamat* and the Head of the *Ketjamatan* Military Government.

When we think of it, we recall that our commanders who head military areas are usually still young without much experience, whilst the civilian head is usually on in years, with much experience and an understanding of the ins and outs of matters concerning his area, especially that he knows the spirit of his people. Indeed the position of local government officials amongst us is that of a service known to have grown up historically with our people in the villages, so that a change in the administrative measures in the village or a change in the hierarchy could easily cause undesirable sentiments. Automatically it would not facilitate the conduct of the military government. It must be noted that any split between the civilian and military heads of a region must be avoided, because it creates a gap which would gives grounds to the enemy for using all efforts to fill it — for example, by making propaganda which enlarges the split, by using, directly or indirectly, the forces of the people's political parties with the objective of overthrowing our government.

Questions of Sentiment and the Working-place.

On the part of both civil and military authorities the question of sentiment does not need to be sharpened. At times a situation is foundfound in which the Military Sub-district Commander who now must hold the wheel in the *Ketjamatan* Military Government feels himself a cut above the *Tjamat (Panewu)* because of his rank and duty; whilst on the other hand the *Tjamat* likewise feels superior to the Commander of the Military Sub-district, because of the former position of the Military Sub-district functionary. Under such conditions, it will surely be difficult to reach good co-operation for the sake of the state. It is recommended that each person places his duty first, especially his obligations as a leader of the struggle in the area of the *Ketjamatan*, because within the bounds of the *Ketjamatan* all activities of those two leaders must be an example to be followed by all of the common people who are under their leadership. How good it would be if the head of the *Ketjamatan* Military Government always used the opportunity to make himself known to the people in that *Ketjamatan* in the company of the *Tjamat (Panewu)*, in order to make close spiritual contact and, in the first place, to see with his own eyes the difficulties being suffered by the people.

For example, every opportunity must be used to come face to face with the people to build their spirit of struggle to a blaze. For instance on anniversaries or national holdays, at times of disaster, and the like.

Conditions of war bring with them the situation that each government agency has its place of work wherever the officials concerned have evacuated, and therefore it does happen at times that the working place of the Military Sub-district Command is very far away from the civilian place of work. In view of the need for speed and especially to avoid the possibility of misunderstandings arising, endeavours must be made to ensure that the offices of the civil and military heads of the military government are united in one place.

275

The Functioning of Autonomy in the Ketjamatan Military Government.

The working instruction for the military government stipulates that the autonomy of Military Sub-districts is a part of the character of *Wehrkreise* of these Sub-districts on the basis of the fact that, in general, the Military Sub-district is the largest compact area.

During the six months in which the military government has functioned it has been shown that:

a. Communications between the pockets are sufficiently ensured so that in general the leadership of the *Kabupaten* Military Government is quickly able to give leadership to the whole or to the greater part of the area of its *Kabupaten*.

b. There is a shortage of staff for the leadership of *Ketjamatan* Military Governments. Because of this development, it is necessary in future to centralise and concentrate authority as far as possible at the level of the *Kabupaten* Military Government for the sake of stability of the administration.

Basically, autonomy for the *Ketjamatan* Military Government operates as follows:

i. The autonomy of the *Ketjamatan* Military Government is a division of the autonomy of the *Kabupaten* Military Government, accorded it because tactical conditions have split up the *Kabupaten* in such a way that it was necessary to delegate that autonomy to lower agencies (the *Ketjamatan* Military Government).

ii. The Military Governors or the Military Region Governments authorised to do so by the Military Governor because of tactical conditions, especially communications, may transfer and decrease the autonomy of the *Ketjamatan* Military Governments by transferring/returning it to the *Kabupaten* Military Government.

EXPLANATION.

On the other side of the coin to the great aptness of the *Wehrkreise* system there is some danger or a shortcoming that may be detrimental, because it gives priority to the interests of lesser regions above the interests of greater regions, and is thus detrimental to a wider affiliation.

Implementation of the automomy of *Ketjamatan* Military Government in the ways outlined above will guarantee the wider interest. In practice, it is usual for the *Kabupaten* Military Government to determine which rights and duties it needs to and can transfer to the *Ketjamatan* Military Government, and similarly also the *Kabupaten* Military Government may alter/annul any of the regulations of the *Ketjamatan* Military Governments which it considers necessary.

By the *Kabupaten* Military Government is also meant those *Kabupaten* Military Governments which have arisen because of conditions, for instance when a Military Region Command becomes cut up into two or more parts, as often happens, with one part led by the Military Region Commander/*Bupati*, whilst the other is led by the Deputy Commander of the Military Region/*Patih*, and the like.

A. The General Section of the Staff sees to:
    a. Organisation
    b. Police
    c. Justice
    d. Communications
    e. Secretariat.

B. The Economic Section of the Staff regulates:
    a. The economic blockade
    b. Economic connections with supply in general
    c. Endeavours concerning finance, equipment and armaments
    d. The defence bank.

C. The Social Section of the Staff regulates:
    a. Social affairs
    b. Education
    c. Information
    d. Public Health.

D. The Defence Section of the Staff regulates:
    a. The Village Home Guard/People's defence
    b. Intelligence investigations.

A. GENERAL AFFAIRS.

THE SPECIAL DUTIES OF EACH MEMBER OF THE STAFF.

a. Organisation.

Personnel and Documentation are included under the Organisation subsection. The Personnel service must pay attention to competence, industriousness, capacity, the actual product of work, the spirit and discipline of members of the staff. To meet this requirement, changes must be made in the personnel (for example, their replacement, removal, dismissal and the increase or decrease of staff). In receiving new personnel it is necessary to exercise very careful watch over their acceptance. Every new member who joins up and is accepted must bring clear references as to why he left his former place and what was his former field of duty (for example, the unit/department is no longer intact and/or how to contact his former superiors, and the like). Should it be shown that he is still needed by his former unit/departement he must be returned to that agency Similarly also with deserters.

Notes.

The placing of labour has very great influence upon the operation of the military government, while the position of the military government is important in the struggle at this time.

Especially is this true with regard to personnel from the Security and Economic sections which at this time constitute the arteries of our military government. The situation here should be corrected as quickly as possible and then the work should be entrusted to those of our soldiers who are honest, capable and have a patriotic spirit. Just and strong measures must be taken against those doing dishonest things.

Experience in military matters, administration, etc, are absolute conditions for carrying out duties.

POLICE.

On the basis of Order of the Day No. 106/MBKD/PTTD/49, Military Government Police are to be set up by means of amalganating the Military Police of the Military Regions and the State Police, with the exception of the mobile units of the Military Police and the Mobile Brigade of the State Police. Full police powers are given to the Military Goverment Police as have been given already to the Military Region Military Police and to the State Police.

The duty of the Military Government Police is to strengthen the guard over security and public order in this time of war, and also especially to use all their powers to save the State from the activities of destructive elements.

When confronting a problem which calls for additional strength, the Military Government Police have the right to ask for assistance from troops of the nearest territorial or mobile command, and this request may not be rejected.

All central equipment and finances of the Military Government Police are seen to by the Central Military Government, whilst their regional equipment and finances are seen to by the Military Governors. It is stipulated that the amalgamation of the Military Region Military Police and the State Police in the Military

Government Police is of a technical character and having to do with instructions, while organisationally-administratively, each group continues to be seen to separately (by the State Police and the Military Region Military Police).

The Military Government Police in the Military Sub-district Command.

In accordance with the joint instruction of the State Police and the Military Region Military Police, a sub-detachment of the Military Government Police is placed in every Military Sub-district, which also has posts of the Military Government Police.

Organisation.

Every sub-detachment of the Military Government Police shall have commander and a deputy-commander. Should the commander be a man from the State Police, his deputy must be drawn from the Military Region Military Police, and vise-versa.

Duties.

Apart from endeavours to ensure that members of the shock-troops are always in readiness, the Sub-detachment Commander must himself lead and give directives to the posts of the Military Government Police. Further, he is also responsible for training the village cadres and the village police in marching and making investigations, in order that they may give their backing to the Military Government Police in watching over destructive elements, secret saboteurs and provocateurs. A guard is mounted night and day in the Sub-detachment. The section for dealing with the investigation of court cases consists of a head and four assistants.

Thirty men are placed in a Sub-detachment, completely armed in the ratio of 1 : 1, to be used as shock-troops and for patrols in brigade formation to places where this is considered necessary.

Fifteen watchmen are placed at each post, who are divided into three shifts if conditions are critical. These posts operate a watch guard under fixed arrangements. Should there be a case to be investigated for forwarding to the courts, it must be sent to the Sub-detachment.

In posts at the front, there must be a front intelligence officer and also a section for the investigation of cases which is seconded to the front Commander for the investigation of cases at the front and then for their submission to a front Judge.

279

Leadership.

The general leadership of the Military Government Police in the Military Sub-district Commands is held by the Commander of the Military Sub-district who entrusts the day-to day leadership to the Sub-detachment Commander of the Military Government Police.

The Sub-detachment Commander of the Military Government Police in the areas under Military Sub-district Commands is appointed by the Commander of the Military Government Police Detachment.

Accountability.

In the day-to-day leadership, the commander of a post of the Military Government Police is responsible to the Commander of the Military Government Police Sub-detachment, while the Commander of the Military Government Police Sub-detachment is responsible to the Commander of a Detachment of the Military Government Police.

In the general leadership, those commanders are responsible to the respective heads of the regional Military Govrnment.

Should there be a difference of opinion about an order on some matter calling for immediate measures between the commanders of the Detachment and Sub-detachment, or between a post of the Military Government Police on the one hand and the head of the regional Military Government (Commander of a Military District/Commander of a Military Sub-district) on the other, the order of the head of the regional Military Government concerned shall be executed in the first place. Then the commander involved has the right to bring the matter before his superios for their consideration. This agency is obliged to investigate and to present its considered opinion to the head of the regional Military Government concerned who must reach a decision and must inform the two parties in the Military Government Police of that decision.

Connections in the Execution of Duties.

It is obligatory for members of the Military Government Police to work as closely as possible with the local government officials and the village officials who are obliged by the Revised Law Code, and other civil servants who are obliged by special statutes, to carry out police duties.

THE ADMINISTRATION OF JUSTICE.

Justice shall be administered in accordance with the Directive of the Commander in Chief on "Emergency Regulation" governing

Military Courts of the Military Government, governing Civil Courts of the Military Government, concerning Special Military Tribunals and concerning the Method of Executing Sentences of Imprisonment."

The following explanation deals only with what concerns the Military Sub-district Commands.

The structure and authority of the military courts of the military government are as follows:

Military courts of the Military Sub-districts operate within the borders of the Military Sub-district.

The seat of the Military Court of a Military Sub-district shall be the same as that of the Commander of the Military Sub-district.

The region under the jurisdiction of the Military Court of a Military Sub-district covers the Military Sub-district. The Military Court of a Military Sub-district consists of the Commander of the Military Sub-district as President, two first officers as members who are appointed by the Commander of the Military District, and a member of the Armed Forces as Clerk of the Court who is appointed by the Commander of the Military Sub-district.

The Military Courts of Military Sub-districts shall bring to justice all cases of crime and infringement of the law which are committed in the area under their jurisdiction by members of the Armed Forces of the rank of non-commissioned officers and soldiers. Should a crime or infringement of the law be committed by a non-commissioned officer or soldier together with an officer, the Military Court of the Military Sub-district shall not have the right to bring that case to justice.

Notes:

1. All cases of crime and infringement of the law committed by members of the Armed Forces with the rank of first officer below that of captain, or committed together with non-commissioned officers or soldiers, or together with a civilian, shall be brought to justice in a Military District Military Court.

2. All cases of crime and infringement of the law committed by members of the Armed Forces with the rank of first officer from that of captain up to and including that of lieutenant-colonel, shall be brought to justice in the Military Governors' Military Courts.

3. What is meant by members of the Armed Forces is members of the Army, the Navy and the Air Force who have been militarised and permanent civil servants who work in the Armed Forces.

Laws and Procedures which are to be Used.

The criminal laws to be applied by the military courts of the military government mentioned above are:

The Military Criminal Code as revised;

The Criminal Code as revised by Statute No. 1/1946;

The Act concerning criminal law (Statute No. 1/1946);

. Other Statutes and Regulations containing provisions for criminal law.

The procedure which is to be used by military courts of the military government is a summary procedure guided by the provisions of Article 3377 of the Revised Law Code.

Concerning the Prosecution at Military Courts of the Military Government.

In the military courts of the military government, the prosecution in those courts shall be conducted by a first officer apointed by the Head of the Sub-detachment of the Military Government Police.

Concerning Judgements of the Military Courts of the Military Government.

No judgement made by the military courts of the military government, whether by the Military Governors' Military Courts, the Military Districts' Military Courts or the Military Sub-districts' Military Courts, can be revised.

All judgements by the military courts of the military government shall be put into effect in a period not exceeding 7 (seven) days after the judgment has been pronounced.

The Prosecutor concerned is the person who must carry into effect the judgement of a military court of the military government.

The Civil Courts of the Military Government.

The civil courts of justice throughout Java and Madura are to be abolished and replaced by Civil Courts of the Military Government.

The Civil Courts of the Military Government are divided into:

a. Kabupaten.

b. Police Courts.

Police Courts.

There shall be a Police Court in every *Ketjamatan (Kepanewon).* The seat of the Police Court shall be the same as that of the

Tjamat (Panewu).

The area under the jurisdiction of a Police Court shall cover the area of the *Ketjamatan (Kepanewon).*

Structure and Powers of the Police Courts.

The Police Courts shall be composed of the *Tjamat (Panewu)* as judge and a civil servant appointed by the *Bupati* as clerk.

The Police Courts shall try all criminal cases which were formerly brought to justice by the District Courts.

Laws and Procedure to be Used.

All regulations which were in force for and were applied by the former District Courts shall be in force for and shall be applied by the Police Courts, with the proviso that the application of those regulations must be adjusted to present conditions and that the summary procedure referred to in Articles 4a to 4c inclusive of the District Court Procedure shall be used in trying cases.

Carrying Out of Judgements by Police Courts.

The person who must carry out the judgments of a Police Court is a member of the Military Government Police who is appointed by the head of the Sub-detachment of the Military Government Police.

Method of Executing Sentences of Imprisonment.

If a sentence of imprisonment cannot be executed in the ordinary way because of present conditions, then the methods of executing that sentence of imprisonment can be replaced by the payment of a fine amounting to Rp. 1000.— (one thousand rupiahs) for every month or part of a month of the prison sentence.

Should the payment of a fine as intended in the articles of the regulation governing the Military Government Judicature likewise not be possible, then the method of executing the sentence of imprisonment may be replaced by forced labour for a period one-half the length of time of the sentence of imprisonment which should be carried out.

Persons undergoing a sentence of forced labour may live in their own village or in the village in which they committed the crime or infringed the law, but they must come every day to give their labour to the Head of the Village in which they live, whilst the type of work which they are to do is to be determined by the *Tjamat* whose area encompasses the said village.

For clarity, please read the Regulation governing Military Government Courts.

COMMUNICATIONS.

By Communications is meant here: the delivery of letters, the distribution and communication of news (verbal of written) by use of permanent couriers or by relay-runners. A chain of communications must be set up in such a way so that, even though the leadership is far from its seat, it will still be able to conduct its leadership and also will at all times be able to control the situation. For this purpose an officer and as many assistants as are needed may be appointed who have the duty of organising, maintaining and controlling the orderly and effective conduct of communication. Because communications are the soul of a Command, attention must be paid to such questions as the following:

   i. Establishing contact with the tactical Commanders asking information from them about the placing of their troops and security conditions in areas through which couriers will perhaps have to pass.

   ii. a. In consideration of the results obtained from poin i. above, a system of relay couriers is to be planned, taking geographical conditions and the situation into account, in which the distance between each relay post shall be a minimun of 5 hours' walking distance.

   ii. b. Giving responsibility for each relay stage to a specific communications post which is to carry out the work of communication.

   iii. Determining fixed times for the (periodical) departure from each courier post.

   iv. Making a selection from among the couriers at present being used; in view of the numbers of personnel who must fulfil the needs of point in ii above, they must be selected and must meet with certain conditions, including:

     a. Must have a great sense of responsibility for the delivery of letters or other things entrusted to them.

     b. Must be able to endure walking long distances at a fast pace.

     c. Must be possessed of considerable initiative and many ideas for surmounting the many difficulties which will possible obstruct their journeys.

   v. Providing information about the codes for classification of the documents, for instance:

284

a. "Express"
b. "Immediate"
c. "Ordinary"

a. *"Express"*

* Orders for tactics which will be useless if they are too late.
* Reports on the conduct of tactics which require answers/ further orders.
* Suggestions to superiors in order to avoid precipitate decisions or decisions which are incorrect due to changed circumstances.
* Tactical reports concerned altered tactical conditions which would be dangerous to those concerned if they do not, or do not yet, know of them.

b. *"Immediate"*

* Tactical Orders which in view of time, distance and geographical conditions would arrive too late by ordinary means (needing a big time margin).
* Ordinary letters which through mistakes in transmission can no longer be delivered in accordance with the schedule fixed.

c. *"Ordinary"*

* Documents not included in a. and b. above.
* Documents not On Service (private correspondence).

vi. Investigating/ordering the investigation of the implementation of regulations or plans which are being/have been carried out, and reporting the results of the investigation.

vii. a. Investigating and making use of the possibility of using transport (bicycles, horses, vehicles, etc) in the respective region to speed up the despatch of news/documents.

   b. Making contact with the respective Staff I concerning the use of enemy vehicles or means of transport. For example, for communication with units cut off by enemy areas endeavours should be made to deliver documents by vehicular transport (the enemy's aircraft, trains, bus services, etc).

viii. Giving pseudonyms to communications posts. This is necessary for the protection of security, and all the more so if the posts lie in an area patrolled or occupied by the enemy. For example, the relay post of an X-post is called "Sastro"; the village cadres only know Mr Sastro and do not need to know what Mr Sastro's function is. The same thing is done with the next post in line and therefore if someone asks, the only answer possible is that a person has "gone to see Mr Sastro", so that somenane's going to a post can be taken to mean a family visit.

Communications Security.

Each post is not an ordinary quarter, but is a place kept secret from the public. The site of the post moves around within its *rayon* in line with battle conditions, but continuing to keep in touch with other posts, units of troops or agencies which are nearby.

Usually a post consists of several houses which are scattered here and there: somewhere for receiving visitors and working, somewhere for sleeping, and a place in reserve. Besides this there are already posts in reserve to north, east, south and west, to be used if it is necessary to move. The posts are hidden and the staff is disguised as ordinary people.

Ordinary letters are to be burnt after the contents have been thoroughly studied and the letter has been registered in code in a book held by the head of the post. Only important documents, such as basic instructions etc, and letters to be forwarded are kept in the post and these are hidden away also.

Commanders should endeavour to decrease the number of letters and to convey news and orders verbally by officers. But for the sake of documentation the posts possess books such as the one mentioned above in which all important incidents are written down in code, so that the head of the post can write a complete report later on when the war is over. It will be proved in the future how important is the documentation of our struggle now.

Couriers

These posts and also the commanders have their own couriers whom they have trained themselves. For the weekly contact between post and post an officer (student) should be used.

Speed

Constant efforts must be made to increase the speed of communications but the absolute condition for communication is that it is fast and exact. By improving the ways of making the journey, the time taken can be shortened.

Always Prepared

Every post must be prepared at all times to face the possibility of a mopping-up action, if necessary it should remove immediately. Clothing, goods and documents must always be ready to be concealed or to be removed.

Codes

Member of a post and the couriers must use different names and a code on their journey in accordance with what is determined by each head of a post for his subordinates.

SECRETARIAT

The composition of the secretariat is to be:

1. Secretary
2. Editor (Order and Correspondence Section)
3. Letter-register clerk
4. Outgoing Letter clerk
5. File clerk
6. Typists
7. Despatch clerk.

The work of these various functions/sections is:

1. Secretary:
   a. To be head of the Secretariat.
   b. To distribute the letters for sections, obtaining receipts in the letter-register book at the instruction of the Head of the Ketjamatan Military Government.
   c. To file personally incoming secret letters in the secret letter files.
   d. To register outgoing secret letters in the secret letter register.
   e. To attend to letters concerning administrative matters.
   f. To sign outgoing letters on behalf of or at the order of the Head of the Ketjamatan Military Government.

2. Editor:
   Editing is devided into two sections:
   a. Correcting documents concerning Orders/Instructions/Decrees/Announcements.
   b. Correcting general correspondence.
   The editor follows the orders/notes etc. in accordance with the directives or points given by the Secretary.

3. Letter-register Clerk.
   a. Registers incoming letters in the Letter Register book.
   b. Find and bundle together related letters.
   c. Distribute letters in accordance with the Secretary's directive.
   d. Keep the Authorities Register, the Business Register and the Reminder Book.

4. Outgoing-letter Clerk.
   a. Registers outgoing letters in the outgoing letter book.

b. Find and bundle together related letters.

c. Give outgoing letters to the Despatch Clerk, after ensuring that they have been numbered, signed, stamped and that enclosures are complete. (In a large Secretariat this work is done by the Control Section).

d. Keep the Authorities Register, the Business Register and the Reminder Book.

Explanation:

Authorities Register.

All incoming and outgoing documents are to be registered in the Authorities Register under the heading of the senders (Date and number of letter register/outgoing letter register number, date and number of letter and contents).

Business Register.

All documents are to be registered in the Business Register under the heading of the subject/contents.

Incoming documents: Date and number of letter register; date and number of incoming document; sender, subject.

Outgoing documents: Date and number of outgoing letter Register, address and subject.

Reminder Book.

Everything is to be entered which it is thought needs to be remembered. (Usually at the directive of the Secretary).

5. File Clerk.

Filing is devided into two parts:

a. Incoming.

b. Outgoing.

The File Clerk puts away incoming and outgoing documents given to him for that purpose by the Letter Register Clerk and the Outgoing Letter Clerk; he sees to the loan of documents at the directives of the Letter Register and the Outgoing Letter Clerk. (If the Letter required is not in the files, it must stated where it is, for example, in Section II, in the Supply Section, etc).

Note:

The File Clerk merely notes the numbers of documents, he does not need to know the contents.

A chit must be given with every request for the loan of a document and must be bundled with the related letters; this must be done even for requests by the Letter Register/Outgoing Letter Clerks.

6. Typitst.
   a. Typing material for the Secretary and Editor.
   b. Check the typing of typed documents.
   c. Lay-out letters in such a way that the contents are clear and easy to read.
7. Despatch Clerk.
   a. Put outgoing letters into their envelopes.
   b. Foreward such envelopes to their addresses through messengers, and be responsible for the speed/lateness of delivery. Examine the despatch book to ensure that letters sent have really reached their addresses.
   c. Know the code-numbers of each address and be responsible should there be any leakage.

Nota Bene

It often happens that the Secretariat is suspected or accused of being bureaucratic and too long-winded because their handling of letters takes rather long. But this occurs because as a matter of fact the Secretariat ought to be accurate and also must know thoroughly the contents of the incoming and outgoing mail so that it can be remembered should there be some questions.

The keeping of letters in bundles is to be avoided, for at a certain moment we will face the difficulty of not knowing in what bundle a certain letter is. (This is apart from those letters concerning a single matter). References (onwards and backwards) are important for the Letter-register Clerk, because if they are not entered as they should be, while the documents concerned are not bundled with later correspondence, they will easily become "lost", and only because the references were forgotten. The Authority and Business Registers should be written up properly and exactly so that at any time it will be easy to find some document when it is asked for.

In a small Secretariat, several posts can be held by a single person. (It often happens in Ketjamatan offices that a single person is Letter-register clerk, Secretary, Typist, etc. all in one.)

B. ECONOMIC AFFAIRS

THE ECONOMIC BLOCKADE

Since 19th December 1948, the Renville Agreement no longer exists, and thus there are no *status quo* lines any more. Although this is so, in fact a line still exists which, however, is confined to a line between areas which are really under the authority of the

Republic and those which are really under the authority or the enemy.

The population living within areas under enemy authority are not our dependants, although they may be our relatives.

Conclusions:

An economic blockade must be conducted all along the line of actual authority (not the *status quo* line of former times). Lessons of the past have taught us two basic facts, namely:

a. In the matter or regulations governing the economic blockade, there must be conformity for the compass of one *Wehrkreise*, without any exceptions.
b. Sanctions must be provided in those regulations for all infringements without exception. Exceptions lie in one pair of hands alone, that is with the person responsible for the compass of the *Wehrkreise*, so that the good and bad of the regulations is the responsibility of the Commander of the *Wehrkreise*.

CONNECTIONS BETWEEN THE ECONOMY AND SUPPLIES IN GENERAL (PEOPLE AND ARMY)

The meaning of supplies in general is service for the carrying out of military duties which takes the form of finance, equipment and armaments. The source of supply is the economy of the region. Thus supply is not the economy, although there is a connection; if the economy is sound, supplies will flow easily! Supplies must be able to go along with strategy!

Information must be given clearly with accompanying illustrations (pictures) of the combination of forces becoming the resultant power to fight.

What is our strategy? It is a strategy of forming a military government. The methods of implementing that strategy include guerilla warfare (small battles), sabotage, scorched earth, ambushing the enemy's supplies (harassing the supply line); gradually to restore the de facto territory of the Republic by our patrols. **These are the tasks of the mobile troops.** The tasks of the Military Sub-district Commands are to remain fast in their regions and, by means of greatly improving the economy, to get supplies ready for the armed forces which are in or which pass through their regions.

The Supply Tasks of the Military Sub-district Commands

1. In each *Ketjamatan* Military Government there is a Supply Section led by a military man (a member of the equipment

section) who is assisted by civilians, the duties of which are to attend to:

a. The keeping of stock books on supply goods to be found within the bounds of the *Ketjamatan*.
b. The keeping of books showing the export of goods from the region (See also point 3. below).
c. An over-all view of the existence of supply goods in the region.
d. To pass on requests from villages in the region which are suffering from a shortage in stocks of foodstuffs or money.
e. To give orders to the villages in the region which are to fulfil the requests from villages which have been passed on (see 1.d. above) in the name of the military government.
f. To submit reports and requests from the *Ketjamatan* Military Government about economic matters (supply).

2. a. It is the *Tjamat* who shall give orders and be fully responsible for the collecting and storage of goods.
   b. The *Tjamat* shall recommed and give orders about such matters to the village military government in order that regulations (instructions) about collection of foodstuffs etc. related to supply will be executed as well as possible.
   c. The village military government must do the work mentioned in points a. and b. above with a full sense of responsibility.
   d. All supply goods which have been collected are stored in the respective villages with the matter of strategy in mind, and these stored goods are the responsibility of the head of the village military government.
   e. The village military government must report all results of the collection and storage of goods or what remains of them to the supply section of the Staff of the *Ketjamatan* Military Government.

3. a. The distribution of supply goods is to be divided into two, namely:

   i. Troops passing through (mobile troops), and
   ii. General.
   b. The place where this distribution takes place is in each village.
   c. Distribution for troops passing through is seen to by the Village Cadres as the assistants of the head of the village military government (the *Lurah*).
   d. In order that mobile troops on furlough in a certain village do not have their upkeep neglected, every village must at

291

all times keep a stock of rice, at the very least one hundred
kilograms, which is earmarked for mobile troops.

e. Should it happen that at some time the total stocks of rice
are only one hundred kilograms, the Village Cadres must
immediately request an addition from the Supply Staff of
the *Ketjamatan* Military Government.

WORK TO BE DONE

The work to be done is divided into three sections, namely:

1. Finance
2. Equipment
3. Armaments

Guide:

These tasks are to be carried out in all fields with the factors
in mind which have been explained in the section on general
economic affairs.

The conditions of the work are that those doing it must be able
to distinguish between personal matters and state affairs.

Explanation. This matter must be reviewed more deeply with
exact definitions. If this is not done, various excesses will arise,
including corruption.

What is corruption? It is a step taken by an individual or a
group which, being linkedt o their official position, makes use of
it for their own interests with the consequence of a loss to the
state. This should be explained through giving examples of what
is meant and what is not. (Cigarettes, etc. from a good friend, etc.).

What is fraud? Fraud is the embezzlement of monies or goods
given by organisations of the state to those made responsible for
their keep.

What is malversation? Malversation is deliberate and incorrect
behaviour to get around the regulations and the prohibitions in
the administration.

Capital

Businesses in all fields operating on the resources in the region
(including from its people) provided they are not of a personal
character, must all be entered in the books and full responsibility
taken (accountability). We must continue to be accountable for
as long as the struggle goes on (usually there is a limit, namely
25 years).

292

The personnel of the Military Sub-district Commands may change a thousand times, and those officials may be brought to law a thousand times by the military government via its courts. (Sanctions).

The work to be done with regard to supply has been laid down in Instruction No. 4/MBKD/49, dated 1-1-'49, namely:

Finance

Village banks are to be revived with capital from the military government or from the population itself.

The purpose is that, by providing the people with loans for commerce (so that they do not merely await the results of the harvest alone) they will be able to fulfil their own needs (salt, oil, etc.).

Method: capital from the military government is to be repaid in installments within 10 (ten) weeks at an interest of 10%, likewise paid in ten installments. This profit is to be used for the purchase of soap, sigarettes, etc., for the troops. When the capital comes from the population themselves, the distribution of the profits will be based upon the following needs:

a. Shareholders.
   For village development
   For defence in the proportions of 25% and 50%
b. Taxes on cigaretts, tobacco, leather, cows must be fixed by regulations promulgated by the commanders of all *Wehrkreise*, applied in conformity with uniform regulations and collected by civil agencies (Opening of a taxation branch in the *Ketjamatan* etc.).
c. An increase in the market tax is to be made by the authorities concerned in all market places (the stalls, not outside) as a contribution by the vendors to the Government for the firm support of a long struggle.
d. An additional rise an forestry licenses is to be applied by the authorities concerned as a contribution from the purchases of timber for commerce or house building.
e. In regions where the population is religious a compulsory alms tax (zakat/fitrah) is to be levied, expecially at harvest time, at the Friday prayers (at mosque), to be applied by the responsible authorities.
f. In regions where the population are prosperous, a popular "Good-works" movement is to be begun for financial contributions given in exchange for a written receipt and with the knowledge of the *Wehrkreise* Commander. This money is to be given

293

voluntarily, it must not be obtained through force or at the point of a gun; it must come from the people's own conviction, and must be properly administered (reports must be made).

g. Charity funds are to be collected when troops are on leave and give a performance (concert etc.) on the seventeenth day of the month. [1])

h. State loans from the population; these may only be arranged by the regional head of the military government. A part of such loans is to be spent and a part invested in some constructive business (trading, bank, etc.) to be paid back in turn to the subscribers to the loan in order that their confidence will not be lost.

i. Trade and commerce is to be undertaken for obtaining goods from any source (both from areas under our authority and from areas occupied by the enemy) provided that it is directed into the regions to increase the stocks of the *Wehrkreise* which must conform with its needs. Useless goods should not be included in these transactions; goods which are in short supply in the regions should be brought in from outside, and the like. These trading ventures may be undertaken by the Military Subdistrict Commands as organisations, and may be undertaken by persons who are not members of the Armed Forces provided that there is an agreement as to division of the proceeds with the person(s) running the venture (fifty-fifty, one-third, etc., depending upon the risks involved and the origin of the capital used). These businesses are constructive and add to the prosperity of the region.

Mobile troops can assist in increasing the goods needed for supply, so long as the men of the unit are able to do the work gladly and provided that, after their own needs have been deducted, there is an obligation to give the balance to the head of their finance section.

Equipment

At bottom this matter cannot be solved within the regions under our own authority, especially with regard to:

a. Medicines
b. Clothing in large wholesale quantities
c. Cigarettes in cartons

---

1. The Proclamation of Independence was made on the seventeenth day of a month (August, 1945) and so it became a favourite day for entertainments, festivities, etc.

d. Soap in large wholesale quantities
e. Oil for lighting
f. Stationery.

These are the things which must become the centre of attention of the trading organisations set up in each Military Sub-district Command, especially in the Military Sub-district Commands which are very close to areas under the enemy.

Whilst we prohibit and control the export of goods from regions under our authority, we must also encourage and give special exemptions to those willing and able to import the above goods and also provide them, for example, with premiums for risks, an escort of mobile troops, and the like. To the single-man vendors (itinerant vendors) information should be given as intensively as possible so that, besides looking for the greatest possible profit, they are reminded of their duty to work for meeting our needs in the areas under the authority of the Republic. This matter should be stressed daily in every economic sector of the Military Sub-district Commands. In this matter of trying to meet our needs, we must also have thought already of locally-made preparations (substitutes) the use of which we can recommed in areas under our control. For example:

a. Javanese herbal remedies
b. House industries for weaving
c. Common tobacco with newsprint as cigarette-paper
d. Not to use soap, but to bath frequently
e. Oil made from soya beans, from the fruit of the rubber tree, etc.
f. Reduction of stationery through greater use of verbal means, or through the use of a sheet of paper on both sides (the paper of old letters used again).

Food

Concerning the endeavour to increase crops, we shall be able to surmount this completely so long as:

a. an orderly control is exercised over the export of foodstuffs;
b. large-scale waste, such as in public kitchens, is abolished and is replaced by family kitchens (billeting to be accompanied by a grant, a quota of raw materials);
c. by making road-blocks in such a way that arable land is increased to be planted with sweet-potatoes, cassava, etc.;
d. superfluous armed personnel from the Armed Services who have no duties should assist in intensifying the product of the rice-fields (by weeding, repairing irrigation ditches for wet rice-fields, making dams, etc.);

e. superfluous personnel is directed to individual market-gardening on waste forest lands, with the permission of the Forestry Service.

In practice, every Military Sub-district Command tries to improve the economy by means which take into account the possibilities and the capacity of the area; however, it has been proved this purpose, and not whether the possibilities are known or not; it may also be that concerned could not make up their minds because they wait for a shortly-forthcoming clash with the enemy.

We must not forget that in this matter the Military Sub-district Commands have a constructive duty, and people must free themselves from such hopes. The people and their villages must be led towards being economically capable of defending themselves when later on we leave that region. Therefore all expert personnel from the various economic fields must be mobilized (recruiting people, if possible, also from the towns) so that, as from now, the aspect of village development must be actively begun and led; in the first place, the work ought to be done by members of the Armed Forces or by an organisation of the Armed Forces. The lacks suffered by the experts (not being with their families, eating at odd hours, being chased by the enemy, being deprived of things usually available in cities) are not very significant when we recall that in the future, the villages throughout the whole territory of the Republic which we have led onwords will be militant and capable of defending themselves economically. Daily necessities, which in colonial times were extremely simple and could be bought for $2\frac{1}{2}$ cents (the famous "sebenggol"), must be increased in the right direction so that the will to increase the things available which exists at present with only modest means to fulfil it will continue to be active, and will eventually be able to make smooth connections with the towns (foreign countries and so forth) and by this means the people will be able to satisfy the economic law of supply and demand without the assistance of other nations (Chinese, Indians and others; the middlemen will be of our own people).

The only other way to obtain the things which we cannot make ourselves is by means of fighting and this is the task of the mobile troops which they conduct especially against convoys, camps and other similar objects. When such successful attacks are made by territorial troops which are part of the Military Sub-district Command, they must be reported to the Military Sub-district Command so that the *Wehrkreise* Commander can also make arrangements for the supply of mobile troops. In such cases, the needs of the territorial troops must first be obtained from the large towns which are controlled by the enemy; this can be undertaken together with well-to-do friends in those places, so that we can buy the licenses issued to Republican civil servants for the distribution of goods. It must not happen that those licenses fall into the hands of people of another nationality.

The principle of the matter is that there are a thousand and one ideas, so long as they are put into practice. Should a thousand ways be tried and fail, there is still another one to be applied.

Armaments

Increasing the strength of our armaments is the duty of the mobile troops alone, to be implemented means of armed force. Up to now, for example during attacks upon camps, convoys and other objects, attacks have been merely disruptive, but gradually, in the light of past experience, those units will gradually merely seize especially their equipment, their arms and ammunition.

When the size of the bullets we need is the same as that of the enemy, it is obvious that it will be easier to attend to a supply of bullets. Remember that our arms in general are the product of our struggle against Japan four years ago, and now the shortage of bullets and ammunition is felt. A past extravagant use of bullets which was not effective has brought about the consequence that is now deeply felt by the fighting members of the armed forces, so that by now every member of the armed forces fully understands the value of bullets.

The basic efforts to be made are:

1. To look for arms whose bullets are of the same size as those of the enemy.
2. To economise in the use of the bullets we have under the slogan: "One bullet for one enemy".
3. A disciplined prohibition against the use if bullets to hunt pig etc.
4. Bullets which are hidden in the regions we control should be exchanged for other things or should be requisitioned.
5. Through our colleagues in the towns to look for connections to obtain bullets from the enemy in exchange for goods or money.
6. Arms for which there are only small quantities of bullets left should be exchanged (through mediation of the Military District Commands) from the guerilla fronts to regions which are more peaceful.

7. To undertake large-scale fighting instead of the tactic of sniping and sharp-shooters.

The above points are taken from the lesson to the cadres in every Military Sub-district Command to be used as guide and in addition to Instruction No. 4/MBKD/49, dated 1-1-'49, with the no that:

a. it is not a matter of knowing the possibilities existing due to the capacities of the region, but

b. of undertaking steps from these thousands and one ways in organised and systematic fashion (not arbitrarily, but disciplined and regulated).

Defence Bank

Basic Considerations

There are very many wealthy people who have an excess of riches which are used only to increase the wealth of individuals.

Great strength is to be found amongst the itinerant vendors who are now involved in connections with money-lenders who should in fact obtain our assistance and be able to make a contribution to defence.

Our defence, the duration of which is not yet certain, requires large expenditures so that we may be fully prepared to face the enemy.

Recally also that the circulation of Republican currency does not go smoothly because there are many farmers who possess no capital, whilts they have time for commerce while waiting for the crops to ripen, the shortages in foodstuffs must be met by means of trade so that the farmers too are able to defend themselves.

Also in view of the Java Command H.Q. Instruction No. 4 dated 1-1-'49 for the establishment of village banks.

Requirements

The wealthy will be able to declare their good will with the existence of the "Defence Bank" — that is, by giving a part of their money to form the Bank's capital; the right to their wealth will not be reduced.

The setting up of the "Defence Bank" will enable us to settle the question of individual money-lenders, which means release for the small itinerant vendors from usury, whilst they will be able to obtain loans at low interest from the "Defence Bank". The profits of the Bank are the manifestation of the good will of the well-to-do, put to work by the small itinerant vendors; what profits exist at present must be availed of and are basically an endeavour which lighters the burdens of the people in general.

Implementation

a. The "Defence Bank" shall have the same composition as the Village Banks which are set up in every village where it is possible to do so, and constitute branchces.
b. The "Defence Banks" shall be in the hands of the villages *(Kelurahan)* themselves.
c. Supervisory control shall be centred in every Sub-district.

Capital

a. Capital shall be obtained by the sale of shares to the people in the areas of the respective *Kelurahan.*
b. The price of the shares is not to be the same but shall be dependent upon the buyer's purchasing power; especially the wealthy shall be asked to buy at as high a price as possible.
c. The funds collected from the sale of shares shall be the capital of a branch of the "Defence Bank" in a *Kelurahan.*
d. There is the possibility of permitting capital to be taken from the village funds (Cash funds, taxes, etc.).

Employees

a. The Sub-district centre shall determine which persons are to be charged with keeping the books — the bank clerks.
b. A bank clerk will have under him a group of 3 to 4 branches of the Defence Bank, depending upon their size.
c. Every branch of the Defence Bank shall appoint assistant bank clerks who are to be recruited from the original village population.
d. The village *Lurah* shall be responsible for the proper functioning of the banks in his area.
e. The *Lurah* shall be responsible with regard to difficulties from those contracting loans.

Interest

a. Interest is fixed at 10 per cent of the amount of the loan. The loan shall be paid back in ten installments amounting to one-tenth of the loan plus one-tenth of the interest at each installment.
b. Loan and interest must be fully re-paid within 50 days.
c. A further loan may be contracted by an individual when former loans have been re-paid.

d. The interest shall be used for: 25% for the shareholders, 25% for the village and 50% for special defence projects.

An honorarium shall be fixed for the Inspector, clerk and his assistants. Supervision of the management lies with the military government in the Sub-district, although the officials concerned are not defence personnel.

The Life of the Defence Bank

a. The Defence Bank shall continue to exist for the duration of our defence against the enemy.
b. In peace-time it shall be altered to become the Village Bank which ought to exist for the special interests of Village Funds; it shall be already by the gradual repayment of capital to the shareholders.

C. SOCIAL AFFAIRS

SOCIAL WORK

Expecially during times when the people, especially the families of our soldiers, are undergoing great sufferings in consequence of Dutch aggression, social work must receive the special attention of the Military Sub-district Command. For this purpose the following shall be undertaken:

a. Recreation centres shall be established where our soldiers can relax and obtain modest entertainment.
b. On holidays and National Days, visits should be made to the Heroes' Cemeteries, to wounded soldiers, who should be provided with some simple treat in the form of food and sweetmeats or letters of appreciation to strengthen their faith and to stimulate the fighting spirit.
c. Assistance in the form of money, foodstuffs, textiles for clothing (if available) should be provided to the families of soldiers and civil servants (if the head of the family is unable to supply them with these necessities), and to the evacuees.
d. Evacuees: Special attention should be paid to the evacuees with regard to their housing, to issisting them with foodstuffs and for their protection. For this purpose there can be arranged, for example:
In every village each family with sufficient means should be obliged to billet evacuees. In compensation, the evacuees should be obliged to give their services for the needs of the village's well-being. (For example, in the fields of farming health, education, information services and the like).

To those evacuees who give clear factual evidence of the contribution of their services in the interests of defence and the
well-being of the village, some small payment of money should
be made or foodstuffs given to lighten the sufferings of their
family. Usually, the evacuees bring with them no small amount
of their valuables to the villages. Under such conditions, they
can be an attraction for thieves/criminals who perhaps live in
the vilage. Experience has shown that not a few of the evacuees
have been the victims of robbery, plundering, theft and the
seizure of their goods. Clearly, this matter must be attended
to by the Security Section of the Military Sub-district Command,
primarily ensuring the legal safety of the evacuees. For this
reason the Military Sub-district Command must make a list of
names, valuables, etc.

Additional

In view of the conditions, places and atmosphere in which our
soldiers live, it is necessary for them at times to be able to go to a
place in an undisturbed area where they can go to feel at peace,
feel healthy and be able relish good food and so on. A resting
place should be made for this purpose which is situated far from
the battlefield, if possible in region where the scenery is good, where
there is a swimming pool, and so forth. How good it will be if at
such times games are held, reading-material provided; and, to
fortify their spirit, there is a need for explaining to them the
history and ideals of our struggle. An endeavour should also be
made to explain spiritual matters to them (a moral re-arming).

EDUCATION

Although we are now in the maelstrom of the struggle, the question of education may by no means be neglected. In this connection,
education may be divided into two parts:

Education on the school bench, and

Education which is obtained from practice (in society).

School Education

Education on the school bench may be divided into two levels,
namely, the level of Junior High School down, and the level of
Senior High School up.

At the first level, education in emergency form can be given in
various places, for instance, in the grounds of a building, in the
rooms of a house which are large enough, in a mosque and so on,
whilst teaching personnel can be recruited from teachers, students

(of a level higher than those to be taught) or from the evacuees (who have sufficient knowledge to equip them for teaching).

For the second level (Senior High and up), endeavours should be made to provide education in the form of front-line schools, that is, by lectures given as in college by teachers and experts in technical and general subjects to students wherever they can gather, or by means of distributing written lectures to the students who are scattered because of their duties.

Practical Education

It is education obtained through practice which in reality is extremely useful at the present time. Amongst the things which can be done to secure this are the following:

If pupils are to be found in the area of the Military Sub-district such as are mentioned below, a division of tasks/work can be arranged for them by the mobilization officer of the Military District Command in the following ways:

A. *For the pupils of General Schools:*

I. For pupils of Classes 1 and 2 of the Senior High School:
   a. Hamlet cadre or Village cadre
   b. Squad leader or head of a section of the *PAGER DESA*
   c. Assistant in the security section of Hamlet/Village/*Ketjamatan*
   d. Health cadre of Hamlet/Village/*Ketjamatan*
   e. At the Communications Posts.

II. For pupils of Class III and graduates of the Senior High School (who have not yet furthered their studies):
   a. In the General Section of the Military Sub-district/Military District Commands
   b. In the Defence Section of the Military Sub-district/Military District Command
   c. Head of a Hamlet or Military *Lurah* (in the battle zones)
   d. In the Security Section of the Military Sub-district/*Ketjamatan*
   e. In Information and Health work (Social Affairs)
   f. Officer's assistant in the Communications Posts.

B. *For the pupils of Specialised Schools:*

I. Trade/Economic Schools (of the same level as Senior High School):

For pupils of Classes 1 and 2:

In the *Kelurahan/Ketjamatan* Sections for Economic Affairs/Prosperity/Finance.

For pupils of Class 3 (and for graduates who have not yet worked):

In the Military Sub-district/*Ketjamatan*/Military District Command/*Bupati* sections for Economic Affairs/Prosperity/Finance.

II. Teachers' Colleges:

For pupils of Class 4 of Lower Teachers Colleges:

a. Teaching in Elementary Schools and for People's Education (anti-illiteracy)
b. Education Staff of the Military Sub-district
c. Information Staff of the Military Sub-district.

For the Upper Teachers Colleges:

(Note: in Republican areas the Upper Teachers Colleges go as far as class II alone):

a. People's Education and Elementary Schools
b. Education Staff of the Military Sub-district/Military District Command
c. Assistant Teacher at Junior High Schools
d. Information Staff of the Military Sub-district/Military District Command.

III. Forestry Schools:

Pupils of Classes 1, 2 and 3 can be mobilized as civil servants assisting Forestry Foremen, or as Forestry Foremen in the *Ketjamatan*.

IV. Agricultural Schools:

Pupils from Classes 1, 2 and 3 can be put to work as employees of the Agricultural Service, as Assistant Agricultural Foremen, or Agricultural Foremen in the *Ketjamatan*.

V. Fisheries Schools:

(Note: the existing Fisheries Schools are only of a level with the Junior High Schools).

Pupils of Class 3 can be mobilized as Fisheries Cadres in the *Ketjamatan*.

VI. Technical Schools:

(Note: Many pupils of these schools have already joined the Technical Units of Brigade 17).

Pupils of Class 6 of Lower Technical Schools:

a. In the Public Works sections of the *Kabupaten.*
b. In the Armaments Sections of the Military Governors/ *Wehrkreise*
c. Seconded to Radio Broadcasting posts at various places (radio and electrical sections).

C. *For the Students of University Faculties:*

I. Technical Faculties.
(Note: many students of these Faculties have already become members of the Command of Brigade 17).
a. In the Resident's Public Works sections
b. In the Armaments Sections of the *Wehrkreise* and *Sub-Wehrkreise*
c. As assistant instructor on sabotage and in the engineering service of the *Wehrkreise,* or as mobile troops
d. Teaching in the front-line schools (in their specialised subjects).
e. As technicians in radio broadcast posts.

II. Medical Faculties.
a. Seconded to hospitals, Red Cross centres and branches
b. Trainers in People's Health
c. Health Section (Social Affairs) of the Military District Command/Military Governor
d. Teaching in the front-line schools.

III. "Gadjah Mada" University.
a. Seconded to the local government officials, from *Tjamat* to Resident/Governor
b. In the General Sections of Military District Command/ Sub-Territorium Commands/Military Governor (in accordance with their level)
c. In the Information Sections of Military District Commands/ Sub-Territorium Commands/Military Governor (in accordance with their level).

IV. Academy for Political Studies.
The same tasks as for the students of "Gadjah Mada", especially to be seconded to local government officials.

V. Teachers Training Academy.
a. Seconded to hospitals, Red Cross centres
b. Teaching in front-line schools (Junior and Senior High Schools)

c. Information Staff of the Military Governor/Sub-Territorium Commands/Military District Commands.

VI. Forestry/Agricultural Academies.

Students of these academies can be put to work in the Staffs of Resident or *Bupati* to work in keeping with their subjects.

VII. Finance Academy.

Students can be put to work in the Finance Staffs of Java Command H.Q./Military Governor/Sub-Territorium Command.

INFORMATION

In view of the present level of the struggle, in which our military government has been properly set up and is working well throughout the whole of the Java Territorium, it is necessary that, apart from considering matters of defence, social welfare, economic affairs and public health, we fulfil our obligation to attend to information.

It is hardly to be denied that our efforts in information have so far been insufficient, and all the more so when compared with the activities of the Dutch and of persons who in this time of many difficulties use every opportunity to poison the spirit of society with instigation and provacation.

The excuse of insufficient equipment and capable personnel cannot be denied; indeed, it is to be greatly regretted, but these conditions are not to become grounds for doing nothing forever. With all our powers we must try to overcome those difficulties and to begin immediately with an orderly and wide-spread information compaign.

In connection with this, therefore, and to carry out what is recommended in the Instruction from H.Q. Java Command No. 1, Section III point c, clause 1 about information, an Instruction has been issued to the Military Governors to give orders to the Commanders under them in their respective regions (Sub-Territorium Commands, Military Districts, Military Sub-districts) so that, as quickly as possible, information work will be carried out which is more orderly and more widely spread than in the past in that field, and with the principle of our old struggle in mind.

In order that there shall be uniformity of system and organisation with regard to information throughout the entire Java Territorium, the following matters must be given proper attention:

I. The Organisation of Information Work

The principles which are to be used in information organisation are:

a. The form and character of the military government and the *Wehrkreise* are to be kept in mind.
b. It must be dynamic and mobile.
c. As far as possible using personnel from amongst the people themselves who have a good influence upon the community.

It must also be recalled that the emphasis of our struggle lies in defence of the villages so that the emphasis of information work also must lie in village information.

For these reasons, the information organisation in the *Ketjamatan* (the information division of the military government of the Military Sub-district) must be composed in the best possible way. Many students and employees of the Information Ministry who have good qualifications can be made use of here. Further, the following points can be used as guide:

The Information Section of the Military Sub-district Military Government

A military man should be appointed as leader; a civilian (Local Government civil servant or employee of the Information Minitry) should be appointed as deputy leader, whilst the secretary should be a civilian appointee (from the Local Government civil service or the Information Ministry). Two information men should be recruited from amongst students, Local Government civil servants or employees of the Information Ministry, from which groups there should also be recruited two administrative personnel.

Information in the *Kelurahan* should be left to the *Lurah* with the assistance of several or the Village Cadres who have received training and also, if possible, with help from student personnel, whilst the general lines of information should be fixed by the Military Sub district Information Section.

Additional

We recognise only one information organisation in the whole of the Java Territorium, and that is the Information Section of the Military Government which covers military and civilian information. In keeping with the formation of the Military Government, all employees of the Information Ministry are included in the information section of the Military Government and work as members of the Military Government and in the name of the Military Government.

Because the information organisation laid down above is based on the territorial structure which will continue to exist, also because the emphasis of information work is placed in the Village which likewise will not be able to be abolished, information work will continue at all times throughout the whole Territorium irrespective of conditions in the information centres (Military Sub-Territoriums, Military Governors, Java Command H.Q.).

With such a form and system of organisation as the above, these information centres constitute planning, supervisory and co-ordinating bodies alone.

II. Information Work

In order to achieve the best possible results from information, three basic things must be obtained:

1. Adequate information equipment
2. Good information material
3. Capable information workers.

Information Equipment

Attempts should be made to obtain (as far as possible):

a. A (battery) radio receiver in every Military District *(Kabupaten)*
b. A duplicating machine in every Sub-territorium Command or Military Governor's staff
c. The greatest possible amount of paper and writing materials
d. A simple printery (hand presses) in every Military Governor's staff.
e. Notice boards in every *Kelurahan.*

Information Material

The following may be used as sources of information:

a. Instructions from the H.Q. Java Command, Armed Forces Staff and similar material from the Armed Forces
b. Decrees/Announcements from the Military Government (Military Governor, Sub-Territorium Commands, etc.)
c. Decrees/Announcements from the Emergency Government of the Republic of Indonesia Central Government Commission in Java
d. Reviews/surveys from the H.Q. Java Command/Armed Forces Staff, Military Governors, etc.
e. Radio news (this needs to be screened and carefully examined before being used)
f. Other materials to be found in the respective areas.

Information Workers

a. Must be able to work on their own
b. Possess sufficient initiative
c. Must think dynamically and must react quickly

307

d. Have the journalist's spirit

e. Must be friendly and mix a great deal amongst the community.

It is to be noted that, when spreading information material in the form of publications (magazines or brochures), an investigation must always be made as to whether that material really does reach the lower-level places (Military Sub-district, *Kelurahan,* and so forth). Because of the close connection with despatch it is also necessary to regulate an organisation of communications as well as to prepare information material. The best possible communication service for this purpose should be built up between the information centre and the farflung information regions.

Apart from this, attention should also be given to the gathering of news about the respective regions to be forwarded to the next higher information organisation, in the form of periodical reports (weekly, monthly, etc.) made out in a fixed and systematic way.

It is surely not necessary for us to remind ourselves that every information worker must have a broad and deep (intensive) understanding of all Instructions and Decrees from Java Command H.Q., the Military Governors, the Sub-territorium Commands and so forth, so that he can give objective and suitable information about them.

Other Points

Special information directed to the mobile troops is primarily the responsibily of the commanders of *Wehrkreise/Sub-Wehrkreise.*

THE PEOPLE'S HEALTH

The Task to be Undertaken by the Military Government in the Wehrkreise.

In view of the present organisation of the struggle, in which our military government is obeyed by the whole people with full trust and confidence in its rule, besides considering questions of defence we must also pay attention to social and economic questions and the matter of our people's health. Being situated in large towns our hospitals are occupied by the enemy, dispensaries (chemist's shops) and health training centres have suffered a similar fate and are being used by the enemy for his own interests. In consequence, the people's health has declined and possibly has become less stable. Added to this, very few specialists, doctors, chemists and analysts are to be found outside the towns.

Theoretically, it will not be possible to care for the people's health properly and this may result in a decline of the potential strength of our defence and our military government.

In connection with all the above, and after conducting an experiment in a people's health system in two *Kabupaten* which were no longer dependent upon conditions in the large towns, an Instruction has been issued to commanders. Cammanders should order the respective doctors of Military Governor's Staffs, Military Region Commands (Sub-territorium Commands), Military DDistrict Commands and Military Sub-district Commands, to carry out the public health system which has been tried out and has run well — it is even the case that this new system, which makes use of the personnel and the materials to be found in the villages, has been more successful in advancing the people's health in several regions than in the three years under the Republic with the old system which ran well in those areas.

Slogans to be Used.

* What is needed is that there should not be many people ill. (Prophylaxis.)

* Medicines are to be made from ingredients that are easily obtainable in the villages and which are understood by all people (popular).

* Hospitals, polyclinics, dispensaries and training centres for paramedical personnel are to be run by *gotong-rojong* (co-operative) methods by the people of the Military District Commands, the Military Sub-district Commands and the Villages together with trained health workers to be found in those regions (mobilization of evacuated medical personnel).

In order that people do not become ill (prophylaxis), education of the people with regard to health is to be undertaken in the following ways:

a. Every village within the bounds of a Military Sub-district Command is to send, at the order of the *Tjamat*, one person to receive a one-week's lightning course of theoretical training to become the village health officer; this person is to bring his own needs, besides which each village is to contribute 10 coconuts to the hospital in exchange for training material and for a living for the training course workers.

b. After the one week's theoretical training is ended, the condidate village health officers are to be seconded to the people's health centres (polyclinics) for practice during one week. In this way two week's training will provide every village in the areas under Military Sub-district Commands with a people's health officer who knows how to make simple diagnoses and to prescribe simple treatment with medicines prepared himself from things which

309

are easily to be found around the village in which he lives. He must also be able to educate the people of his village in preventive measures (prophylaxis) and to train one person in every hamlet to become his assistant in that hamlet.

The dispensary in the Military Sub-district is to be under the control of the Head of the Military Sub-district Command Health Service. Evacuees can be helped to find work by being placed in this medicine making concern. The kinds of medicines made should be capable of being kept for a long time and be in the form of tables and powders (care should be taken about moulds and fungi). As there are no containers to hold the oils of ointments to prevent them drying up, ointments also should be in powder form which can be later mixed and cooked with coconut or peanut oils or with fat to make the ointment. Members of the Health Service must give information as to the potency of these medicines and the advice of the doctors must also be heeded by the dispensers. Apart from preparing medicines already known to be effective, the chemists must also try to improve their potency and their quality from a technical point of view, and must also try to find new medicines which, before being put into mass production, should be tried out in consultation with the doctors; only then, if the results prove good, should they be put into production on a large scale.

The village health officers who are the product of the lightning training are to report on the people's health conditions in their village, and to report upon his experiences to the nurse who is head of the Health Service in the area covered by a Military Sub-district Command. In turn this nurse receives instructions from doctors, assistent doctors and the head of the Health Service of a Military District Command. Thus within the bounds of a Military District Command *(Kabupaten)* one doctor is needed; should there be no doctor available, a nurse of many years' standing with a wide experience will do, provided that he/she is supervised by the *Kabupaten* doctor or the Army doctor in that area. The area of a Military Sub-district Command needs one nurse, whilst in a village there should be a health officer from the lightning training course who is assisted by helpers in each of its hamlets, whilst one senior nurse is needed to control health in the territory of a *Kabupaten* (Military District Command.)

In the way outlined above, the health instructions given by the Head of the Health Service of a Military District Command can be executed amongst the entire people. This system was certainly never practised in the Dutch period, the Japanese time nor under the Republic of Indonesia before this second aggression by the Dutch.

310

The village health officer who is the product of the lightning training course can be called a practical health officer.

The subjects to be taught in the training of these village health officers are:

The theory and practice of

a. Hygiene (scientific but popular)
b. Prophylaxis
c. Pathology (scientific but popular)
d. Diagnosis
e. Therapy
f. Dispensing (from ingredients popular in the villages)
g. Administration of polyclinics
h. Surgery (primarily first aid)
i. Ordinary polyclinics.

For the manufacture of medicines from ingredients to be found around the villages, a dispensary must be set up that is able to distribute its products to the polyclinics (people's health centres) throughout the whole area of the Military Sub-district Command. to establishi this dispensary, money is to be borrowed (or contributions taken) for the initial purchase of medicines and ingredients. The perfection and speed of development of this dispensary will depen upon the conviction and desire for social advance by the people of the Military Sub-district Command concerned. Undergraduate assistant chemists can be put at the disposal of such a dispensary whilst they continue their practical studies.

There follow a few prescriptions which have proved to bring good results.

AILMENTS OF THE INTESTINAL TRACT.

1. *Beras Ketan* (the grain of a glutionus variety of rice)
   to be baked and then pounded fine   100 grams
   Kunir (Curcuma Longa L.), to be baked and then
   pounded fine   1 grams
   To be mixed together.

   Dosage: Three teaspoonfuls (desertspoonfuls) three times a day.

   Note:

   The quantity of *kunir* to be used depends upon the gravity of the ailment (amount of diarrhoea). The dosage for children is measured in teaspoons, for adults in desertspoons.

2 Mature papaya (pawpaw) leaves   2 grams

Toasted coffee-beans (the bean inside the skin
should be no more than half-cooked)   10 grams
To be pounded fine and mixed.

Dosage: One tea/desert-spoonful three times a day.

Note:

The quantity of mature papaya leaf depends upon the gravity
(blood and mucus) of the dysentery.

3. Roots of a mature (but not too old) coconut palm   5 grams
    Water   100 cc.
    Boil together.

    Dosage: (infusion on decoction) One glass (50 cc) to be drunk
                 three times a day.

Note:

This mixture may be kept for no longer than 25 hours. The
amount of the coconut palm root depends upon the gravity of
the diarrhoea.

For diarrhoea, the patient can also be ordered to drink strong tea
without sugar. And to alleviate the pain, hot ashes wrapped in cloth
can be laid over the stomach and the patient instructed to eat *djadah*
(a cake made from glutinous rice). Because it is difficult to find
gram weights in the villages, it is sufficient if the proportions of
the above quantities are used.

COUGHS.

Mature leaves of the Betel (Chavica Betle Miq., Chavica
Mature leaves of the Betel (Chavica Betle Miq.,
Chavica Siriboa Miq.)   3 leaves
    Brown coconut sugar   3 desertspoonfuls
    Ginger root (Zingiber Officinale Rosc.)   As ordered
    Crush and mix.

Dosage: One tea/desert-spoonful three times a day.

Note:

The size of mature Betel leaves is almost the same everyere; it
is the leaf used for betel-chewing; the brown sugar is to be sliced
fine and only then measured. The amount of ginger root depends
upon the amount of mucus to be removed from the throat and
internal passages.

Children should be given a teaspoonful, adults a desertspoonful.
Apart from coughs, this preparation is also good for influenza,
laryingitis, bronchitis and espedially for whooping cough in children.

312

MALARIA.

Mature leaves of the papaya (pawpaw)	200 grams
Leaves of the *Ketepeng* (Cassia Alata L.)	100 grams
Water	100 cc.

To be boiled together.

Dosage: (infusion or decoction) One glass (100 cc.) three times a day.

Note:

As *Ketepeng* leaves are diffiicult to find, there are many kinds, and the names vary from place to place, it may be better not to use these but only ordinary papaya leaves; as with treatment by quinine, this decoction/infusion of papaya leaves should be taken for several months (days). The dosage for children is one half to one third that for adults, depending upon age.

BASIC MEDICINE FOR PURIFICATION OF THE BLOOD FOR EXTERNAL DISEASES (VENEREAL DISEASES IN WOMEN) AND OTHER COMPLAINTS ARISING FROM VENEREAL DISEASES.

Leaves of the *Kumis Kutjing* (Orthosiphon-Grandiflorum)	1200 grams
Water	100 grams

To be boiled together.

Dosage: (infusion or decoction) One glass (100 cc) to be drunk three times a day.

Note:

Because the *Kumis Kutjing* is at times confused with the *Pis Kutjing* (Jovonese) as the flowers are similar, it is better to say *Remudjung* leaves and to show example when explaining.

In connection with the cure of the chemical symploms olthough the blood is still contaminated, so that the disease has not been completely eradicated, this infusion/decoction of *Remudjung* leaves should be used for a number of days or several months. A woman with an infected womb (most of these infections originate with men) should also take the *Remudjung* course of treatment.

SKIN DISEASES (ESPECIALLY ITCHES)

Sulphur

1 part each of:
Rice flour
Betel leaves (Chavica Betle Miq; Chavica Siriboa Miq.)

Kunir (Curcuma Longa L.)

Laos (Alpinia Galanga Sw.)

Mix together over a slow fire with coconut oil or fat. For external use.

Note:

Take a bath and soap well to ensure cleanliness; dry the body with a towel; then rub the medicine in with cottonwool, pinching out the pus so that the medicine can penetrate the wounds made by the itch. Each day the rubbing with medicine should be increased until no more pustules are visible and the rash is dry. Whilst taking this caurse of treatment (3 to 5 days) until the rash is dry, the patient may not bath. When the rash has dried and the pustules healed, a bath with a good soaping should be taken and an examination made to ensure that no pustules remain.

Especially in the case of *Gudig*, much sulphur is to ne used and the mixture is to be cooked over a slow fire; rice flour is used to give body to the medicine. For *Kadas (Panu)* much *Kunir* and *Laos* is to be used with only a little sulphur and betel. *Kadas* is treated by first violently rubbing the pustules until a little blood comes out and only then applying the ointment. For *Koreng* which originates in infected wounds or for Ulcus Tropicum, which are plentiful in the villages, there should be a great deal of betel leaves used and only a little of the other ingredients, and without the addition of rice flour. Treatment is given after washing the wound with water in which betel has been boiled, then putting the medicine on. For bandages, strips of dried banana leaf or Betel leaves can be used after they have been boiled.

EYE DISEASES

Mature leaves of the Betel (Chavica Betle Miq.; Chavica Siriboa Miq.)	3 leaves
Water	200 cc.

To be boiled together. For external use.

Dosage: (infusion or decoction) To be used twice a day to wash the eyes.

Note:

As there are no pipettes, either capok or cottonwool is used in washing the eyes, and to make an eye compress, the leaves of the *Tapak Liman* (Elephantopus Scaber L.), examples of which should be shown when explaining.

Of course, for the radical cure of trachoma the patient must be sent to a doctor with complete medical supplies and equipment.

DISEASES OF THE MOUTH AND TEETH

Mature Betel leaves	5 leaves
Water	200 cc.

To be boiled together. For external use.

Dosage: (infusion/decoction) To wash the mouth three times daily after meals.

Note:

For diseases of the mouth (wound in the mouth) and the jaws and for sprue, it is enough merely to wash the mouth.

For diseases of the teeth, while rinsing the mouth, the medicine is to be sucked around the diseased tooth (dentitis dificilis, pirodentitis, gangrene) and the gums are to be poulticed with hot ash in a cloth three times a day.

For pulpitis (a diseas of the tooth nerve) and caries (medium or deep), the cavity is to be cleaned with some simple homemade instrument and then filled with cotton steeped in oil of cloves (or cloves pounded into powder).

DISEASES OF THE NOSE AND EARS

Betel leaves	1 leaf
Peanut oil	2 cc

To be pounded togethe and cooked over a slow fire until it reaches 40 degrees Centigrade. For external use.

Dosage:

Three times a day three drops are to be put into the ear (nose).

Note:

Because there are no pipettes, cotton is to be used. The drops are to be given after the ear (nose) has been washed with salted water which has previously been boiled to 100 degrees Centigrade.

SUBSTITUTE FOR BORACIC COMPRESS

Mature Betel leaves	3 leaves
Lime water	100 cc.

To be boiled together over a slow fire.
For external use.

LIQUID FOR CLEANSING NEW AND OLD WOUNDS

Betel leaves	7 leaves
Kunir (Curcuma Longa L.)	1 part
Water	200 cc.

Make a decoction or infusion of the above.
To be used twice a day to wash wounds.

TO PURIFY COTTON

Cotton is to be picked from the plants and cleaned of seeds, etc. it must then be boiled for half an hour at 100 degrees Centigrade and dried in the sun (it should be left to dry in a high place to avoid its becoming dirty). It can be sterilised in the usual way using simple utensils (the *dandan:* the rice- steaming pot).

Other prescription recipes will be provided bit at a time.

Method of Establishing and Operating Polyclinics

Polyclinics are established for the following purposes:

a. To diagnose of the patient after his examination and so that the patient understands his own disease; after receiving the doctor's advice about treatment and the medicines to be used the village health officer can make the medicine himself. Only if the patient can not be treated by medicines of his own making as the ingredients for them are not available (pneumonia, tuberculosis, nephritis, madness, paralysis, trachoma) should he be given medicines made from foreign ingredients (international drugs, injections, serum).

b. For a once weekly or once monthly control; the patient returns to the polyclinic.

c. To report that the diseases has been cured or that there are new symptoms (complications).

Whilst medical personnel (doctor, nurse, people's health officers, dispenasary officer) treat or control patients and listen to their reports, they are also able to draw conclusions about iprovement of their work (a more simple method, the way of treating a certain case). Chemists must look for new medicines and perfect their techniques. The polyclinic is to be built by *gotong-rojong* (co-operative) methods and through contributions and loans from the villages of the Military Sub-district Command for its establishment. It must be maintaned through the people's own resources (be self-supporting). Its costs must come from donors (rich people) and every patient, according to a classification of his weath, must give goods in exchange (eggs, coconut, rice, salt, tea, coffee) for his medicinces and his treatment at the clinic. The poor do not need to pay. The incoming goods are sold to pay for the running of the polyclinic.

Method of Establishing and Operating People's Hospitals

As a beginning, a People's Hospial should be set up (what is meant is a special place for this purpose) where patients can be accommodated (for hospital treatment). The capacity should be for 200 patients which must meet the needs of one Military Region Command and *Kabupaten*.

Donors (rich people) should assist co-operatively and provide anything from washbasins to houses. All equipment should be very simple, whatever can be used for a particular purpose; if such equipment should be very simple, whatever can be used for a particular purpose; if such equipment is not available it should be home-made so that the hospital becomes a practical people's hospital. As there are no large houses in the villages to accommadate all sections of a hospital under one roof, each section needed (surgery, gynaecology, children's diseases, skin and veneral diseases, internal diseases, infectious diseases, office and stores, mortuary) can be housed in a separate building. Thus the hospital is situated in a village or a hamlet with its office and stores in the midst. The doctor's house or that of the senior nurse (the doctor's assistant) is to be in one viillage with the hospital. Especially the sections for gynaecology, veneral diseases and the mortuary should be situated near a river, while the office and store should be near a road, and the infectious diseases section should be in an isolated house surrounded by a thick hedge. Funds for advance payment in cases where patients have not yet brought any goods can be obtained from loans or contributions from the people of the region within the nursing district of the People's Hospital.

A social fund, to pay for the needs of poor people can be obtained from donors (the Social Section of the Military District Command).

The Fuids of the People's Hospital

Payment by the patients in keeping with their economic standing is the fund used to pay for the employees of the People's Hospital and for whatever is needed to improve the hospital. The goods received in payment from the patients should be put up for trade so that the expenditures of the People's Hospital can be met.

The midwife attached to the People's Hospital is concurrently Head of the Training Course for the *Dukun* [1]) living within the Military District Command, so that the *Dukun* become assistant village midwives. Minor or easy operations are performed in the

317

People's Hospital; major operations are done in surgical hospitals
by a surgeon whose treatment district is that of one Military Region
Command or that of several Military District Commands.

Surgical hospitals are also situated in places meeting very modest
requirements, but the doctor's equipment and medicines meet
internattional requirements, for if there are serious lacks in the
surgery the patient's life can easily be lost.

Conclusions to be Drawn

Through this system, which has been operating in several *Kabupaten* with good results, a complete programme of people's health
can be quickly put into practice using modst and co-operative
1) Dukun: Herbalists and midwives who have had considerable experience
      but have not been trained in scientific medicine.
methods, so that the military government can guarantee that the
people's health is not dependent upon foreign countries and so that
the whole of the people become hygiene-minded.

With the existence of surgical hospitals, people's hospitals,
polyclinics, polyclinics, people's · health officers, people's health
assistants, *Dukun*, assistant village midwives, officers for medicines
(a dispensary industry), and the training of village officers for
people's health, all of them under the leadership of diplomaed
surgeons, doctors, senior nurses, midwives, and assistant chemists,
the doctors and otherr medical personnel, apart from having the
satisfaction of participating in the development and strengthening
of our Republic, will be able to raise the levels of their skill for
the interests of their science and the well-being of the people as
true members of the medical profession.

D. DEFENCE

The "People's Total Defence" has already been built up in the
villoges under the leadership of the *Lurah* and with the assistance of
his staff. For the improovdment of this system, it has been determined
that the Village Cadres are territorial personnel, side by side with
the *Lurah*, to do the work of co-ordination and to activate in military
fashion all kinds of civilian tasks.

Past experience shows clearly that the Dutch system of spreading
their wings widerr and controlling conditions is always by means
of propaganda, by distributing food-stuffs, medicines and the like.
Those goods have originated in seizure and theft from the population
of otherr areas to be used for winning the hearts of the people
elsewhere. This Dutch endeavour is pioneered by patrols aimed at:

a. Destruction of our guerilla units which are scattered amongst the villages (the capture of our youth and the seizure of weapons).
b. The capture of leaders of the local government civil service for the perfecting of their puppet administration.
c. The plundering of foodstuffs and the valuables belonging to the ordinary people who have evacuated to other areas.

They have also set up permanent guards at strategic places and also where there are important military constructions. Thus it is evident that, because they lack enough trops, the Dutch can not possible occupy the villages and towns which are not so important. The village, therefore, may experience three kinds of situations:

When a village is visited by an enemy patrol

When it is occupied by the enemy

When it is neither occupied by the enemy nor is there an enemy patrol.

Measures to be taken in trying to surmount these three kinds of situation are dealt with in the brochure entitled "Village Defence" (by Col. A H. Nasution). In broad lines, they are that, when the enemy comes on patrol, the population must make temporary evacuation taking their valuables and domestic animals with them. Especially must the local government leaders who live in that area hide themselves in order to avoid being pounced upon by the enemy. Should a village be occupied, it must be seen to that every effort to set up a puppet administration is brought to nothing. Further, the occupying forces must be gradually disrupted so that the enemy becomes unnerved and does not feel secure there.

A region that is still at peace must make all preparations and keep on holding training a such a kind that it is at all times ready to face all kinds of eventualities.

Amongst the enemy's efforts to bring chaos to the countryside and to unnerve the population is the organisation of robbers who terrorise everywhere. In most case under such conditions, the local government and village administrative officers seem to be defenceless. They are not able to act because they wait for an armed cover. In fact, with the existence of the Village Guard troops, it is this eradicating confusion which is their task together with the whole of the people.

a. PAGER DESA

It has been proved everywhere that Dutch actions (night and day, but especially at night) against places we occupy often come without our prior knowledge so that the continued occupation of our military centres is threatened. It frequently occurs that many members of the army and many young men of the settlements are captured and taken off by the Dutch because of confusion as to whether to take preventive measures or to put up opposition. This happens primarily because the enemy's approach is known only very suddenly so that panic and demoralisation may occur among the troops and especially among the people. This also happens because news between guard or patrol pasts is not yet well regulated and running smoothly.

To overcome these conditions it is necessary to revive the questions of Intelligence and Security and to attend to them properly. Besides this pickets must be set up in the Military Sub-district Commands and *Kelurahan* and a Guard Leader appointed in the hamlets to ensure security in their respective territories.

Further, the following matters should be given attention and ought to be carried out.

SECURITY IN THE HAMLETS:

1. A watch/guard is to be established in every Hamlet, especially those beside main roads which are frequently used by the enemy.
2. The watch/guard is to be under the leadership of a Chief Guard.
3. The Chief Guard is to be a member of the Village Guerilla Troops.
4. The post of Chief Guard is to be taken in turns for spells of one day/night at a time. (The appointment and relief is to be regulated by the leader of the Guerilla Troops of the Hamlet or Head of the Hamlet).
5. The Chief Guard acts as the foremost advance post for the Military Sub-district Command for watching and passing on news about enemy conditions.
6. The Chief Guard also organises the village guard within his Hamlet.
7. The Chief Guard is to report every in his Hamlet to the Picket of the *Kelurahan*.

THE KELURAHAN PICKETS:

1. The Chief Guards are led by the Picket of the *Kelurahan*.
2. The *Kelurahan* Pickets are composed of members of the *PAGER DESA* (Village Guerilla Troops) who take this duty for spells of three days at a time under instruction of the Head (Commander) of the *PAGER DESA*.
3. *Kelurahan* Pickets consist of two persons: a Picket Chief and a Deputy.

4. In the field of security the *Kelurahan* Pickets have the following duties:

   a. To guarantee security of the territory of their *Kelurahan*.
   b. To guarantee the security of the Staff of the Military Government of the *Kelurahan*.
   c. To see to it that the Hamlet Posts are always under guard.
   d. To make watch-guard patrols within the territory of their villages.
   e. To see to it that the intelligence and security instruction of the Military Government are put into effect by the people of their villages.
   f. To report day to day events to the Picket of the Military Sub-district Command.

THE MILITARY SUB-DISTRICT COMMAND PICKETS:

1. The *Kelurahan* Pickets are under the leadership of the Military Sub-district Command Pickets, and the latter are under the leadership of the Military District Command Pickets.
2. The Military Sub-district/District Command Pickets are composed of members of their respective staffs who take this duty for spells of three days at a time.
3. The Military Sub-district/District Command Pickets consist of two persons: a Picket Chief and his deputy.
4. The tasks of the Military Sub-district/District Command Pickets are the same as those for the *Kelurahan* Pickets in their respective regions (see points a. to f. above).

Note:

The Chief Guard, the *Kelurahan* Picket and the Military Sub-district Command Picket make contact with one another at any time something happens or there is important news.

The pickets are responsible for the security of the guard centres and for the security of our military and civilian leaders living in their area. At any time something happens which might endanger them, they are to be informed so that they can make preparations to ensure that their positions are not threatened.

General Duties for Pickets and Chief Guard

Apart from the tasks mentioned above, they also have the following duties:

1. The Pickets are the Deputy Commanders each attending to the day to day happenings in their respective territories. For the Chief Guard this duty is to be the Deputy in his Hamlet for the *Kelurahan* Picket.

2. When troops or fighting units arrive suddenly at a certain place, the Picket/Chief Guard is to make the first arrangements for their accommodation which will be attended to later on by the Supply Section.

3. It is the responsibility of the Picket to restore order should there be a serious disturbance in his territory. If the disturbance has been made by an ordinary member of the population, the matter should be turned over to the police; if it has been caused by military personnel it should be handed over to the Military Police, and if it has been caused by enemy accomplices or spies, it should be turned over to the Intelligence Section.

Note:

In the *Kelurahan,* the representative of the police is the *Lurah* himself.

There are also similar representatives in the *Ketjamatan*/Military Sub-district Commands.

4. To regulate the relay communication in the delivery of letters.

Explanation

With these Pickets we can depict the territories of the Military District Commands, the Military Sub-district Commands down to the *Kelurahan* as being like a hostel inhabited by a single family which is composed of the ordinary people and the army who together fight against the Dutch. The army does the actual fighting (conducts operations) and the people supplement their work and provide them with what is needed; the Military District/Sub-i district Commands act like a headquarters and attend to all the needs of the hostel.

Naturally, it is the duty of the Picket to attend to order in the hostel. The guards of the hostel are the members of the population who perform the task of watch-guard; the head of the watch-guard is the Chief Guard of each Hamlet respectively. It goes without saying that, should something untoward happen in the hostel, whether it is caused by someone from outside the hostel or by a member of the hostel itself, it is the Picket which attends to it in the first place. Should troops or fighting units come, they should report to the Picket, which will then see to food and accommodation for them and the like. And also, for example, should the hostel be under threat of attack from an enemy it will be the guard post of the Picket which must face the attack first in order to ward it off. And so on. Each Picket should picture to itself that its territory is a hostel which is under its care.

With picket duties being performed in the Military District Command, the Military Sub-district Command and the *Kelurahan* there will be additional guarantees of security within the territory of each Military District Command. Therefore, with the issue of this Instruction, the Military Sub-district Commands and the *Kelurahan* are required to establish Pickets for their respecctive areas.

INTELLIGENCE

The tactic of fighting taken by our people and army is that of the guerilla, which means a tactic of hitting at the enemy wherever he is weak and of avoiding him wherever he is strong. In order to carry out this tactic with simple means all leaders need information about the enemy. This information is to be obtained by sending out investigators to ask for news from the population. In this matter the common people can assist the fighting personnel.

Information which is needed by the leadership is:

1. The strength of the enemy: the number of men, the weapons, the means of communication, the means of transport and other equipment such as tanks, carriers, cannon.
2. The enemy's nationality: Dutch, Chinese, Japanese, Indonesian (in the latter case, from which area).
3. The enemy's habits: The times at which they sleep, eat, bath, relax, go out on the move, where they are and the roads.
4. Important enemy sites: army centres, barracks, officers' quarters, machine depots, ammunition dumps, stores and other things such as sentinel posts.
5. The roads: Bridges and other constructions which have been damaged, or which have been repaired again, or which also need to be destroyed.

All members of the population, men or women, the old, the young and the children, have the obligation of collecting this information and of passing it on to the Head of the Hamlet, the *Lurah*, the Military Sub-district Command, the Military District Command, to Intelligence officers from the Staff of the *Wehrkreise*. Only persons with the rank of Head of Hamlet upwards are permitted to give such information to troops who need it, and then only after those troops (or a member of them) thow their letters of identification.

Every Military Sub-district Command has the obligation of collecting such information and news from the *Kelurahan*.

SECURITY

What is meant by Security here is the safety and security of the leadership (both civilian and military) and of the troops. Ensuring such security involves:

The question of a better guard upon secrets, and

The question of the eradication of enemy spies.

Under ordinary conditions (when there is no confusion or disturbance) every person wishing to come into a Hamlet can be required to register his name, address, purpose of the visit, how many hours he wishes to remain, etc. By this means, each Head of a Hamlet will know how things stand in the area under his authority and will be able to capture enemy spies immediately if there are any.

It is more difficult if there are many evacuees in a place and their arrival has coincided with an attck. Under conditions of great disturbance such as those it is very difficult to refuse entry to enemy spies. The best way is for the Military Sub- district Command to fix beforehand certain villages which are solely for evacuees, and in this way the identity of enemy spies can be established.

Wherever there are army centres, barracks and so forth the guard against enemy must be intensified.

Finally, the perfecting of Intelligence and Security depends upon the conviction, skill and cleverness of the whole of the population.

———————